Praeger Handbook on Understanding and Preventing Workplace Discrimination

Praeger Handbook on Understanding
and Preventing Workplace Discrimination

Volume 1
Legal, Management, and Social Science Perspectives

Volume 2
Best Practices for Preventing and Dealing with Workplace
Discrimination

Praeger Handbook on Understanding and Preventing Workplace Discrimination

Volume 2

Best Practices for Preventing and Dealing with Workplace Discrimination

Michele A. Paludi, Editor

Foreword by D. Gayle Loftis

 PRAEGER

AN IMPRINT OF ABC-CLIO, LLC
Santa Barbara, California • Denver, Colorado • Oxford, England

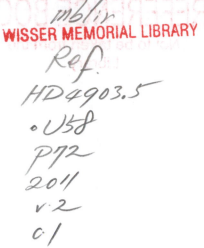
Library of Congress Cataloging-in-Publication Data

Praeger handbook on understanding and preventing workplace discrimination / Michele A. Paludi,
Carmen A. Paludi, Jr., and Eros R. DeSouza, editors.
    v. cm.
    Includes bibliographical references and index.
    Contents: v. 1. Legal, management, and social science perspectives—v. 2. Best practices
for preventing and dealing with workplace discrimination.
    ISBN 978-0-313-37974-1 (hardcopy : alk. paper)—ISBN 978-0-313-37975-8 (ebook)
    1. Discrimination in employment—United States. 2. Discrimination in employment—United
States—Prevention. I. Paludi, Michele Antoinette. II. Paludi, Carmen A. III. DeSouza,
Eros. IV. Title: Handbook on understanding and preventing workplace discrimination.
    HD4903.5.U58P72 2011
    658.3008—dc22   2010012556

ISBN: 978-0-313-37974-1
EISBN: 978-0-313-37975-8

15   14   13   12   11   1   2   3   4   5

This book is also available on the World Wide Web as an eBook.
Visit www.abc-clio.com for details.

Praeger
An Imprint of ABC-CLIO, LLC

ABC-CLIO, LLC
130 Cremona Drive, P.O. Box 1911
Santa Barbara, California 93116-1911

This book is printed on acid-free paper ∞

Manufactured in the United States of America

One day our descendants will think it incredible that we paid so much attention to things like the amount of melanin in our skin or the shape of our eyes or our gender instead of the unique identities of each of us as complex human beings.

—Franklin Thomas

To Antoinette and Michael, my parents. Thank you for encouraging me to speak and write about workplace discrimination.

—Michele A. Paludi

Volume 2 Contents

Foreword

Discrimination occurs in many forms. It is not a new issue, just one about which the public has become more aware. Unfortunately, awareness of its existence does not equate with an understanding of the multitudes of ways that persons and organizations can engage in discrimination, react to discrimination, or respond to an allegation of discrimination against a person or organization. Retaliation for making the complaint, whether the claim is found to be justified or not, has become even more common in recent years.

The investigation of claims of discrimination or retaliation requires an understanding of more than just how to ask a question. How should an employer train the workforce to be sensitive to discrimination, to prevent it, and to deal with such an allegation when made? Do the reactions and damages claimed by the plaintiffs have any basis in social science or studies?

As an attorney who has worked on numerous such cases over the last thirty years, both in state and federal courts, it has become clear to me that more understanding of "the nature of the beast" is required. Education in the subject matter and the processes that operate in both the prevention and elimination of discriminatory or hostile workplaces is needed not only for the legal practitioner, but also for the individuals who are in the trenches of the workplace. The costs for business and government when prevention and elimination are not seriously undertaken by the employer are significant. They include emotional damages and medical care for the victim, distraction of the employer's employees from their business in order to participate in litigation discovery and testimony, and counsel fees for defense as well as for the successful plaintiff. Furthermore, seldom is there only one victim. The uneducated and untrained duplicate their errors repeatedly, and the costs may even escalate due to the failure to address obvious problems of discrimination in the workplace. Frequently, the offender creates a pool of victims even if the victims may not be aware of each other's existence.

I have been fortunate to work with Dr. Michele A. Paludi, who has demonstrated to me that understanding discrimination and working to eliminate it requires more than just a knowledge of how to litigate for damage that has occurred, and that a victim of discrimination is not alone in the social science that has addressed this subject. The chapters compiled by the editors in this work can serve as a reference for every human resource office and law firm that must deal with these subjects. It is to be hoped that the greater understanding that can be derived from works such as this can ultimately result in money being spent by businesses to train and educate for prevention, rather than as damages and attorneys' fees to victims.

We can only aspire to that day.

D. Gayle Loftis, Esq.
Hackensack, New Jersey

Acknowledgments

Michele A. Paludi

Change does not necessarily assure progress, but progress implacably requires change. Education is essential to change, for education creates both new wants and the ability to satisfy them.

—Henry Steele Commager

I thank Jeff Olson and Brian Romer at Praeger for extending me this opportunity to edit a second volume to the *Praeger Handbook on Understanding and Preventing Workplace Discrimination*. I also thank the contributors to this volume who have shared their expertise and experience in promoting fairness and respect in organizations. I have learned a great deal from their work.

The following deserve my appreciation for their support and encouragement during the preparation of this volume: Rosalie Paludi, Lucille Paludi, Carmen Paludi, Jr., Paula Lundberg-Love, Kevin Nadal, Steve Earle, Tony LoFrumento, and Tony Deliberti. Thank you.

As first-generation Americans my parents were faced with discriminatory treatment because of their ethnicity and, in my mother's case, because of her gender as well. Rather than teaching me to accept this reality, they instead encouraged me to understand prejudice and discrimination and to speak out on behalf of those whose voices were silenced because of the discrimination. I learned also by observing how they treated people. They embraced the differences in individuals while simultaneously valuing the similarities among us.

I am always reminded of Charlie, a man who attended my father's wake in 1980, who told my mother, sisters, and me how my father had affected his life. Charlie, an African American man, told us my father was the only co-worker (both were skilled workers at General Electric) who treated him fairly, did not talk with him in a derogatory manner, and stopped others from making racial slurs and epithets.

I am also reminded on almost a daily basis of my maternal grandfather, John Peccichio, who, at my graduation from Union College in 1976, showed me where he helped construct buildings at the college years earlier. He was an immigrant to the United States from a small village near Naples, Italy. He was proud that his granddaughter was a graduate from the college he helped build, an opportunity denied to his daughters since the college had been previously all male. I am reminded of my grandfather as I now am a professor and teach in the very buildings he helped construct. I have requested rooms in these buildings for teaching my courses to honor him. He arrived in Schenectady, New York, as did my paternal grandparents and maternal grandmother and was met with prejudice. Pascucci (1984) recounted ways in which Italian immigrants were discriminated in Schenectady. For example:

A more blatant, crude form of restriction, but with similar results, was found in real estate ads such as the one placed by a city realtor in the *Union Star*, that offered a free trolley ride to inspect a new tract of building lots. . . . The headline announced that the sites were "For Americans" only, but, lest anyone misunderstand, the lengthy advertisement further specified that "land sold only to white Americans of English speaking, German or French decent." If any doubts were still to remain, the realtor advised, in conclusion, that "no lots will be sold to colored people or undesirable foreigners." That the press had no compunctions about printing such offensive comments indicates that either prejudices were common and openly expressed or that paying advertisers were not to be discouraged. (p. 13)

In my courses on human resource management, I discuss change management, including the importance of working for change and being committed to this effort because it does take time. I share with students my personal experiences of living in the United States before the passage of the 1964 Civil Rights Act. I tell them that my parents told me to "pay attention" when President Kennedy started working on civil rights legislation, which then was continued by President Johnson. I grew up in a pro-union family (my father was a union member) and saw people ban together in workplaces using a collective voice to protect their rights as employees before the passage of Title VII. And in my lifetime, I have seen changes in workplaces since its passage. I know that change is possible. I also know that change is met with resistance. And I understand what Kurt Lewin once stated, "If you want to truly understand something, try to change it."

It is because I believe that change is possible that I wanted to edit this second volume on workplace discrimination. The contributors describe strategies to accomplish change through effective and enforced policies, investigatory procedures, and training programs. They rely on empirical research from the social sciences as well as management theory and case law to guide their programs. They are all change agents.

Whenever I become concerned about change with respect to civil rights legislation taking too long to be accomplished, I am reminded of what Dr. Bernice Sandler once told me, "A woman's work is never done."

This second volume is part of the work I must continue to honor the change for which my grandparents, parents, and so many others worked tirelessly to end discrimination.

REFERENCE

Pascucci, R. (1984). *Electric city immigrants: Italians and Poles of Schenectady, New York, 1880–1930*. Retrieved September 9, 2009, from http://www. schenectadyhistory.org/resources pascucci/1.html.

Introduction to Volume 2

Michele A. Paludi

> This is how change happens, though. It is a relay race, and we're very conscious of that, that our job really is to do our part of the race, and then we pass it on, and then someone picks it up, and it keeps going. And that is how it is. And we can do this, as a planet, with the consciousness that we may not get it, you know, today, but there's always a tomorrow.
>
> —Alice Walker

In 2007 I had the opportunity to cofacilitate training programs with Carmen A. Paludi, Jr., on "coping with change" for coordinators of Employees Assistance Programs (EAPs) throughout New York State. The objectives of this program were to assist coordinators with the following: (1) identifying the characteristics of personal and organizational change; (2) understanding the psychological, physical, behavioral, and organizational consequences of dealing with personal and organizational change; (3) understanding strategies for managing transitions and coping with change; and (4) identifying interviewing, assessment, and referral strategies for employees coping with changes in their lives.

EAPs provide help to employees whose work performance has suffered as a consequence of a personal (death, move, personal illness, divorce) or organizational (layoffs, new job, new supervisor) problem (Smith & Mazin, 2004). The majority of problems can be resolved before an organization loses a valuable employee or that employee causes problems for the organization. The EAP coordinator's role is to assist employees while they correct their work performance. Thus, the EAP is designed to increase productivity, enhance morale, increase employee retention, and reduce absenteeism and turnover rates. During the training programs, we discussed stages of change: denial ("It will never happen to me"), resistance ("I really don't see why I need to change"), exploration ("We can do this. I'm certain of it"), and commitment ("I feel confident working here now") as well as barriers to change, reactions to change, self-assessment, resources for being a change manager, and change management techniques (see also Bovey & Hede, 2001; Gilley, 2005; Mercer, 2000).

From my work as a management consultant, I have witnessed two situations in which the coping with change model and training program we developed for EAP coordinators were useful for organizations and individuals dealing with workplace discrimination: (1) training EAP staff to assist complainants, accused, and witnesses involved in a complaint process; and (2) assisting the organization with understanding individuals' reactions to their discrimination and harassment management program and ensuring a successful initiative in enforcing change to achieve a discrimination- and harassment-free and retaliatory-free work environment. I briefly address each of these situations.

EAPs can be trained to assist employees who are parties to a complaint through their employer's policy and procedures. This approach was used by the Hunter College Sexual Harassment Panel during the late 1980s and early 1990s when I co-chaired the panel with Richard Barickman (Helly, 1990). We provided training to their EAP staff about workplace and academic sexual harassment, including the following: legal definition, behavioral examples, incidence and impact on individuals' emotional and physical well-being, career development, interpersonal relationships, and self-concept. We discussed Hunter College's policy and procedures for filing and resolving a complaint of sexual harassment. Since investigators of complaints of sexual harassment at Hunter College (or any organization) must not provide emotional support for parties to the complaint, we engaged EAP staff to offer this needed service (see Paludi & Paludi, 2003). EAP staff may provide support for employees seeking resolution for other forms of workplace discrimination and harassment (see volume 1 for a description of all protected categories).

We identified an ecological approach for conducting training programs on sexual harassment for organizations (see Paludi & Paludi, 2003).

This approach, applicable for other forms of discrimination and harassment, stresses that workplace discrimination training be provided in a sequence that ensures optimum assistance for all parties in a complaint resolution. We identified the sequence as follows:

- Investigator(s) of Complaints
- Employees Assistance Program
- Trainers
- President and Vice Presidents
- Managers and Supervisors
- Employees

It is documented in the social science literature (see Cortina & Wasti, 2005; Dansky & Kilpatrick, 1997) that flashbacks may occur during training sessions on workplace discrimination. Therefore, we recommended that investigators and EAP counselors be trained initially so that employees will have an outlet for filing complaints and receiving emotional support during the complaint process.

In this training with EAPs, we include a unit on how to manage stages of change employees encounter when dealing with workplace discrimination and harassment, for example:

- Managing Denial
  - Encourage employees to vent their anger and frustration
  - Be supportive
- Managing Resistance
  - Explain the transition in dealing with discrimination and harassment for employees
  - Help employee focus on the positive aspects of change
  - Give clients space
- Managing Exploration
  - Ask employees for input
  - Reinforce employees who are managing change in positive ways
  - Be flexible with employees
- Managing Commitment
  - Offer employees positive feedback on the transitions they are making
  - Assist employees in reevaluating their goals and objectives
  - Help employees set new challenges for themselves

This strategy is based on common responses to discrimination and change, for example, fear, anger, helplessness, sadness, and anxiety that take place during the course of seeking resolution for a complaint of workplace discrimination or participating in an investigation of workplace discrimination (Paludi & Paludi, 2003).

The change model and training program may be used to assist employees and managers with an understanding that change is inevitable in organizations, including dealing with workplace discrimination through effective and enforced policies, investigatory procedures, and training programs. The change model also provides organizations with (1) the knowledge that denial and resistance eventually will be replaced by commitment and (2) suggestions for helping management guide employees through the process of change by initiating strategies to help employees work through their resistance and achieve commitment (Mercer, 2000). In essence, the model assists with the fundamental transformation of organizations. It is based on planned, strategic, and long-range efforts.

An organization that moves from having no policy on discrimination or harassment of a protected category to initiating a policy starts a change cycle for its managers and employees. For example, with Genetic Information Nondiscrimination Act (GINA) becoming effective on November 21, 2009, organizations with 15 or more employees had to revise their policies and training programs to include this new federally protected category (see volume 1, chapter 4). This change included the following tasks:

1. Revising the employees' handbook to include GINA;
2. Updating all policies and procedures that pertain to discrimination;
3. Educating investigators about genetic information discrimination in general, the EEOC guidance and the organization's responsibilities for preventing and dealing with GINA discrimination and harassment;
4. Displaying the required EEOC posting;
5. Educating managers and employees about their rights and responsibilities under GINA;
6. Educating interviewers of job applicants about legal and illegal questions to ask individuals regarding genetic information;
7. Monitoring how staff treats an employee after learning about the manifestation of a disease in an employee's family to avoid adverse employment action toward this employee; and
8. Monitoring that genetic information, like other medical information, is maintained in a file for an employee that is independent from their personnel file.

Such changes promote stress for employees and employers who are concerned with the need for additional policies and training (for example, "Is the company being sued?" or "Are we going to have more complaints from employees after we provide the training?") or who mistrust their employer—that is, they may feel that their organization is policing them once again (Barling, 2004). Employees may be concerned with being retaliated against should they speak out to their employer about the changes being made in the organization. Still others may worry about perceived threats to their power. Some employees are accustomed to doing things a certain way; change challenges their comfort zone. Few of us deal with change without feeling unruffled. Change is difficult. Individuals experience a loss of what is familiar and known, loss of control, and loss of their identity. Loss is a central theme of experiencing change in one's job as well as in one's personal life (Gilley, 2005).

A change in an employee's life may produce what is only a minimal reaction at the time it is initiated. However, resistance to change surfaces weeks, months, or even years later. Reactions to change build up and then explode. What surfaces is a response to an accumulation of previous changes (Trader-Leigh, 2002).

Organizations must take "reasonable care" (see volume 1, chapter 14) with federally and state protected categories through effective and enforced policies, procedures, and training programs. We thus recommend the change management model for organizations implementing reasonable care with respect to workplace discrimination and harassment. Responses to change, most notably, resistance, can be reduced by communicating with employees to help them see the logic of the change.

The first step in this model is to conduct a change audit, which examines the organization's history of discrimination and harassment management, the current state of its management, and its future capabilities (Gilley, 2005; Smith & Mazin, 2004). An audit will diagnose barriers to successfully implementing reasonable care and will suggest recommendations for improving the organization's policies, investigatory procedures, and training programs. Sample audits are offered in volume 1 for sex discrimination (chapter 10) and national origin discrimination (chapter 5). In this volume, an audit is discussed with respect to age discrimination and intergenerational conflict. Sample audit questions for GINA, the newest protected category include the following (also see volume 1, chapter 4):

1. Does the employer have a policy statement for dealing with genetic information discrimination and harassment?

2. Does the policy prohibit discrimination and harassment from peers, or is it limited to discrimination and harassment by managers?

3. Is the policy statement well publicized? Is it circulated periodically among all members of the company?

4. How do employees learn to whom they should report complaints of genetic information discrimination or harassment?

5. Are remedies clear and commensurate with the level of discrimination or harassment?

6. Does the company have procedures to inform new employees about genetic information discrimination and harassment?

7. Does the company facilitate regular training programs on genetic information discrimination and harassment?

8. What services are available at the company to employees who have experienced genetic information discrimination or harassment?

9. Does the workplace foster an atmosphere of prevention by sensitizing individuals to the topic of genetic information discrimination and harassment?

10. Is the employer following state laws with respect to genetic information discrimination and harassment as well as federal law?

11. Has the employer modified its nondiscrimination policy to include the new GINA, which became effective November 21, 2009?

12. Does the employer use nondiscriminatory recruitment and selection procedures for applicants?

All stakeholders should be involved in the change audit, including the human resource department, employees, managers, and administrators. Anonymous surveys requesting information about the discrimination and harassment management of the organization can be useful. In addition, focus groups may be used to obtain more in-depth responses about the organization's discrimination and harassment management program (Barbazette, 2006; Jones, 2000). Sample questions for the anonymous survey and focus groups include the following:

1. In the past, what was the culture of the organization with respect to discrimination and harassment management (for example, successful, inconsistent, resistant)?

2. What types of changes have occurred in policies, procedures, and training programs?

3. Are the policies, procedures, and training programs on discrimination and harassment congruent with the organization's goals, mission, and values?

4. What barriers exist to maintaining a discriminatory- and harassment-free work environment and a retaliatory-free work environment?

5. What do you believe must occur for change in this area to occur successfully?

In addition to conducting an audit, human resource scholars and consultants have recommended conducting a SWOT (strengths, weaknesses, opportunities, and threats) analysis or a barrier analysis (see volume 1, chapter 5; Dineen & Bartlett, 2002; Williamson, Cooke, Jenkins, & Moreton, 2003). The SWOT analysis classifies internal aspects of the organization as strengths or weaknesses and the external situational factors as opportunities or threats. Using this analysis, the organization can leverage its strengths associated with its discrimination management program (for example, enforcement of policy statement prohibiting GINA), correct weaknesses in its program (for example, lack of an annual training program for managers and employees), capitalize on opportunities (for example, assistance from EAP), and deter devastating threats to the program's success (for example, failure to have confidential procedures for filing a complaint of sexual harassment).

A barrier analysis may be used when an employment issue—for example, a policy, procedure, training program, hiring practice, or performance evaluation—limits opportunities for members of a protected group. Through this analysis, an investigation of the triggers found in the employment issue are identified and resolved, for example, lack of promotion for women employees, or high separation rate of employees who are disabled. Barriers may be found in all functions of human resource management, including recruitment, hiring, promotions, training, incentive programs, and disciplinary actions.

Following the completion of the audit, SWOT analysis, or barrier analysis, the organization must implement, enforce, evaluate, and monitor its policies, procedures, and training programs (see volume 1, chapter 14). Employers must recognize that change in their organizations, including change in their management of workplace discrimination and harassment, is difficult and is met with resistance. The following recommendations have been offered for human resource directors and consultants working with employers who are effecting change in their organizations (Gilley, 2005, p. 109):

1. Change in preventing and dealing with workplace discrimination is nonlinear.

2. Employees may be resistant at first to being told to follow the harassment and discrimination management program.

3. An organizational culture must be established that values and supports change.

4. Buy-in from all stakeholders in the organization, especially employees must be achieved.

5. All changes with respect to discrimination and harassment management must be provided to all members of the organization (for example, via e-mails, newsletters, at company-wide meetings).

6. Feedback from employees and managers must be obtained regarding their perceptions of the changes being made in the way their organization prevents and deals with workplace discrimination and harassment.

7. Procedures must be in place that describe the organization's responses to employees who are resisting change.

8. Resistance may be signaling lack of communication or ineffective communication about the organization's responses to discrimination and harassment.

9. Changes to reasonable care must be executed in small increments.

10. Monitor the changes made toward the ultimate goal. Make any refinements that are necessary.

11. Reward employees and managers who are engaging in change.

Carmen Paludi, Jr., and I have presented our clients with a checklist for managing change, including change in their discrimination and harassment management:

1. Have you studied the changes carefully and identified who is likely to lose, including what you are going to lose?

2. Do you understand the subjective realities of these losses to the people who experience them, even when they seem like an overreaction to you?

3. Have you acknowledged these losses with sympathy?

4. Have you permitted people to grieve and express your own sense of loss?

5. Are you giving employees accurate information?

6. Have you defined clearly what is over and what is not?

7. Have you found ways to acknowledge the changes?

8. Are you being careful not to denigrate the past but, when possible, find ways to honor it?

9. Have you made it clear how the changes you are making are necessary to protect the continuity of the organization?

10. What actions can you take to help people deal more successfully with the changes that are taking place in the organization?

Finally, organizations must be trained to understand that change is a lengthy process that evolves with considerable time. As Gilley (2005) noted:

> Much of successful change depends on relationships, collaboration, and trust. Trust takes a long time to develop, yet can be destroyed in a matter of seconds. Creating an environment that supports change requires dedication and commitment, often in light of pressure for immediate results. (p. 110)

GOALS OF THIS VOLUME

The contributors to this volume offer recommendations for assisting organizations with change in terms of establishing and maintaining reasonable care with respect to preventing and dealing with workplace discrimination. Contributors include labor attorneys, human resource managers, scholars, management consultants, and management professors, all of whom are committed to creating a healthy environment of change for organizations with respect to discrimination and harassment. This volume integrates legislation, management theories, empirical social science research, and practical applications relevant to preventing and dealing with workplace discrimination. Part I offers recommendations regarding legal enforcement and compliance. Part II offers recommendations for policies and training programs in managing discrimination in the workplace. Part III offers suggestions for meeting strategic challenges, including viewing diversity training as meeting the organization's competitive advantage and organizational efforts needed to support diversity programs.

Sample policies are offered, as well as outlines of training programs for managers or employees on sexual harassment, age, sexual orientation, disability, and race. The recommendations offered in volume 2 are grounded in the case law, human resource management, the Equal Employment Opportunity Commission's guidelines, and social science research addressed in volume 1.

It is my hope that employers implement the recommendations identified in this volume in their programs on reasonable care to maintain a healthy, safe, and empowering work environment, thus ensuring that Alice Walker's sentiment, quoted at the beginning of this introduction, can be realized.

REFERENCES

Barbazette, J. (2006). *Training needs assessment: Methods, tools and techniques.* New York: John Wiley & Sons.

Barling, J. (Ed.). (2004). *Handbook of work stress.* New York: Sage.

Bovey, W., & Hede, A. (2001). Resistance to organizational change: The role of defense mechanisms. *Journal of Managerial Psychology, 16,* 534–549.

Cortina, L., & Wasti, S. (2005). Profiles in coping: Responses to sexual harassment across persons, organizations, and cultures. *Journal of Applied Psychology, 90,* 182–192.

Dansky, B., & Kilpatrick, D. (1997). Effects of sexual harassment. In W. O'Donohue (Ed.), *Sexual harassment: Theory, research and practice.* Boston: Allyn & Bacon.

Dineen, M., & Bartlett, R. (2002). *Six steps to root cause analysis.* Oxford: Consequence.

Gilley, A. (2005). *The manager as change leader.* Westport, CT: Praeger.

Helly, D. (1990). Institutional strategies: Creating a sexual harassment panel. In M. Paludi (Ed.), *Ivory power: Sexual harassment on campus* (pp. 231–250). Albany: State University of New York Press.

Jones, C. (2000). Levels of racism: A theoretical framework and a gardener's tale. *American Journal of Public Health*, 90, 1212–1215.

Mercer, M. (2000). *Absolutely fabulous organizational change: Strategies for success from America's best-run companies.* New York: AMACOM.

Paludi, C., & Paludi, M. (2003). Developing and enforcing effective policies, procedures and training programs for educational institutions and businesses. In M. Paludi, & C. Paludi (Eds.), *Academic and workplace sexual harassment: A handbook of cultural, social science, management and legal perspectives* (pp. 176–198). Westport, CT: Praeger.

Smith, S., & Mazin, R. (2004). *The HR answer book.* New York: AMACOM.

Trader-Leigh, K. (2002). Identifying resistance in managing change. *Journal of Organizational Change Management, 15,* 138–156.

Williamson, D., Cooke, P., Jenkins, W., & Moreton, K. (2003). *Strategic management and business analysis.* Burlington, MA: Butterworth-Heinemann.

Introduction to Volume 1

Michele A. Paludi and Carmen A. Paludi, Jr.

Education is important because, first of all, people need to know that discrimination still exists. It is still real in the workplace, and we should not take that for granted.

—Alexis Herman

In 2005, Paul Haggis wrote and directed the movie, *Crash,* which asked its viewers to consider the complexities of tolerance. The movie's synopsis included the following description:

A Brentwood housewife and her DA husband. A Persian store owner. Two police detectives who are also lovers. An African- American television director and his wife. A Mexican locksmith. Two car-jackers. A rookie cop. A middle-aged Korean couple. . . . They all live in Los Angeles. And during the next 36 hours, they will all collide. . . . Diving headlong into the diverse melting pot of post-9/11 Los Angeles, this compelling urban drama tracks the volatile intersections of a multi-ethnic cast of characters' struggles to overcome their fears as they careen in and out of one another's lives. In the gray area between black and white, victim and aggressor, there are no easy answers. . . . CRASH boldly reminds us of the importance of tolerance as it ventures beyond color lines . . . and uncovers the truth of our shared humanity. (Celebrity Wonder, 2005)

Crash left unanswered more questions than it answered for its viewers, for example:

- What are the origins of discrimination?
- What prevents individuals from challenging their prejudices about race, ethnicity, age, national origin, disability, and sex?
- How can institutions, such as workplaces, in this society assist individuals in overcoming stereotypes and prejudices about co-workers who are "different" from themselves because of religion, race, national origin, sex, and sexual orientation?
- Under which conditions is race stereotyping likely to occur?

This handbook addresses these questions. The questions stem from our consulting work with academic institutions and businesses as well as from our understanding of the following cases related to workplace discrimination, which received prominent attention in the national media during the preparation of this handbook:

1. In 2009, President Obama signed the Lily Ledbetter Fair Pay Act of 2009. This act allows employees to claim back pay for a period of up to two years before the filing of the claim with the Equal Employment Opportunity Commission. In addition, the act is retroactive, with an effective date of May 28, 2007.

2. On September 25, 2008, President George W. Bush signed a bill amending the Americans with Disabilities Act, which became effective on January 1, 2009.

3. In June 2008, the Supreme Court ruled in favor of 28 employees who lost their jobs during cutbacks at a federal research laboratory in upstate New York, Knolls Atomic Power Laboratory. Twenty-seven of the employees were at least 40 years old, the age at which protections begin under the Age Discrimination in Employment Act.

4. In March 2008, 15 African American and Latino airport employees in Dallas settled a lawsuit for $1.9 million. They alleged that their white co-workers created a hostile work environment by intimidating them with swastikas, nooses, and other racist symbols.

5. In August 2008, Video Only, a home-electronics retailer in Seattle, Washington, was ordered by a Portland judge to pay $630,000 to employees at one of its stores in Jantzen Beach. The employees alleged religious and racial slurs, including a doll with its face and hair painted black, which was hog-tied and hung by a nail in a break room.

6. In November 2008, a federal district court judge in Arizona entered a consent decree for nearly $2 million and remedial relief to resolve a class-based

religious bias lawsuit against the University of Phoenix and Apollo Group, Inc. The suit alleged discrimination against non-Mormon employees.

7. In September 2008, Faiza Abu, who was employed at the Best Western Airport Execuetl in Sea Tac, Washington, refused to take off her hijab, a Muslim head scarf, when her manager informed her the hijab did not work with their new uniforms. She wore the hijab because of religious reasons. According to the lawsuit, Shawn Walters, Ms. Abu's manager stated: "Either you're going to take it off or I'm going to fire you."

Ms. Abu stated: "I didn't take it off—and he fired me."

8. On October 8, 2008, the U.S. Supreme Court heard arguments in *Crawford v. Metro Gov't of Nashville and Davidson County, Tenn.* Vicky Crawford had cooperated in an internal investigation of sexual harassment filed against a human resources director, Gene Hughes. Hughes received no discipline. However, Crawford and three other employees who cooperated with the investigation were fired.

WORKPLACE DISCRIMINATION LEGISLATION

Under Title VII of the Civil Rights Act of 1964, the Americans with Disabilities Act, and the Age Discrimination in Employment Act, it is illegal to discriminate in any aspect of employment, including the following:

- Hiring and Firing
- Compensation, Assignment, or Classification of Employees
- Transfer, Promotion, Layoff, or Recall
- Job Advertisements
- Recruitment
- Testing
- Use of Company Facilities
- Training and Apprenticeship Programs
- Fringe Benefits
- Pay, Retirement Plans, and Disability Leave

In addition to federal legislation, states prohibit discrimination as well (see Volume 1, Appendix B). For example, New York enacted SONDA legislation, the Sexual Orientation Non-Discrimination Act, which prohibits discrimination on the basis of actual or perceived sexual orientation. California, Massachusetts, New Hampshire, New Jersey, and Vermont have similar legislation with respect to sexual orientation.

As another example of state-protected categories, Oregon includes marital status. New Jersey and California added gender identity as a protected

category. New Jersey also includes domestic partnership status and atypi-
cal hereditary cellular or blood trait as protected categories. Rhode Island
and Missouri include AIDS testing as a protected category. Louisiana
includes sickle-cell trait as a protected category. As a final example, political affiliation is a protected category in the District of Columbia.

Discriminatory practices under federal and some state laws also include
the following:

- Harassment on the basis of race, color, religion, sex, national origin, disability, or age
- Retaliation against an individual for filing a charge of discrimination
- Participation in an investigation or opposing discriminatory practices
- Employment decisions based on stereotypes or assumptions about the abilities, traits, or performance of individuals of a certain sex, race, age, sexual
orientation, religion, or ethnic group, or individuals with disabilities
- Denial of employment opportunities to a person because of marriage to, or
association with, an individual of a particular race, religion, or national origin, or an individual with a disability, including HIV/AIDS

HOSTILE WORK ENVIRONMENTS

Behavioral examples of discriminatory treatment include the following:
racial slurs or epithets, unwelcome sexual advances, sexual graffiti, telling jokes pertaining to protected categories, sexually suggestive posters
and engaging in threatening, and intimidating or hostile acts toward an
individual because that person belongs to or is associated with any protected categories.

A hostile work environment may exist for employees when (1) verbal
and or nonverbal behavior in the workplace occurs because of an individual being a member of a protected category, (2) the behavior is
unwanted and unwelcome, and (3) the behavior is severe or pervasive
enough to unreasonably affect the employee's work environment. In
addition, a hostile work environment can be created by an individual's
peers; it does not have to occur only between individuals of unequal
power in the workplace. Furthermore, the hostile environment must be
more than trivial; it has to affect the conditions on an employee's work.
Hostile work environments can occur although the individuals are of the
same race, sex, age, sexual orientation, and so on.

"REASONABLE CARE" IN PREVENTING WORKPLACE DISCRIMINATION

Employers have a legal responsibility to prevent hostile work environments by exercising "reasonable care" through an effective and enforced policy statement, effective and enforced investigatory procedures, and training programs on discrimination and hostile work environments for all members of the workplace. California, Connecticut, and Maine have mandated training, for example, on sexual harassment. California also has defined what it considers to be a qualified trainer—that is, an individual who "either through formal education and training or substantial experience can effectively lead in person (training) or webinars" (Johnson, 2005).

Furthermore, all employers must investigate complaints of discrimination when a complaint is filed and when a supervisor or manager is told of the discrimination, even if this individual is not the official designated complaint officer and even if the complaint is not made in an "official" manner. Thus, once the employer knows, the requirement of responsive action begins. The employer knows when an employee with organizational authority is made aware of the alleged complaint.

The Equal Employment Opportunity Commission (EEOC) demands that investigations be completed promptly, confidentially, and with impartiality. Employers must take measures to ensure that the employee who was subjected to the hostile work environment is "made whole," the legal term for being put into the position they would have been had the harassment not occurred. Once the remedy is undertaken, it is vital that the employee who experienced a hostile work environment know that her or his employer will continue to monitor the situation and pay attention to actions taken with regard to her or his employment situation.

RATIONALE FOR THIS HANDBOOK

Despite these guidelines for investigating complaints of discrimination and establishing preventative measures, statistics indicate that employers may not be properly implementing antidiscrimination laws in their organizations. Individuals may seek resolution through the EEOC after they have exhausted internal procedures. In January 2010, the EEOC published its report dealing with the number of charges of workplace discrimination filed with this agency in 2009 (see Table 1).

These statistics and the cases summarized at the beginning of this Introduction underscore problems that exist in U.S. workplaces. Employees

Table 1
EEOC Complaints of Workplace Discrimination, 2009

Protected Category	Number of Complaints Filed with EEOC in 2009
Age	22,778
Disability	21,451
Equal Compensation	942
National Origin	11,134
Pregnancy	6,196
Race/Color	33,579
Religion	3,386
Retaliation	33,613
Sex	28,028
Sexual Harassment	12,696

Source: EEOC 2010.
Note: Statistics regarding complaints of genetic information discrimination were not available for 2009; this form of discrimination became illegal in November 2009.

experience (1) harassment and discrimination because they are members of protected classes, and (2) retaliation for bringing to their employers' attention their perceived discrimination or harassment. Thus, assistance is required for organizations, including their human resource managers and presidents, to understand how to prevent and deal with workplace discrimination and harassment.

This two-volume handbook seeks to accomplish this goal. Volume 1 of *The Praeger Handbook on Workplace Discrimination* provides an overview of workplace discrimination through an examination of federally protected categories, including age, disability, equal compensation, genetic information, national origin, pregnancy, race/color, religion, sex, and sexual harassment. In addition, the volume includes a discussion of retaliation. Furthermore, Volume 1 offers guidance on state laws that prohibit discrimination and harassment because of individuals' sexual orientation. An overview of state protected classes is presented. The role of the EEOC in seeking resolution for complaints of discrimination and harassment is also discussed. Volume 1 also presents chapters on employers' legal responsibilities to prevent workplace discrimination and to investigate complaints brought to their attention.

Volume 2 offers strategies related to "reasonable care" in terms of preventing workplace discrimination through policies, procedures, and training programs. These strategies are grounded in case law, management theory, and empirical research in the social sciences that are discussed in Volume 1. Resources such as Web sites and organizations devoted to workplace discrimination issues are also provided for the reader.

Chapters in both volumes are written by noted attorneys, human resource managers, scholars, consultants, and academicians who have published extensively in the area of workplace discrimination. Attention is paid to scholarly research, case law, and human resource practices for implementing the law and management theories in the workplace with respect to each type of discrimination. It is a goal of this handbook that the strategies for policies, procedures, and training programs stimulate additional research, advocacy, and legislation in the area of workplace discrimination.

Schingel (2006) noted, with respect to the movie *Crash:* "Until we as a society can take the time to understand the roots of discrimination and take a good look at our own thought patterns, we'll never move forward."

In keeping with Schingel's sentiment, the major goal of this handbook is to provide companies with the tools necessary to prevent as well as deal with all types of discrimination in the workplace.

REFERENCES

Celebrity Wonder. (2005). *Synopsis.* Retrieved September 6, 2009, from http://www.celebritywonder.com/movie/2005_Crash.html.

EEOC (Equal Employment Opportunity Commission). (2010). Retrieved April 18, 2010, from http://www.eeoc.gov.

Johnson, M. (2005). California requires sexual harassment training. *Legal Report,* January-February. Retrieved April 18, 2010, from http://www.usc.edu/ schools/medicine/faculty_staff-resource/equity/calif.pdf.

Schingel, R. (2006). *How the movie Crash illustrates race and ethnic relations in America.* Retrieved September 6, 2009, from http://www.associatedcontent.com/article/18187.

I

Legal Enforcement and Compliance

1

Practical Strategies for Avoiding and Properly Responding to Complaints of Workplace Discrimination

Harry R. Hayes

"Area Erectors, Inc. to Pay $630,000 to Class of Black Workers in Race Discrimination Lawsuit"

"Extra Space Management to Pay $95,000 for Disability Bias Against Employee with Cosmetic Disfigurement"

"Duane Reade to Pay $240,000 to Settle EEOC Lawsuit for Sexual Harassment and Retaliation"

"Ceisel Masonry to Pay $500,000 for Harassment of Hispanic Workers"

"Maverick Tube to Pay $175,000 to Settle EEOC Retaliation Lawsuit"

—from the Equal Employment Opportunity Commission Web site

A random visit to the Equal Employment Opportunity Commission (EEOC) Web site, or any other news resource that reports on employment and workplace litigation, certainly would justify a belief that employers still have a lot to learn about preventing and dealing appropriately with workplace discrimination.[1] During times like the present of contracting economic activity and rising unemployment, history shows that workplace discrimination claims tend to increase. Indeed, the EEOC statistics for federal fiscal year 2008 report a total of 95,402 complaints filed compared with 82,792 in 2007, a 15 percent increase. Proactive employers need to be concerned about two distinct areas when it comes to workplace discrimination. First, do you have proper policies, procedures, and training programs in place *now* before a claim is made, and, second, if a claim is made charging workplace discrimination, do you have adequately trained staff who know how to respond and investigate the claim? Employers with insufficient workplace discrimination avoidance practices or who are unaware of the correct way to handle a discrimination complaint significantly increase their chances of being held liable by courts and juries for unlawful workplace discrimination.

Since the U.S. Supreme Court decisions in *Burlington Industries, Inc. v. Ellerth,* 118 S. Ct. 2257 (1998) and *Faragher v. City of Boca Raton,* 118 S. Ct. 2275 (1998), employers have been on notice of the importance of an effective antiharassment and discrimination policy and, in the event a complaint is made, an appropriate and thorough investigation. If the right policy is in place and "practiced," and a quality investigation occurs, an employer can prevail in certain discrimination cases even if an employee has been victimized by unlawful conduct. That is so in part because Title VII of the Civil Rights Act, according to *Burlington Industries*, "is designed to encourage the creation of anti-harassment policies and effective grievance mechanisms" (*Burlington Industries, Inc. v. Ellerth,* 1998). The Supreme Court phrased the two prongs of the affirmative defense as requiring, first, that employers exercise reasonable care to *prevent* and *promptly correct* the harassment and, second, that employees must make a reasonable effort to take advantage of the employer's preventative or corrective opportunities.[2]

THE EFFECTIVE WORKPLACE POLICY

The first prong of the employer's defense can only be met if the employer has in place a reasonably designed and effective antiharassment policy. No one-size-fits-all policy will protect employers across the board regardless of industry, culture, organizational structure, and size. However, 10 plus years of court cases since *Burlington Industries* and *Faragher* have painted a clear picture of the elements of an effective antiharassment policy.

No workplace discrimination policy should be without a definition of what constitutes "harassment" based on the protected characteristics (age, disability, and so on). Although the policy should have a separate definition of sexual harassment, it is a mistake to draft the policy so that it appears it is applicable only to sexual discrimination. That leaves the employer exposed to a claim that it considers sexual harassment complaints to be more serious or deserving of more protection than other forms of workplace discrimination. The employer's policy should state that employees are strongly encouraged to report any conduct they perceive to be workplace discrimination or harassment.

The policy also should be written in language that will be understood by the intended audience, namely, the average employee, with consideration for age, language, and other factors. If the majority of an employer's workforce consists of teenagers, for example, the complaint procedures are not reasonable if they cannot be understood by the average teenager.[3] An owner of a Burger King franchise, after a claim for sexual harassment was brought against a general manager of the store by a 16-year-old employee, received the following assessment of its complaint procedure from a federal judge:

> An employer can avoid liability under Title VII for harassment (on a ground, such as sex, that constitutes a form of discrimination that the statute forbids) of one of his employees by another by creating a reasonable mechanism by which the victim of the harassment can complain to the company and get relief but which the victim failed to activate. . . .
>
> The mechanism must be reasonable and what is reasonable depends on "the employment circumstances," . . . and therefore, among other things, on the capabilities of the class of employees in question. If they cannot speak English, explaining the complaint procedure to them only in English would not be reasonable. In this case the employees who needed to be able to activate the complaint procedure were teenage girls. . . .
>
> Ignoring this point, the company adopted complaint procedures likely to confuse even adult employees. The employee handbook that new employees are given has a brief section on harassment and states that complaints should be lodged with the "district manager." Who this functionary is and how to communicate with him is not explained. The list of corporate officers and managers at the beginning of the handbook does not list a "district manager," or for that matter a "general manager," but instead a "restaurant manager"; and there is evidence that employees confuse "district manager" with "restaurant [or general] manager"—that is, Wilkins, the harasser. There is a phone number on the cover of the handbook, and if you call it you get a receptionist or a recorded message at V&J's headquarters. But an employee would not know whom to ask for at headquarters because she is not told who her district manager is or the district of the restaurant at which she works.[4]

The court in *EEOC v. V&J Foods* (2007) expressed additional difficulties with the employer's complaint mechanism but the lesson is evident. The policy must spell out an effective and understandable complaint procedure for employees. At a minimum, employees should be given more than one avenue of making a complaint outside the employee's own chain of command. If an employee's supervisor is the only choice provided, and the supervisor is the alleged harasser, the complaint process is deficient. At a minimum, an employer ought to designate by name and contact information at least two other individuals authorized to receive such complaints, including the chief human resources staff person. A small business of up to approximately 75 employees should also allow employees to bring discrimination complaints directly to its chief executive officer or president.

An additional point deserves emphasis when it comes to the employer's avenues for employee complaints. It is common for larger companies to offer employees a toll-free number to call if they have problems in the workplace or to emphasize that they follow an open-door policy through which employees are free to approach managers at any time with their concerns. Providing employees with those types of options to bring forward all forms of general complaints does not satisfy an employer's obligation to have in place an effective complaint process for dealing with workplace discrimination. "Progressive claims that its 'open door policy' and company 'hotline' were both avenues for processing such complaints. . . . Such avenues of complaint, geared not specifically towards sexual harassment complaints, but instead to any run-of-the-mill behavior an employee deems inappropriate, are insufficient" (*Bennett v. The Progressive Corporation,* 2002).

In the policy, always spell out what disciplinary measures will be taken if harassment has taken place and assure employees that the employer will take prompt and immediate corrective measures when discrimination has occurred. As in all cases of inappropriate workplace behavior, discipline should be graduated and progressive. Harassment that is primarily verbal, for example, may not need to be dealt with as harshly as harassment that involves physical contact. A supervisor who uses his or her position of authority to compel a sexual relationship out of an unwilling subordinate should in most cases be disciplined more severely than an employee who tries to force a personal relationship on a co-worker. The policy should be clear that the employer reserves the right to impose any discipline deemed appropriate under the circumstances, up to and including termination of employment.

The end of the policy should include a statement that no retaliation will be taken or tolerated against anyone who brings a good-faith complaint of discrimination or harassment. Some employers include a provision that employees who make false or unsubstantiated complaints are subject to discipline, including termination of employment. That is better left out of any written policy because it can easily be interpreted as a subtle threat or at least a dissuader. The point is made by stating the protection extends to "good-faith" complaints. Employees should be assured that, to the extent possible, complaints of discrimination and harassment will be treated with confidentiality. Complete confidentiality cannot and should not be promised, even when an employee requests that a complaint or concern "stay between us" or not be reported up the chain of command.

A workplace discrimination and harassment policy must be disseminated to employees.[5] A variety of methods can accomplish this, including making sure new hires are given a copy, posting the policy throughout work areas on bulletin boards, featuring it on an employee intranet site or web portal, and highlighting it during training sessions. Redistribute the policy on a regular basis with the employee handbook. Effective dissemination means that if any employee subsequently makes a complaint, the employer is in the position to prove that more likely than not, the complaining employee was aware of the policy. It is sufficient to have a signed acknowledgment of receipt of an employee handbook that contains the policy or a new hire orientation form signed off by a human resources manager stating the policy was discussed and explained. Oral testimony that the company's workplace harassment policy was contained in a handbook or manual, and that it was company practice to give all new employees a copy of the manual, is not sufficient, particularly in the absence of a signed receipt.[6]

Like any employee handbook policy, training managers on workplace discrimination and the employer's specific policy should not be overlooked. An untrained manager can derail the employer's ability to defend a discrimination claim in a myriad of ways. Managers should be coached on how to recognize potential harassment; they should know the importance of responding to or reporting immediately any potential situation that could lead to a discrimination complaint; they should be able to explain the complaint process to an employee and direct them to appropriate company officials with their complaints if necessary, and they should refrain from judging on their own the validity of potential claims that should undergo the employer's investigation process. Employers should never assume that managers are equipped to handle potential discrimination in the workplace just because they have been given a copy of an employee handbook with the employer's policy.

INVESTIGATING COMPLAINTS

Employers continue to lose workplace discrimination cases simply because they fail to conduct a quality investigation after receiving a complaint. It is wrong to automatically assume that human resources personnel are up to the task of investigating such claims. Discrimination complaints, particularly complaints of sexual harassment, typically are difficult to resolve unless the accused comes right out and admits to the offending conduct. Hostile environment harassment cases, in which nonphysical behavior is involved, are never simple, quick, or easy to investigate, even for someone with prior experience. Dropping such a complaint on the desk of an employee who has no training or experience in conducting an investigation of similar complaints is guaranteed to result in an inadequate investigation and legal difficulty for the employer.[7]

Many commentators on this issue recommend that employers hire an attorney to investigate a workplace discrimination claim or at least oversee the investigation. As a practicing attorney, I have heard legitimate arguments for and against doing that. One difficulty with using outside counsel in such a situation is that employees who are interviewed as part of the investigation can feel intimidated, nervous, or reluctant to be completely candid. It seems a better option, if available, is to use an investigator from inside the company who most people will perceive as objective and unbiased because chances are that witnesses will be more forthcoming and accurate with their recollections under that scenario.

Skilled investigators have solid writing and interpersonal skills, as well as some degree of expertise, knowledge, or experience in conducting investigations. They should be good listeners and have been with the company long enough to be familiar with its culture, policies, politics, and staff. Investigators ought to have received some training or education in discrimination laws, particularly Title VII. They must have an understanding and appreciation for the concept of confidentiality. At the onset of the investigation, a road map or methodology should be established for how the investigation is going to be conducted. People who are going to interview witnesses, which will include the person making the complaint and the alleged harasser, need to have a general format to follow for conducting interviews. And more important, the employer's investigator must be a credible witness if the matter ends up in litigation.

In cases in which a fact-finding investigation is necessary, it should be started as soon as possible. In some instances, it makes sense to separate the complainant and the accused during an investigation, particularly if a small office setting is involved. If that is appropriate, the person making the complaint should not be the one who is transferred or taken out of their normal work location because that could be viewed as unlawful retaliation later. Temporarily transferring the accused, adjusting work schedules, or extending the accused a nondisciplinary leave with pay are better options.

Interviews of witnesses should be conducted away from the workplace and in a confidential and comfortable location. All interviews should be conducted by the company's primary investigator, but at least two company representatives should be present to remove the chance that an important fact will be missed in the note-taking. Witnesses should never be interviewed in a group. Every witness should be told that their statements probably will have to be shared with attorneys for the company at some point and will be the basis for a final report after the investigation is over. Taking written notes during the interview is far more preferable to tape or video recording the sessions, which seems to put most people under stress. If necessary, witnesses can be told that they may be asked to sign a typed version of their statement.

The EEOC has issued guidelines that in part address how to conduct an adequate investigation of discrimination claims.[8] A portion of those guidelines include suggested questions to pose to the person making the complaint, any witnesses, and the accused. An effective investigator is one who focuses on uncovering the facts, namely, what happened, who was involved, and when, where, and how the incident occurred. According to the EEOC guidelines, appropriate questions include the following:

- **For the employee making the complaint:** Who, what, when, where, and how: Who committed the alleged harassment? What exactly occurred or was said? When did it occur and is it still ongoing? Where did it occur? How often did it occur? How did it affect you? What response did you make when the incident occurred? Has your job been affected in any way? Did anyone witness any of the incidents? Did you tell anyone about it? Did anyone see you after it took place? Do you have any notes, physical evidence or other documents regarding this? Do you know if this person has harassed anyone else? How would you like to see the situation resolved?

- **For the employee accused of improper behavior:** What is your response to the allegations? Why would the person making the complaint lie about this? Do you know of any potential witnesses or people who would have relevant information? Do you have any notes, physical evidence, or other documents that relate to this?

- **For witnesses:** What did you see or hear? When did it occur? Describe the accused's behavior toward the complainant. Did the complainant tell you anything about this? What and when? Do you know of any witnesses to this? Did anyone else talk to you about it? Do you have any other relevant information about this?

An investigator should not say a number of things during these interviews. Other than telling the accused what the accusations are, a statement by a witness should not be disclosed to another witness. An investigator should refrain from offering a witness any personal opinion as to how the investigation is progressing, the merits of the complaint, the believability of other witnesses, or the likelihood of any particular outcome.

After all the relevant witnesses have been interviewed and the investigator has reviewed whatever pertinent information came to light during the investigation, a written report summarizing his or her findings should be prepared. The report should recite the allegations, the relevant statements of the witnesses, the response of the accused, the existence of documents or other evidence bearing on the matter and why they are significant, and the facts that can be reasonably determined as a result of the investigation.

On that last point, perhaps the most difficult part of drafting the report will be resolving conflicting versions of what took place. Investigators often are required to resolve credibility determinations, and harassment cases frequently have a "he-said, she-said" aspect to them. If the two conflicting versions have to be resolved in the report (not all will), look for testimony from other witnesses or documentary evidence that supports one version over another. Make a mental note during interviews as to the demeanor of the witness during the questioning. Which ones seemed candid and genuine as opposed to those who appeared nervous, seemed anxious, or avoided eye contact? Does the witness statement make sense, particularly when it is reviewed in context with all the other information? Does anyone have a motive not to tell the truth or to withhold any information? Have the witnesses been involved in any other workplace situations that reflect on their credibility? Have other people complained about the same employee accused in this case?

The investigator should avoid coming to a conclusion in the report as to whether workplace discrimination has occurred or recommending a resolution of the matter. Management should make the ultimate decision as to whether the company's policy has been violated and what steps will be taken going forward. The input of the investigator, including the report, will need to be a part of that process.

Not every investigation will enable management to come to a definitive conclusion as to what happened or whether the company's policy has been violated. Investigators should allow for that possibility before they even start their work. That does not mean the employer should do nothing. After a complaint is made, even one determined not to have violated company policy, the employer can revisit its employee training and keep an eye on the interactions between the complainant and the accused. If the employee who brought the complaint was adversely affected in any way by the conduct of the accused, the employer ought to try to remedy that situation (for example, additional paid leave if work time was lost). Regardless of the final determination by management, both the complaining party and the accused should be told the results of the investigation and management's decision. Other witnesses do not need to know the outcome.

In those cases in which management concludes that its workplace discrimination policy was violated, the employer's obligation is to come up with a remedy that is designed to stop the offending behavior and ensure that it not take place again. The severity of these remedial measures will depend on the conduct. An employee with no history of offending behavior who e-mails a sexually suggestive joke to a co-worker probably requires nothing more severe than a verbal reprimand and a refresher on the company's e-mail and harassment policy. Someone who has engaged in a persistent campaign of offensive and severe harassment against an individual because of gender, race, or age may require a suspension without pay or termination of employment. The goal for the employer is to demonstrate that workplace discrimination will not be tolerated and that, when it takes place, management will react immediately and appropriately.

NOTES

1. "Workplace discrimination" for our purposes includes claims tracked by the EEOC based on race, sex, national origin, religion, retaliation, age, disability, and claims filed under the Equal Pay Act.

2. Burlington and Faragher involved sexual harassment, but the decisions have been applied to other forms of workplace discrimination.

3. See EEOC v. V&J Foods Inc., 507 F.3d 575 (7th Cir. 2007).

4. Ibid.

5. See Hill v. The Children's Village, 196 F. Supp.2d 389, 399 (S.D.N.Y. 2002).

6. Bennett v. The Progressive Corporation, 225 F.Supp.2d 190 (N.D.N.Y. 2002).

7. "[T]he person alleged to be the central figure in the investigation into plaintiff's complaint . . . had no experience investigating sexual harassment complaints, and had only been working at Progressive for four or five months." Bennett v. The Progressive Corporation, 225 F.Supp.2d 190 (N.D.N.Y. 2002).

8. *EEOC Guidance on Vicarious Employer Liability for Unlawful Harassment by Supervisors*, EEOC Notice No. 915.002 (June 18, 1999).

REFERENCES

Bennett v. The Progressive Corporation, 225 F.Supp.2d 190 (N.D.N.Y. 2002).

Burlington Industries, Inc. v. Ellerth, 118 S. Ct. 2257 (1998).

EEOC (Equal Employment Opportunity Commission). (1999). *EEOC Guidance on Vicarious Employer Liability for Unlawful Harassment by Supervisors*. Washington, DC: U.S. Government Printing Office.

EEOC v. V&J Foods Inc., 507 F.3d 575 (7th Cir. 2007).

Faragher v. City of Boca Raton, 118 S. Ct. 2275 (1998).

Hill v. The Children's Village, 196 F. Supp.2d 389, 399 (S.D.N.Y. 2002).

2

Resources for Targets of Sexual Harassment

Margaret S. Stockdale and Lynda M. Sagrestano

Given the prevalence and insidious effects of sexual harassment in the workplace and in academic environments, it is essential for everyone to have clear information about how to handle incidents of unwanted social-sexual behavior regardless of whether it is labeled as sexual harassment. Moreover, according to U.S. law, employers may not be held liable for harassing conduct that does not affect a tangible employment consequence, if the employee filing a claim of harassment "unreasonably failed to take advantage of any preventive or corrective opportunities provided or to avoid harm" (*Burlington Industries, Inc. v. Ellerth,* 1998, p. 745). Therefore, employees who want to preserve their option of pursuing a legal claim of sexual harassment need to understand how to mobilize the preventative or corrective opportunities available to them in their organizations.

In this chapter, we discuss the strategies and resources that targets of sexual harassment may rely on to deal with incidents of harassment. First, we discuss options for targets to attempt to resolve the problem within their institutions. Second, we outline the basic steps for filing a legal claim of sexual harassment against one's employer or academic institution. Third, we discuss alternative dispute resolution mechanisms for resolving complaints of sexual harassment.

COPING AND RESPONDING TO SEXUAL HARASSMENT WITHIN THE INSTITUTION

Strategies for dealing with sexual harassment have been the focus of a fair amount of discussion but little empirical research on their relative effectiveness. Building on theoretical and descriptive research categorizing various ways that targets handle harassing conduct, Knapp, Faley, Ekeberg, and Dubois (1997) offered a two-dimensional framework of target responses to sexual harassment (described below). Empirical research by other scholars has largely supported the view that targets tend to respond to harassment in unassertive ways, and that they reserve assertive, confrontational responses for more severe forms of mistreatment (Cortina & Wasti, 2005; Magley, 2002).

The first dimension in Knapp et al.'s (1997) model distinguished between the mode of response, handled by one's self or with support from others, and the focus of the response—toward the self or toward the initiator. This conceptualization resulted in four types of responses. The first, least assertive category of responses is labeled *avoidance-denial*. Here, the target "goes it alone" and focuses only on her (or his) reaction to the harassment. This is a common response among those who fear retaliation or negative repercussions for taking more assertive action. Although the avoidant strategy appears to be both common and ineffective, self-focused, self-managed response strategies may have a role. Positive self-talk in which the target engages in self-affirming behavior that reminds herself (or himself) that she or he is not to blame for the harassing treatment may mobilize the target to take more assertive and effective actions.

The second category of responses to sexual harassment includes strategies that remained focused on the self (target of harassment) but involve getting help from other people. This category is called *social coping* (Knapp et al., 1997) or *support seeking* (Cortina & Wasti, 2005). Such strategies involve seeking help from friends, co-workers, or even professionals to help the target make sense of the harassment and perhaps devise strategies for responding more effectively or to manage the negative personal consequences of harassment such as depression, anxiety, and post-traumatic stress disorder. Supportive others can provide more instrumental help by agreeing to go with targets to discuss their concerns with a supervisor or compliance officer or to confront the initiator directly. Progressive organizations may facilitate social coping methods by having trained sexual harassment advisors, ombudsmen, or affinity groups such as a "women's council" with whom targets can speak confidentially and obtain advice on various options (Kihnley, 2000).

Confrontation/negotiation is the third category of responses identified by Knapp et al. (1997), in which the target of harassment deals directly with the initiator through such strategies as telling the person directly that the behavior is unwelcome and unwanted, threatening to report the person to authorities, or engaging in some other direct behavior toward the initiator. Although direct confrontation may appear risky to the victim (Cortina & Magley, 2003), statutory protections are in place against retaliation, and because the victim could file a claim of retaliation (West, 2002), courts generally do not accept a plaintiff's "fear of retaliation" for not taking assertive action to attempt to end the harassment. Effective direct confrontation typically occurs when the offensive behavior includes speech and expression, and the organization encourages and supports direct intervention (Rowe, 1996). In addition, targets should not wait for the harassment to escalate before confronting the initiator. A tactful mention that one's actions were offensive, unwanted, or uninvited when the harassing conduct first occurs may nip the harassment in the bud while allowing the target and the initiator to save face and preserve their working or academic relationship.

The final category of response strategies discussed by Knapp et al. (1997), *advocacy seeking*, represents an initiator-focused, supportive mode of response. With these strategies, targets rely on institutional support and remedies, such as filing a formal complaint against the initiator. As with direct confrontational/negotiation strategies, advocacy-seeking strategies are considered to be effective but rarely are used (Knapp et al., 1997). For employees to preserve their option of filing a federal Title VII claim of sexual harassment against their institution (that did not result in a tangible job consequence), it is critical for them to take advantage of their institutions' resources, such as a complaint procedure. We turn our attention next to options that targets may pursue outside of the institution in which the harassment occurs.

RESPONDING TO SEXUAL HARASSMENT BEYOND THE INSTITUTION

Persons who believe that their rights to harassment-free work or educational environments have been violated may file a complaint with an agency that will either investigate and possibly file a lawsuit on behalf of the complainant or permit the complainant to file his or her own law-suit. In this section, we outline the basic steps for filing a complaint of sexual harassment with a federal or state agency for both employment and educational contexts. Furthermore, we discuss alternative dispute resolution processes that are used to resolve sexual harassment (and other discrimination) disputes.

Filing a Legal Complaint of Workplace Sexual Harassment

The Equal Employment Opportunity Commission (EEOC) is the federal agency that enforces employment discrimination laws. Most states also have laws against employment discrimination, including sexual harass-ment, and have Fair Employment Practices Agencies (FEPAs) that pro-cess claims of sexual harassment and other forms of discrimination. According to federal law, an individual must file their complaint within 180 days of the last alleged act of discrimination or harassment. If their claim is also covered by a state or local law, that deadline is extended to 300 days. Most states have a work-sharing agreement with the EEOC such that a claim filed with the EEOC is simultaneously filed with the ap-plicable state FEPA and vice versa (EEOC, 2007). To file a complaint, individuals can complete a questionnaire (available at https://apps.eeoc. gov/eas/) that screens complaints for the appropriate law, and requires that complainants provide their name and contact information, name and con-tact information of the institution in which the alleged harassment occurred (respondent employer, employment agency, or union), a short description of the harassing situation(s), and the date(s) of the alleged ha-rassment. Employers with fewer than 15 employees are exempt from EEO law. Federal employees or applicants for federal jobs have different filing requirements and should consult their local EEOC office or visit this Web site for more information: http://www.eeoc.gov/facts/fs-fed.html.

Once the EEOC or state FEPA receives the complaint, they will deter-mine whether the allegations warrant an investigation. In some cases, the EEOC will conduct the investigation itself and may decide to litigate on behalf of the complainant, in which case the plaintiff now becomes the EEOC. Typically, the EEOC or FEPA will not investigate the com-plaint, but instead will issue a "right to sue" letter to the complainant indicating that the complainant has fulfilled their duty to file with the EEOC/FEPA and therefore can pursue litigation as a private citizen. Before the EEOC pursues litigation, however, they will urge the parties to attempt to resolve the case through mediation. Mediation is a form of *alternative dispute resolution* (ADR) in which a trained, neutral third party helps the disputing parties achieve a voluntary, negotiated agreement. ADR is discussed in more detail in the next section, "Alternative Dispute Resolution."

If a mediated agreement or settlement is unavailing and the EEOC or the complainant decides to litigate her or his claim of sexual harassment, both the plaintiff (the party bringing the lawsuit) and the defendant (the party defending against the lawsuit) can use a number of procedural, legal maneuvers to try to advance or stop the case from proceeding to trial. It is beyond the scope of this chapter to explain these procedures in detail, but parties considering litigation should understand that only a small proportion of cases of employment discrimination (sexual harassment or otherwise) make it to trial. Research finds that only about 6 percent of employment discrimination claims (of which sexual harassment is a type) make it to trial (with plaintiffs winning only one-third of the time) (Nelson, Nielsen, & Lancaster, 2007).

Alternative Dispute Resolution

ADR is a class of mechanisms by which disputes may be settled outside of the official legal system, including negotiations, settlement conferences, mediation, and arbitration. Whereas negotiations and settlement conferences can be conducted between the disputing parties or their representatives (for example, attorneys), mediation and arbitration involve a neutral third party who either helps the parties reach an agreement that settles the dispute (mediation) or determines the outcome for the parties (arbitration). The EEOC and many FEPAs provide mediation services when they deem a claim to be meritorious, and the EEOC's mediation program is free if both the complainant and the employer agree to participate. Beiner and O'Connor (2007) recently comprehensively summarized the role of mediation and arbitration in sex discrimination cases. We highlight their main points here.

Mediation   Mediation is a form of a settlement conference and all information revealed in such conferences is considered confidential and cannot be used in court if the case is eventually litigated. As such, with the help of a trained, neutral facilitator the parties in the dispute, which may be aided by their own legal counsel, tend to open up and develop creative, satisfactory solutions. Indeed, many solutions do not involve a monetary outcome and may be as simple as a sincere apology from the employer

(Beiner & O'Connor, 2007, citing an EEOC evaluation of their mediation program). Mediation involves both face-to-face interactions in which the parties discuss their own concerns and possible solutions, as well as "caucuses" in which the mediator meets privately with each party so that confidential information may be discussed that a party does not wish to reveal to the opposing party. Evaluators of the EEOC mediation program note that the revelation of important information during the mediation process as well as openness, flexibility, and a problem-solving demeanor on the part of both parties are important factors for reaching effective solutions (McDermott, Obar, Jose, & Polkinghorn, 2001). Other studies of mediation find that charging parties (employees) tend to be more willing to engage in mediation than defendants (employers), but of those who have participated in mediation, 96 percent stated that they would be willing to do so again (McDermott, Obar, Jose, & Bowers, 2000). Finally, Beiner and O'Connor (2007) remind us that parties may utilize mediation programs other than those provided by the EEOC.

Arbitration   Arbitration is a quasi-legal process that lies somewhere between mediation and litigation (Beiner & O'Connor, 2007). Like mediation, the process involves a neutral third party (arbitrator), is usually quicker than litigation, and is less costly than a formal trial. Like litigation, there is a winner and a loser, and parties can be represented by legal counsel, present evidence, and cross-examine witnesses. Employees and employers can agree to arbitration after or before the dispute arises, such as by an employment contract or collective bargaining agreement. Arbitration agreements usually are not overturned by a court unless the arbitrator completely disregarded the law, although courts have not always enforced employment contracts that require arbitration for employment discrimination disputes. The costs of arbitration can be split by both parties (often with the employer footing more of the bill) or entirely by the employer, but concern has been raised that impartiality may be jeopardized if one party pays the entire bill (Beiner & O'Connor, 2007). Employers may be at an advantage if the arbitrator is one they have worked with before (Bingham, 1998), and therefore it is important that complainants be fully apprised of the factors that potentially may bias an arbitrator's decision against them. Having legal representation when entering or contemplating an arbitration agreement, therefore, is important.

Although ADR (such as mediation and arbitration) has many advantages over traditional litigation, it also has drawbacks. In particular, Beiner and

O'Connor (2007) argue that because the disputes are settled informally and confidentially, no one but the immediate parties benefit (or suffer) from the outcome. Findings that may serve as a deterrent for other would-be harassers or as an incentive for other would-be complainants to bring their cases to light are not made public. Furthermore, no legal precedent is established that may guide the legal interpretation of future cases. Despite these concerns, however, ADR is often considered a preferred way to manage employment discrimination cases, including sexual harassment.

CONCLUSION

Sexual harassment is a difficult but not insurmountable problem to tackle. People who believe that they have been sexually harassed minimally should seek the advice and support of a knowledgeable and trusted co-worker or official to help them consider either informal or formal ways to resolve their concerns. If efforts fail to resolve the problem through the organization's complaint resolution procedures, then aggrieved parties should seek redress through legal means. State fair employment practices agencies or local EEOC offices should be consulted for filing employment discrimination claims. Armed with a reasonable understanding of the personal, organizational, and legal means to resolve sexual harassment complaints, individuals should be well equipped to effectively end the offending behavior and enjoy the privileges of a productive work environment.

NOTE

This chapter is adapted from Stockdale, M.S., & Sagrestano, L. M. (in press). Strategies and resources for institutions and targets of sexual harassment in employment and education. In M. Paludi, & F. Denmark (Eds.), *Victims of sexual assault and abuse: Resources and responses for individuals and families.* Westport, CT: Praeger.

REFERENCES

Beiner, T. M., & O'Connor, M. (2007). When an individual finds herself to be the victim of sex discrimination. In F. J. Crosby, M. S. Stockdale, & S. A. Ropp (Eds.), *Sex Discrimination in the workplace* (pp. 19–56). Malden, MA: Blackwell.

Bingham, L. B. (1998). On repeat players, adhesive contracts, and the use of statistics in judicial review of employment arbitration awards. *McGeorge Law Review, 29,* 223–259.

Burlington Industries, Inc. v. Ellerth, 524 U.S. 742 (1998).

Cortina, L. M., & Magley, V. (2003). Raising voice, risking retaliation: Events following interpersonal mistreatment in the workplace. *Journal of Occupational Health Psychology, 8,* 247–265.

Cortina, L. M., & Wasti, S. A. (2005). Profiles in coping: Responses to sexual harassment across persons, organizations, and cultures. *Journal of Applied Psychology, 90,* 182–192.

EEOC (Equal Employment Opportunity Commission). (2007). *Filing a charge of employment discrimination.* Retrieved May 18, 2009, from http://www.eeoc.gov/charge/overview_charge_filing.html.

Kihnley, J. (2000). Unraveling the ivory fabric: Institutional obstacles to the handling of sexual harassment complaints. *Law & Social Inquiry, 25,* 69–90.

Knapp, D. E., Faley, R. H., Ekeberg, S. E., & Dubois, C. L. Z. (1997). Determinants of target responses to sexual harassment: A conceptual framework. *Academy of Management Review, 22,* 687–729.

Magley, V. J. (2002). Coping with sexual harassment: Reconceptualizing women's resistance. *Journal of Personality and Social Psychology, 83,* 930–946.

McDermott, E. P., Obar, R., Jose, A., & Bower, M. (2000, September 20). *An evaluation of the Equal Employment Opportunity Commission mediation program.* Retrieved May 27, 2009, from http://www.eeoc.gov/mediate/report/index.html.

McDermott, E. P., Obar, R., Jose, A., & Polkinghorn, B. (2001, August 1). *The EEOC mediation program: Mediators' perspective on the parties, processes, and outcomes.* Retrieved May 27, 2009, from http://www.eeoc.gov/mediate/mcdfinal.html.

Nelson, R. L., Nielsen, L., & Lancaster, R. (2007, July). Uncertain justice: The determinants of outcomes in federal employment discrimination litigation, 1987–2003. *Paper presented at the annual meeting of the Law and Society Association, Berlin, Germany.*

Rowe, M. P. (1996). Dealing with sexual harassment: A systems approach. In M. Stockdale (Ed.), *Sexual harassment in the workplace* (pp. 241–271). Thousand Oaks, CA: Sage.

West, M. S. (2002). Preventing sexual harassment: The federal courts' wake-up call for women. *Brooklyn Law Review, 68,* 457–523.

II

Managing Discrimination in the Workplace: Policies and Training Programs

3

Responding to Racial, Gender, and Sexual Orientation Microaggressions in the Workplace

Kevin Leo Yabut Nadal

Previous literature has suggested that while overt discrimination is still pervasive in present U.S. society, discrimination has taken more subtle and indirect forms (Nadal, 2008; Nadal, 2010; Nadal, Rivera, & Corpus, in press; Sue et al., 2007; Swim & Cohen, 1997; Swim, Mallet, & Stagnor, 2004). Given that political correctness has become omnipresent in contemporary times, it is less acceptable for people to be overtly racist, sexist, or heterosexist. Individuals may still hold prejudices on the basis of race, gender, sexual orientation, and other identities, however, that manifest unconsciously in their interactions with others (Nadal, 2008).

Several terms have been used to define the "new" form racism that has become more present in our society. Modern racism (McConahay, 1986), symbolic racism (Sears, 1988), and aversive racism (Dovidio, Gaertner, Kawakami, & Hodson, 2002) all emphasize that racism is likely to be masked and subtle, in comparison to how it may have been 30 years ago. While cross burnings, lynchings, and racial slurs may have been common in the 20th century, these types of behaviors are looked upon negatively, particularly for whites who consider themselves "good, moral, and decent human beings" (Sue et al., 2007, p. 275). Although whites may not condone or participate in racial hate crimes or other forms of conscious racism, they may not recognize the racial prejudices they still hold subconsciously. For example, although many whites may have voted for Barack Obama in the 2008 election, some still may object to their children entering interracial relationships with African Americans.

Sexism also has taken more implicit forms and may be hard to identify (Nadal, 2010). Covert sexism is less obvious in that sexist thoughts and acts are often unconscious by the enactor (Swim & Cohen, 1997). This can be demonstrated by a man who asserts himself as a "liberal" yet still expects women to maintain traditional gender roles. Subtle sexism refers to incidents, thoughts, or behaviors that are considered normative because they generally are acceptable and tolerated by members of society (Swim et al., 2004). For example, while many in society may realize that women get paid less than men in the same position, this reality may be accepted as normal or nondebatable. Benevolent sexism is defined as a chivalrous ideology in which men encourage women to embrace conventional roles (Glick & Fiske, 2001). When a man offers to help a woman carry a box, he believes he is being polite, yet he is sending the message that woman are physically incapable or inferior. Finally, hostile sexism is defined as antagonism toward women who are viewed as taking away men's power (Glick & Fiske, 2001). This can be demonstrated by a man who feels threatened by a female supervisor's power and tries to belittle her or damage her reputation.

This same type of subtle heterosexist discrimination is also widespread toward lesbian, gay, bisexual, and transgender (LGBT) persons. Some common terms that are used are sexual prejudice, sexual stigma, antigay harassment, and heterosexist harassment (Nadal et al., in press). Sexual prejudice and sexual stigma involve negative thoughts, feelings, and stereotypes that individuals may have about LGBT persons (Herek, 2007). For example, when heterosexual people believe that LGBT people are "immoral" or "abnormal," they hold negative thoughts that affect their behaviors and interactions with LGBT persons. Antigay harassment is classified as "verbal or physical behavior that injures, interferes with, or intimidates lesbian women, gay men, and bisexual individuals" (Burn, Kadlec, & Rexer, 2005, p. 24), while heterosexist harassment is defined as "insensitive verbal and symbolic (but non-assaultive) behaviors that convey animosity toward non-heterosexuality" (Silverschanz, Cortina, Konik, & Magley, 2007, p. 179). Both of these terms involve behavioral discrimination that may occur toward LGBT persons (for example, someone yelling a homophobic slur at an LGBT person or someone who stares at a LGBT couple in disgust).

As a result of all of these terms, a new concept has been introduced to describe the covert and indirect forms of discrimination that occur in contemporary society. Microaggressions are "brief and commonplace daily verbal, behavioral, or environmental indignities (whether intentional or unintentional) that communicate hostile, derogatory, or negative racial slights and insults toward members of oppressed groups" (Nadal, 2008, p. 23). Originally modeled from research on racial microaggressions (see Sue et al., 2007), microaggressions may exist toward all oppressed or target groups, including racial and ethnic minorities, women, LGBT persons, persons with disabilities, and religious minorities (Nadal, 2008). The purpose of this chapter is to discuss racial, gender, and sexual orientation microaggressions and their potential impacts on the workplace. While acknowledging that other microaggressions exist (for example, religious microaggressions, ability microaggressions, and social class microaggressions), the chapter will review the literature on racial, gender, and sexual orientation microaggressions and provide practical strategies and interventions on how to confront microaggressions in workplace settings.

PREVIOUS RESEARCH ON RACIAL, GENDER, AND SEXUAL ORIENTATION MICROAGGRESSIONS

Previous literature on racial microaggressions identifies three forms of microaggressions: microassaults, microinsults, and microinvalidations (Sue et al., 2007). These types of microaggressions may apply to gender and sexual orientation as well. Microassaults are overt forms of discrimination in which perpetrators knowingly act or behave in racist, sexist, or heterosexist ways; this is similar to "old-fashioned" discrimination. Microinsults are statements or behaviors in which perpetrators unknowingly send racist, sexist, or heterosexist messages to members of oppressed groups. For example, when a store owner follows a black or Latino customer around a store (but does not follow white customers), she or he is sending the message that African Americans or Latinos are criminals. Microinvalidations are statements that negate or nullify the realities of members of oppressed groups. For example, when a man tells a woman that sexism does not exist, he is invalidating and denying her experiences with sexism.

Previous literature has revealed various categories or themes of microaggressions that may be directed toward people of color, women, and LGBT persons. Examples of racial microaggressions include *assumptions of intellectual inferiority* (when people of color are assumed to be less intelligent or capable than whites); *pathologizing cultural values* (when people of color are criticized for their communication styles, behaviors, or styles of dress); and *assumptions of criminality* (when people of color are assumed to be dangerous or deviant; Sue et al., 2007). Gender microaggressions that women may encounter on a regular basis include the following: *sexual objectification* (when a woman is treated as a sexual object); *invisibility* (when men are given preferential treatment in a company); *assumptions of traditional gender roles* (when an individual assumes that a woman needs to uphold traditional gender roles); and *assumptions of inferiority* (when a woman is assumed to be physically or intellectually less competent than men; Nadal, 2010). Sexual orientation microaggressions include the following: *use of heterosexist terminology* (when heterosexist language like "faggot" or "dyke" is used to degrade LGBT persons); *endorsement of heteronormative culture and behaviors* (when LGBT persons are expected to be or act like heterosexuals); *discomfort with or disapproval of LGBT experience* (when LGBT individuals are treated with disrespect or condemnation because of their sexual orientation or gender presentation); and *assumption of sexual pathology and abnormality* (when LGBT persons are presumed to be oversexualized, to be sexual deviants, or to have HIV/AIDS; Nadal et al., in press). Environmental microaggressions, which are directed toward people of color, women, LGBT persons, and other oppressed groups, are systemic and institutional forms of discrimination that send negative messages toward and about members of these target groups (Nadal, 2008). For example, when the media negatively portrays people of color, women, or LGBT persons in stereotypical ways, or when educational institutions focus primarily on white, European American history, individuals of these oppressed groups are made to feel inferior, exoticized, or invisible.

Literature on microaggressions has suggested that the intersections of microaggressions may influence the severity or intensity of microaggressions. Women of color may experience dual microaggressions, as a result of their gender and race (for example, an Asian woman who is ignored service because of both her race and gender, or when a white co-worker tells an African American woman that her hairstyle is "unprofessional"). Similarly, LGBT persons of color may experience dual microaggressions. For example, when a black lesbian was the victim of a hate crime and the news media did not cover or publicize it as much as when a white gay male was a hate crime victim, an indirect message is sent that one individual is valued over the other (Nadal et al., in press).

PRACTICAL APPROACHES TO GENDER AND SEXUAL ORIENTATION MICROAGGRESSIONS

Given the various forms of microaggressions, what is someone supposed to do when she or he is the victim of a microaggression? In an article on racial microaggressions, Sue et al. (2007) discussed the catch-22 that people of color experience when they witness or are victims of micro-aggressions. For instance, one may question whether a microaggression really occurred, and if the victim believes it did, she or he has to debate whether to take action. This type of process would likely be similar for gender and sexual orientation microaggressions. Thus, a person of color, woman, or LGBT person who experiences a microaggression may ask her or himself the following:

- Did this microaggression really occur?
- Should I respond to this microaggression?
- How should I respond to this microaggression?

This next section will attempt to answer some of these questions and provide suggestions for women and LGBT persons when they experience microaggressions.

DID THIS MICROAGGRESSION REALLY OCCUR?

Sometimes microaggressions may be so glaringly obvious that a person can identify them easily. For example, a woman who notices a male co-worker visibly staring at her breasts when he talks with her may be able to identify this as a microaggression. She knows that he is treating her like a sexual object and feels uncomfortable or dehumanized. Similarly, when a white employer consistently mixes up the names of his Latino employees, the employee may recognize this as being racially motivated, because the employer does not confuse the names of whites in the office.

In many incidents, individuals may question whether a microaggression even happened. For example, if a gay male hears someone yell "Faggot!" as he walks down the street, he may wonder to himself, "Did that really just happen or am I hearing things?" Similarly, if an employer makes a seemingly racist comment to her or his employee of color, the recipient might question whether she or he heard the employer correctly. When microaggressions are experienced in the presence of other people, it would be easy for an individual to ask someone else whether they heard, saw, or experienced the same incident. But when an individual is alone, she or he may be confused or even feel paranoid about whether something really happened. In this case, it may be helpful to (1) trust one's instincts, (2) ask someone (for example, bystanders or passers-by) if the potential microaggression really occurred, or (3) seek support from others for validation. For example, if a person of color, a woman, or an LGBT couple is ignored or receives substandard service to men or heterosexuals, it may be helpful to trust one's instincts (that is, question whether it is obvious the customer service workers are not paying attention to you, while they are pleasant, helpful, and courteous to other whites, men, or heterosexuals). In the workplace, individuals can ask other bystanders if they observed the behaviors (for example, when an employee of color feels like she or he receives substandard treatment by her or his white supervisor, she or he can ask other co-workers of color if they noticed the interaction, if they experience similar treatment, or both). Finally, individuals may seek support and validation from loved ones outside of the workplace (for example, she or he can explain the situation to a loved one to receive a second opinion, receive advice and encouragement, or both).

SHOULD I RESPOND TO THIS MICROAGGRESSION?

If an individual is confident (or fairly confident) that a microaggression existed, she or he has two more questions to ponder:

- If she or he responds to this person, what are the potential risks and consequences?
- If she or he does not respond to this person, what are the risks and consequences?

The victim must consider several other factors when deciding whether or not to respond to the microaggression. First, there is the issue of safety. If a person of color, woman, or LGBT person reacts, one must take into account the likeliness of putting oneself in physical danger. For example, if a group of heterosexual men yells derogatory remarks at an LGBT person as she or he walks down the street, it is possible that responding to the microaggression may lead to a physical assault or confrontation. Therefore, when deciding whether or not to respond, one can consider two factors: (1) the environment that they are in (whether they are in a public setting with others around) and (2) the perceptions of the perpetrators' physical threat (the physical size and stature of the perpetrators, the number of perpetrators present, and the aggression levels or personality styles of the perpetrators).

In addition to physical safety, one may consider the psychological consequences of responding to microaggressions. If a person of color, woman, or LGBT person confronts the individual on the microaggressive behavior, the likelihood exists that the perpetrators will be defensive and argumentative, which potentially may lead to another microaggression. For example, if a woman tells a man that she believes his "chivalrous" behavior is a gender microaggression, he may angrily accuse her of being a feminist who complains about sexism too much, or he may resort to name calling. As a result, the original microaggression may trigger a microinvalidation (that is, by telling her that she complains about sexism too much, he is negating her experience as a woman), or it may trigger a microassault (that is, by calling her a bitch, he is consciously attacking her through harsh, insulting words). Additionally, the victim might consider whether she or he wants to engage in a potential argument or conflict. If a microaggression occurs in public, taking action may lead to time and energy that she or he did not want to waste. If a microaggression occurs in a workplace setting, responding may cause potential conflict or distance in working relationships, as well as potential threats to one's job security or promotion opportunities. As a result, individuals may not be willing to confront microaggressions directly, and microaggressions in the workplace may persist.

Finally, when considering whether to respond, one must ponder the consequences if she or he does not respond to the microaggression. If a person of color, woman, or LGBT person ignores the microaggression or chooses not to say anything, she or he may ruminate about the situation and regret not saying something. The individual might be disappointed in her or himself and feel guilt in allowing the microaggression to occur. In fact, one may feel compelled to confront the microaggression to teach the perpetrator about her or his behaviors, in hopes of preventing future microaggressions toward others.

HOW SHOULD I RESPOND TO THIS MICROAGGRESSION?

If an individual decides to take action when a microaggression occurs, she or he must consider how they want to react. If they are confrontational in their approach, it is likely that the perpetrator will be defensive and reply in a confrontational way. For example, angrily yelling at someone when they commit a microaggression may result in a loud and aggravating argument, in which both parties are unable to listen or fully communicate with each other. This may be counterproductive because the perpetrator may not be able to learn from the experience and may continue to enact this behavior in the future. Sometimes recipients of microaggressions may want to be confrontational because they are frustrated with the accumulation of microaggressions and discriminatory behaviors they have experienced throughout their lifetime. For example, if a person of color is consistently treated as an inferior, a woman gets catcalled on a regular basis, or an LGBT person hears offensive terms frequently, it may be understandable as to why she or he may react irately. Recipients of microaggressions may want to be aggressive in response to the perpetrators to show their strength and ability to stand up for themselves. For example, because people of color, women, and LGBT persons have been taught to be submissive to whites, men, and heterosexuals, they may want to fight for themselves by confronting microaggressions directly.

Another approach to dealing with microaggressions when they occur is to engage in a composed and deliberate dialogue with the perpetrator after a microaggressive incident occurs. Using this approach, the recipient of such a microaggression may inform the perpetrator about how they feel about the situation and how they would like to be treated in the future. For example, if a woman feels like her male employer treats her differently than her male co-workers, she may want to talk to him and share her perceptions with him. If she feels unable to do so by herself, she may want to share her feelings with other female co-workers who feel similarly, whom in turn may also want to calmly confront their employer on his behaviors. Another example may include an LGBT person who talks to co-workers about being treated differently (for example, their co-workers tell them to "tone down their behavior" or avoid asking about their personal and family lives in the same way they ask heterosexual co-workers). It is clear that these types of discourses may be more successful in some environments than in others (that is, it would be easier to confront someone with whom an individual has an existing relationship than a stranger on the street). Having these discussions may be necessary for whites, men, and heterosexuals to become aware of microaggressions and to prevent future microaggressions.

Finally, an important practice to dealing with microaggressions is to seek support and to process one's emotions after a microaggression has occurred. Seeking support can include practical support (for example, if one experiences microaggressions at a workplace, one can file a complaint with human resources), as well as social support (for example, finding an LGBT networking group to validate one's experiences). Processing one's emotions is also important, because microaggressions have been known to lead to an array of mental health problems including depression, anxiety, and trauma (Nadal, 2008). Therefore, individuals who experience microaggressions may find it helpful and necessary to discuss their cognitive and emotional reactions with their loved ones or mental health professionals. In doing so, individuals may avoid accumulating negative and detrimental feelings, which may be beneficial to their mental health.

REFERENCES

Burn, S. M., Kadlec, K., & Rexer, R. (2005). Effects of subtle heterosexism on gays, lesbians, and bisexuals. *Journal of Homosexuality, 49*(2), 23–38.

Dovidio, J. F., Gaertner, S. L., Kawakami, K., & Hodson, G. (2002). Why can't we all just get along? Interpersonal biases and interracial distrust. *Cultural Diversity and Ethnic Minority Psychology, 8*, 88–102.

Glick, P., & Fiske, S. T. (2001). An ambivalent alliance: Hostile and benevolent sexism as complementary justifications for gender inequality. *The American Psychologist, 56*(2), 109–118.

Herek, G. M. (2007). Confronting sexual stigma and prejudice: Theory and practice. *Journal of Social Issues, 63*(4), 905–925.

McConahay, J. B. (1986). Modern racism, ambivalence, and the Modern Racism Scale. In J. F. Dovidio, & S. L. Gaertner (Eds.), *Prejudice, discrimination, and racism* (pp. 91–126). Orlando, FL: Academic Press.

Nadal, K. L. (2008). Preventing racial, ethnic, gender, sexual minority, disability, and religious microaggressions: Recommendations for promoting positive mental health. *Prevention in Counseling Psychology: Theory, Research, Practice, and Training, 2*(1), 22–27.

Nadal, K. L. (2010). Gender microaggressions and women: Implications for therapy. In M. Paludi (Ed.), *Feminism and women's rights worldwide* (pp. 155–175). Westport, CT: Praeger.

Nadal, K. L., Rivera, D. P., & Corpus, M. J. H. (in press). Sexual orientation and transgender microaggressions in everyday life: Experiences of lesbians, gays, bisexuals, and transgender individuals. In D. W. Sue (Ed.), *Microaggressions and marginalized groups in society: Race, gender, sexual orientation, class, and religious manifestations.* New York: Wiley & Sons.

Sears, D. O. (1988). Symbolic racism. In P. A. Katz, & D. A. Taylor (Eds.), *Eliminating racism: Profiles in controversy* (pp. 53–84). New York: Plenum.

Silverschanz, P., Cortina, L. M., Konik, J., & Magley, V. J. (2007). Slurs, snubs, and queer jokes: Incidence and impact of heterosexist harassment in academia. *Sex Roles, 58*, 179–191.

Sue, D. W., Capodilupo, C. M., Torino, G. C., Bucceri, J. M., Holder, A. M., Nadal, K. L., & Esquilin, M. E. (2007). Racial microaggressions in everyday life: Implications for counseling. *The American Psychologist, 62*(4), 271–286.

Swim, J. K., & Cohen, L. L. (1997). Overt, covert, and subtle sexism: A comparison between the attitudes toward women and modern sexism scales. *Psychology of Women Quarterly, 21*(1), 103–118.

Swim, J. K., Mallett, R., & Stangor, C. (2004) Understanding Subtle Sexism: Detection and use of sexist language. *Sex Roles, 51*(3–4), 117–128.

4

Men's Empathic Accuracy in Sexual Harassment Training

William E. Schweinle and Christopher P. Roseman

INTRODUCTION

Sexual harassment is a pervasive (Gruber, 1997) dysfunctional organizational behavior (Griffin, O'Leary-Kelly, & Collins, 1998; O'Leary-Kelly, Paetzold, & Griffin, 2000). The negative consequences for the victims of sexual harassment are well documented and can include negative perceptions of job performance (Glomb, Munson, Hulin, Bergman, & Drasgow, 1999), work satisfaction (Gruber & Bjorn, 1982), and traumatic stress (Woods, Buchanan, & Settles, 2009). Male and female observers of sexual harassment can experience reduced well-being, more burnout, and more thoughts of leaving the organization (Miner-Rubino & Cortina, 2007). These consequences affect not only victims and witnesses. Organizations lose productivity, employee retention and, potentially, money to victim-plaintiffs. Therefore, organizations should benefit from reductions in the incidence and magnitude of sexual harassment activity in the workplace. And, to this end, several workplace sexual harassment prevention training programs have been designed and implemented (Newman, Jackson, & Baker, 2003).

Some authors have argued that strong, pervasive sexual harassment policies and legislation are effective means of prevention (Dekker & Barling, 1998; Gruber & Smith, 1995; Pryor, LaVite, & Stoller, 1993). As a result, carefully articulated sexual harassment policies, legislation, and worker training protocols have been enacted.

Other authors, however, suggest that empirical evidence is lacking to support the efficacy of policy-based sexual harassment prevention (Grundmann, O'Donohue, & Peterson, 1997; Lengnick-Hall, 1995; Newman et al., 2003). And, more recent findings by Tinkler, Yan, and Mollborn (2007) indicate that sexual harassment policies may activate some men's belief that women are inferior and ultimately may increase sexist or paternalistic sentiments among men. Therefore, it is important to continue to develop and implement sexual harassment training methods that are most likely to reduce the incidence of men's sexual harassment behaviors, avoid workplace sexism, and possibly even reduce sexism in the workplace.

This chapter is based on empirical findings and theory relevant to men's sexual harassment of women and empathic accuracy. Specifically, we argue on the basis of empirical findings that employees' sexual harassment training should incorporate elements designed to improve men's empathic accuracy for women's thoughts and feelings. The expectation is that men's improved empathic accuracy will lessen the frequency and severity of their sexual harassment behavior. And, men's improved empathic accuracy may help communication and working relationships throughout an organization.

DEFINITION OF "EMPATHIC ACCURACY"

The awareness of others' thoughts and feelings is known as *everyday mindreading* (Ickes, 2003). Bierhoff (2002) suggests that everyday mindreading about the thoughts, feelings, and intentions of others are centrally important to human social interaction, including interaction that occurs in the workplace. *Empathic accuracy* is the extent to which everyday mindreading accurately captures the thoughts and feelings of other people (see Ickes, 1997). Farrow and Woodruff (2007) argue that empathic accuracy is an essential aspect of emotional intelligence and that it is a fundamental skill that affects people's social adjustment in various domains.

LINKING EMPATHIC ACCURACY TO SEXUAL HARASSMENT ISSUES

Intuitively, sexual harassment–prone men are deficient in their empathic accuracy because these men do not accurately comprehend women's empathic cues during their interactions. Were the men able to more accurately infer women's thoughts and feelings, the men could adjust their behavior toward more appropriate and effective social and work discourse. This conclusion is supported by findings that better empathy is associated with lower sexual harassment proclivity among men (Bartling & Eisenman, 1993; Bingham & Burleson, 1996; Dekker & Barling, 1998; Pryor, 1987). Similarly, Keyton and Rhodes (1999) found that men's ability to take other peoples' perspectives is positively related to the men's ability to recognize verbal sexual harassment cues. And, when men are forced to consider the perspective of a woman being ogled—an objectification-of-women type of sexual harassment (Quinn, 2002)—men tended to better understand the harm caused by men's ogling behavior (Quinn, 2002). For these reasons and others Brunswig and O'Donohue (2002) and Dobrich and Dranoff (2000) argue that empathy training in sexual harassment training is particularly effective in reducing repeated occurrences of sexual harassment.

Empathy and *perspective taking* are more behavioral or internal in nature, whereas empathic accuracy refers to the accuracy of inferences made and perspectives taken. Some recent empathic accuracy research has revealed that men's biased, inaccurate inferences of women's criticism and rejection are associated with men's maltreatment of women, specifically with men's wife-directed aggression (Schweinle & Ickes, 2007; Schweinle, Ickes, & Bernstein, 2002). Furthermore, Schweinle, Cofer, and Schatz (2009) found that more abusive husbands are more likely to sexually harass women in general. These findings support the assertion by O'Leary-Kelly et al. (2000) that sexual harassment exists somewhere along the continuum of sexual aggression rather than along the continua of harassment or seduction behaviors.

Therefore, it is reasonable to conclude that empathic accuracy is an important component of functional interaction between men and women. Schweinle et al. (2009) found a positive relationship between men's propensity to sexually harass women and men's bias to inaccurately over-infer women's criticism and rejection. Taken together, these findings plausibly demonstrate the link between men's deficient empathic accuracy and men's sexual harassment of women. This speaks to correlation, not causation, however, and the link between men's sexual harassment of women and men's deficient empathic accuracy is unclear.

Some relevant findings may help explain this association and support the design of a sexual harassment training program to improve harassment prone men's empathic accuracy. For instance, Gardner (1995) and Quinn (2002) found that men who ogle women tend to deem women's feelings about being ogled as irrelevant. Quinn (2002) speculated that this objectification suppresses men's empathy for women and that when men ogle women, the men are acting actively rather than passively to ignore the feelings of women who are being ogled or sexually harassed. Similarly, Schweinle (2002) found a positive, but insignificant ($r = 0.21$, $p < 0.075$, $n = 78$), correlation between men's sexual harassment of women and men's attentional disengagement, that is, the extent to which men actively look away, from a woman on a standardized videotape. Taken together, these findings suggest that more harassment prone men tend to actively "tune out" women's thoughts and feelings rather than be ignorantly unaware of them.

Other findings further support this conclusion. Specifically, Schweinle and Ickes (2007) reported a significant correlation ($r = 0.27$, $p < 0.05$) between men's attention to a woman on a standardized videotape and the men's accuracy when inferring whether she was having critical or rejecting thoughts or feelings. It therefore follows that improvements in men's attention to women's expressions will result in improvements in the men's accuracy when inferring women's critical or rejecting thoughts and feelings.

It stands to reason, then, that if sexually harassment prone men actively tune out women's thoughts and feelings, then these men can be motivated to actively tune them in and improve their empathic accuracy for women's thoughts and feelings. Empirical findings show that empathic accuracy can be improved through greater motivation to be accurate (Ickes, Gesn, & Graham, 2000; Ickes & Simpson, 2004). Empathic accuracy can also be improved through feedback about the actual thoughts and feelings of the empathy target (Marangoni, Ickes, Garcia, & Teng, 1995). A sexual harassment training curriculum that includes improved empathic accuracy would do well to consider these two findings.

SUMMARY

Based on the findings and synthesis presented thus far, it is reasonable to conclude that men's empathic accuracy can be improved through better motivation to be accurate and through improved attentional engagement in women's emotional and cognitive expressions. Men's improved empathic accuracy, in turn, should result in reduced sexual harassment behavior, because the men are able to correctly infer when women find men's behavior offensive. Men can then use this information to adjust their behavior accordingly—and avoid sexually harassing women. Based on these conclusions, improving men's empathic accuracy should be among the central themes of sexual harassment training.

REFERENCES

Bartling, C., & Eisenman, R. (1993). Sexual harassment proclivities in men and women. *Bulletin of the Psychonomic Society*, *3*, 189–192.

Bierhoff, H. W. (2002). *Prosocial behavior*. New York: Psychology Press.

Bingham, G., & Burleson, B. (1996). The development of a sexual harassment proclivity scale: Construct validation and relationship to communication competence. *Communication Quarterly*, *44*, 308–325.

Brunswig, K., & O'Donohue, W. (2002). *Relapse prevention for sexual harassers*. New York: Kluwer Academic/Plenum.

Dekker, I., & Barling, J. (1998). Personal and organizational predictors of workplace sexual harassment of women by men. *Journal of Occupational Health Psychology*, *31*, 7–18.

Dobrich, W., & Dranoff, S. (2000). *The first line of defense: A guide to protecting yourself against sexual harassment*. Hoboken, NJ: Wiley.

Farrow, T. F. D., & Woodruff, P. W. R. (2007). *Empathy in mental illness*. Cambridge: Cambridge University Press.

Gardner, C. (1995). *Passing by: Gender and public harassment*. Berkeley: University of California Press.

Glomb, T., Munson, L., Hulin, C., Bergman, M., & Drasgow, F, (1999). Structural equation models of sexual harassment: Longitudinal explorations and cross-sectional generalization. *Journal of Applied Psychology*, *84*, 14–28.

Griffin, R., O'Leary-Kelly, A., & Collins, J. (Eds.). (1998). *Dysfunctional behavior in organizations*. Greenwich, CT: JAI Press.

Gruber, J. (1997). An epidemiology of sexual harassment: Evidence from North America and Europe. In W. O'Donohue (Ed.), *Sexual harassment: Theory, researchn and treatment* (pp. 84–98). Boston: Allyn & Bacon.

Gruber, J., & Bjorn, L. (1982). Blue collar blues: The sexual harassment of women autoworkers. *Work and Occupations*, *93*, 271–298.

Gruber, J., & Smith, M. (1995). Women's responses to sexual harassment: A multivariate analysis. *Basic and Applied Social Psychology*, *17*, 543–562.

Grundmann, E., O'Donohue, W., & Peterson, S. (1997). The prevention of sexual harassment. In W. O'Donohue (Ed.), *Sexual Harassment: Theory, researchn and treatment*. Boston: Allyn & Bacon.

Ickes, W. J. (Ed.). (1997). *Empathic accuracy*. New York: Guilford Press.

Ickes, W. J. (2003). *Everyday mind reading: Understanding what other people think and feel*. Amherst, NY: Prometheus Books.

Ickes, W., Gesn, P., & Graham, T. (2000). Gender differences in empathic accuracy: Differential ability or differential motivation? *Personal Relationships*, *7*(1), 95–109.

Ickes, W., & Simpson, J. (2004). Motivational aspects of empathic accuracy. In M. Brewer and M. Hewstone (Eds.), *Emotion and motivation* (pp. 225–246). Malden, MA: Blackwell.

Keyton, J., & Rhodes, S. (1999). Organizational sexual harassment: Translating research into application. *Journal of Applied Communication Research, 27,* 158–173.

Lengnick-Hall, M. (1995). Sexual harassment research: A methodological critique. *Personnel Psychology, 484,* 841–864.

Marangoni, C., Garcia, S., Ickes, W., & Teng, G. (1995). Empathic accuracy in a clinically relevant setting. *Journal of Personality and Social Psychology. 68*(5), 854–869.

Miner-Rubino, K., & Cortina, L. M. (2007). Beyond targets: Consequences of vicarious exposure to misogyny at work. *Journal of Applied Psychology, 92,* 1254–1269.

Newman, M., Jackson, R., & Baker, D. (2003). Sexual harassment in the federal workplace. *Public Administration Review, 63*(4), 472–483.

O'Leary-Kelly, A., Paetzold, R., & Griffin, R. (2000). Sexual harassment as aggressive behavior: An actor-based perspective. *Academy of Management Review, 25,* 372–388.

Pryor, J. (1987). Sexual harassment proclivities in men. *Sex Roles, 17,* 269–290.

Pryor, J., LaVite, C., & Stoller, L. (1993). A social psychological analysis of sexual harassment: The person/situation interaction. *Journal of Vocational Behavior, 42,* 68–83.

Quinn, B. (2002). Sexual harassment and masculinity: The power and meaning of "girl watching." *Gender and Society, 16*(3), 386–402.

Schweinle, W. (2002). The role of men's "overattribution bias" and affect in wife abuse and sexual harassment. *Dissertation Abstracts International, 63,* 04-B.

Schweinle, W., Cofer, C., & Schatz, S. (2009). Men's empathic bias, empathic inaccuracy, and sexual harassment. *Sex Roles, 60,* 142–150.

Schweinle, W., & Ickes, W. (2007). The role of men's critical/rejecting over-attribution bias, affect, and attentional disengagement in marital aggression. *Journal of Social and Clinical Psychology, 26*(2), 175–199.

Schweinle, W., Ickes, W., & Bernstein, I. (2002). Empathic inaccuracy in husband to wife aggression: The overattribution bias. *Personal Relationships, 9,* 141–158.

Tinkler, J., Yan, E., & Mollborn, S. (2007). Can legal interventions change beliefs? The effect of exposure to sexual harassment policy on men's gender beliefs. *Social Psychology Quarterly, 70*(4), 480–494.

Woods, K., Buchanan, N., & Settles, I. (2009). Sexual harassment across the color line: Experiences and outcomes of cross- vs. intra-racial sexual harassment among black women. *Cultural Diversity and Ethnic Minority Psychology, 15*(1), 67–76.

5

Red Light, Green Light: A More Effective Approach to Preventing and Responding Productively to Workplace Harassment

Michael Kaufman

When it comes to the issue of workplace harassment, it seems that corporations, government departments, and professional firms often get stuck between two extremes. At the one end, they virtually ignore the problem until it is too late—doing little more than saying a few of the right things, adopting a policy, and, perhaps, letting employees and managers know that such a policy exists (which they can find somewhere on their intranet, that is, if they happen to have a degree in computer programming). Perhaps they'll do some perfunctory training. At the other extreme (and often by the very same organizations), when harassment does occur, they will swoop in as if it were a police investigation of murder.

Lost at both extremes are effective forms of staff education to prevent harassment from occurring in the first place, effective training of managers on their role in preventing harassment or responding productively if it occurs, effective ways of helping staff and managers learn from occurrences of harassment, and, finally, effective ways to restore workplaces that are polarized by a charge of harassment and the subsequent investigation and punishment.

This chapter sets out an approach to fill these gaps—this approach has been used at the United Nations for which I designed the online training for 55,000 staff in the United Nations Children's Fund (UNICEF), United Nations Development Program (UNDP), World Food Program, and others, as well as developed the live training program for the United Nations Educational, Scientific, and Cultural Organization (UNESCO), both in its Paris headquarters and field offices. I have taken this approach into government departments, professional firms, and corporations. (And although responses by managers, both in human resources and other staff, have been uniformly positive, I should add that it has not been independently evaluated.)

This short article highlights several features of this approach. My focus in this article is on sexual harassment (including homophobic harassment), which is one of my major areas of work. Most of the material in this chapter, and certainly this entire approach, can be used for the full range of harassment, including harassment based on race, ethnicity, religion, country of origin, mother tongue, physical and mental differences, and so forth.

RED LIGHT, GREEN LIGHT

Day in and day out at our workplaces by far the most common form of sexual harassment is not harassment that borders on sexual assault nor *quid pro quo* harassment—that is, offers (or threats) in exchange for sexual favors. Most is far more banal, often subtle, and often open to interpretation. Is it harassment or is it friendly collegial behavior when I compliment a colleague on her new blouse or how fit she is looking? When I ask someone out on a date? Flirt with someone? Tell a joke or make a comment with an extremely mild sexual innuendo or reference? Pat someone on the back or shoulder?

The answer is very clear: it depends. It depends on my tone of voice and body language, the context, the exact content (of a comment), on our reporting relationship, on our personal relationship, on who else is present and who might hear, and on the frequency of my action. Most of all, it depends not on my intent, but on the impact of my words or actions, that is, on how they make someone else feel.

Of course, that list of possibly inappropriate and harassing areas is not a list of things that are black and white (as is *quid pro quo* harassment). Most actions that are experienced as harassment, to use one metaphor, are in the gray area. Unfortunately, the implicit assumption of most approaches to workplace harassment is that the matter is black and white.

By focusing on harassment as a set of absolutes, as a list of things you must not do, we set up a major disconnect with the very staff and managers that we, as those concerned about harassment, hope to reach. People know that many forms of behavior that end up on those endless lists of harassing behavior are simply part of human (including work-place) interaction. As a result, training (when it exists) usually is not cred-ible and is dismissed easily. Rules and instructions to managers are, often, impossible to enact.

The metaphor or image that is the focus of my own training and policy work (both of managers and staff) is a traffic light.

The green light refers to things that always are acceptable at the workplace. Green light means keep going!

The red light are actions that are always inappropriate and always constitute harassment, no matter who is present. This includes certain words or derogatory comments about someone based on her or his gen-der, sexual orientation, race, religion, and so on. It also includes *quid pro quo* harassment. It includes posting or distributing e-mails that show explicit sexual images. It includes jokes of an explicitly sexual nature. The list is actually rather small. The red light means stop! Do not pro-ceed with that action or, if you are a manager, make sure it stops right away.

Where most staff get in trouble and managers feel unable to respond is not about those things. It is on the third light, the yellow, or orange or amber light (whatever you want to call the middle light). These are things such as compliments, flirting, casual touching, and many forms of humor.

Just like in driving, what the amber light tells us is this: It doesn't mean stop, and it doesn't mean go. It means proceed with caution and be prepared to stop.

In my training, a series of exercises helps participants identify these "amber zone" behaviors. It helps people identify the factors that might make that action harassing or not.

And what tells us we should stop? In some cases, it is simply that we should know that a certain behavior is not appropriate, that it crosses a line from amber to red. In other cases, a realization that we should stop is based on the reaction of others—that is, the imagined or perceived impact. By raising awareness about the amber zone, the real area where most people get in trouble, people learn to keep their eyes open when they enter this zone, just like the driver learns to pay particular attention when the light turns from green to amber.

START WITH THE MANAGERS

My work, following the lead of Charles Novogrodsky—my partner for that portion of my work that is based in Canada—is that it is critical to always start with the managers. If we want harassment-free workplaces, then we must ensure that managers have the knowledge, tools, and commitment to set an example; to conduct ongoing, often informal, education of staff; and to respond quickly, fairly, and effectively when they receive a report of possible harassment or witness behavior that they think is inappropriate.

When it comes to managers, as important as understanding the issues and the policy, is teaching the practical skills and giving managers the tools they need to respond to harassment, to carry out fact-finding, and to restore a harassment-fee workplace.

In many cases, I have been asked to train managers and staff together. I say this is not the best first step. For one thing, it sets up a situation in which many staff members will not feel comfortable speaking out about the issues they face. It also may prompt some managers to go out of their way to prove to their staff that they are "one of the boys" and that they, too, think this is all nonsense. And it means that managers are not properly prepared for their own responsibilities once training is done.

Instead, I like to start with training of managers, and this can be anywhere from a half-day to a two-day session. Anything less than a half-day means that managers will neither have the understanding nor the practical skills to prevent or respond to harassment. (And I do half-day sessions only under duress. One or, when possible, two days is really required). Only then would we conduct staff training sessions, which last anywhere from two hours to a full day. In some cases, we then bring staff and managers together for a final session, ranging from two hours to one day. This joint training reinforces the messages of the separate training sessions, focuses on some of the problems that occur in that workplace (but not on individual cases or individual grievances), and develops group commitments and action plans.

AN ADULT-EDUCATION MODEL

We are dealing with some challenging, contentious, and, for some, even traumatic issues. It is a topic about which people often have preconceived ideas and a lot of feelings. We also know that people often use humor, compliments, and flirting to make their workplace tolerable. Any training that requires managers to come down on their staff like a drill sergeant is not going to work. Similarly, any training that hopes that staff will remember 50 PowerPoint slides that recite the policy or lists of "dos and don'ts" is simply not going to work.

This approach is an adult education model. This approach to training is experiential, that is, it is based on people's actual experiences of workplace life. They *know* that a joke or casual touch can be just fine, but they also need to know when it is not or, at least, they need to know *how* to figure out if it is not. I use a lot of (appropriate) humor, focus on individual and group exercises, and make the training fun. Managers and staff do not like to feel as though they are being treated as recalcitrant children, nor as stupid. They are valued for what they know and are challenged on what they have not yet thought about.

EDUCATION MUST BE ONGOING

This approach stresses that education must be ongoing. It is not just once-and-then-you're-done training—it also is orientation of new staff; reminders from managers in the form of posters, e-mails, and short items at staff meetings; longer items at meetings or special meetings if a problem has occurred; and repeat training for all staff every few years. Whatever the financial cost of this training, it pales in comparison to the financial cost of investigations, settlements, lost work time, and an office environment embittered and polarized over a harassment incident and its aftermath.

Often the most effective education is the everyday remarks by managers to those they supervise. A comment that is near the borderline (between amber light and red) might occasion a playful remark such as "I see an amber light flashing." Done with a light touch and even (appropriate) humor, this not only can prevent a staff member from crossing a line, but also reinforce the training without making anyone feel put down or stupid.

HAVING THE TOOLS TO RESPOND TO HARASSMENT

Managers require practical tools for responding to a report of possible harassment or a situation of harassment that a manager observes. What are the protocols and tools for fact-finding? How can they be fair, non-judgmental, and impartial? How can they be supportive of someone who makes a complaint without siding with them before getting all the facts? When should they get help or support from another manager or human resources? How should they conduct themselves if an outside investigation is taking place?

A second thing I stress not only in my training, but also in helping institutions develop more effective policies, is to explore alternatives to traditional forms of punishment. In the most serious cases, the most serious forms of redress are important, including suspensions without pay or dismissal. But, in many cases, this form of punishment is not useful. It can be an overreaction. It can be rightly perceived as scape-goating the person who was caught, rather than changing a form of behavior that is endemic in the workplace. And, it is only punitive, doing nothing to change the individual who committed the harassment.

In terms of alternatives, some of the work that I do is one-on-one coaching (often, gender-sensitivity coaching) with the individual (or individuals) who was found responsible for workplace harassment. In some cases, this is combined with or following a suspension; in others cases, it is an alternative to a suspension. Either way, the premise is to turn the situation of harassment into a learning opportunity. Employers often are startled by the changes an individual undergoes through the coaching process.

A third thing I stress is the importance of restoring the workplace. In the work I do, for example, with Charles Novogrodsky and Associates, we have people who specialize in working with management and staff to restore a fractured, embittered, polarized workplace to a productive and harmonious environment.

GENDER PERSPECTIVE

One thing that is curiously missing from much education on sexual harassment (including homophobic harassment) is a clear gender perspective. By this I do not mean a fatuous "men are from Mars, women are from Venus" or "she says/he says" approach that assumes that much harassment is simply misunderstanding based on supposedly different male and female brains.

Rather, the focus I believe is most useful is to look at the impact on male-female workplace behavior (that is, male-male, male-female, *and* female-female relations) based on how we raise boys to be men and girls to be women in the context of male-dominated societies. It looks at the relationship of men and women to personal, institutional, and social power. It looks at how we value domination. It looks at how our different gendered experiences *do* lead to differences in our brains and our (average) capacity to be empathetic, something that is critical if we are to *feel* how our words or actions affect a co-worker.

Participants usually find that this aspect of one-on-one coaching and longer group training sessions is fascinating and illuminating about their own lives.

6

What Do We Really Know about Sexual Harassment Training Effectiveness?

Caren B. Goldberg

Although a handful of states currently require private sector employers to provide sexual harassment training, many organizations presumably do so in an effort to reduce the incidence of sexual harassment or to prevent incidents from escalating into lawsuits. Even before California jumped on the mandatory training bandwagon, organizations were spending billions of dollars per year on sexual harassment training (Bisom-Rapp, 2001). Yet, despite the money and energy being put into such training, the number of systematic studies that have examined the effectiveness of sexual harassment training is woefully small. As Perry, Kulik, and Field (2009) recently noted, "we know surprisingly little about when and why sexual harassment training is effective." The purpose of the current chapter is to summarize the academic literature on the effectiveness of sexual harassment training.

The extent to which such training has been shown to be effective depends on how one defines "training effectiveness." Training researchers (Kraiger, Ford, & Salas, 1993; Noe, 2002; Tracey, Hinkin, Tannenbaum, & Mathieu, 2001) have argued that training effectiveness can be assessed in terms of cognitive outcomes, skill-based outcomes, and affective outcomes. Cognitive outcomes are measures that are used to "determine the degree to which trainees are familiar with principles, facts, techniques, procedures, or processes emphasized in the training program;" skill-based outcomes are those that are, "used to assess the level of technical or motor skills and behavior;" and affective outcomes are those that "include attitudes and motivation" (Noe, 2002). The effectiveness of sexual harassment training on each of these outcome categories is discussed below.

TRAINING EFFECTS ON COGNITIVE OUTCOMES

Because individuals may engage in harassing behavior without realizing it, a fundamental objective of many sexual harassment training programs is to increase employees' knowledge with respect to the behaviors that constitute harassment. Studies by Blakely, Blakely, and Moorman (1998); Moyer and Nath (1998); and York, Barclay, and Zajack (1997) have found that subjects who received training (or who received more training) were more likely to judge ambiguous situations as harassing than were subjects who received no training (or less training). The consistent support for the effectiveness of training on perceptions of harassment suggests that training may heighten the salience of some behaviors such that subjects would be more likely to perceive these situations as sexually harassing after the training than before the training. Ironically, while this is a desirable outcome, it has deterred many organizations from providing training. A Commerce Clearing House (1998) report noted that, "many small and mid-sized employers made a conscious decision not to have a sexual harassment policy for fear that it would oversensitize their workforce and create complaints (p. 1)."

Aside from perceptions of sexual harassment, little research has tested the impact of training on cognitive outcomes. However, Perry, Kulik, and Schmidtke (1998) found that the effect of sexual harassment training on knowledge about sexual harassment issues was statistically significant for individuals who had a high likelihood of sexually harassing, but not for those were less inclined to harass.

TRAINING EFFECTS ON SKILL-BASED OUTCOMES

Researchers who have focused on skill-based outcomes have examined the effectiveness of sexual harassment training on the behaviors of both perpetrators and victims. Findings from these studies are mixed. On the perpetrator side, Perry et al. (1998) found that sexual harassment training had no effect on trainees' likelihood of engaging in sexual harassment. On the victim side, Goldberg (2007) examined the impact of sexual harassment training on four potential responses to harassment: formally reporting the behavior, confronting the harasser, seeking a transfer and quitting, and seeking legal counsel. Training did not affect the likelihood of engaging in any of these responses, when trainees were faced with what researchers term "gender harassment" (offensive behavior not directed at a particular individual—for example, jokes and cartoons). Training, however, did increase the likelihood that trainees would confront the perpetrator, when they experienced "sexual attention" harassment (behavior directed at a particular individual—for example, repeatedly giving suggestive looks and sending romantic letters). Notably, training did not have a significant effect on formally reporting, transferring or quitting, or seeking legal counsel. Thus, concerns that training may create problems that previously did not exist is unfounded.

TRAINING EFFECTS ON ATTITUDINAL OUTCOMES

Research on the effectiveness of sexual harassment training on attitude change has been sparse; however, Perry et al.'s (1998) findings suggest that training is not effective at changing attitudes. The lack of support for training effects on attitude change is not terribly surprising. Attitudes regarding sexual harassment stem from norms regarding men's and women's sex roles (Gutek, 1985). Because these attitudes develop over a lifetime, they are unlikely to be altered by a single sexual harassment training program.

SUMMARY

Given the resources being poured into sexual harassment training, the dearth of controlled studies of training effectiveness is surprising. The few studies that have attempted to measure the effects of sexual harassment training suggest that training does increase knowledge about sexual harassment. This is encouraging news, because a number of people likely engage in behaviors that are sexually harassing without realizing it. Having knowledge and using it are two distinct issues, however. Thus, the real litmus test is whether sexual harassment training affects behavior. The research in this area suggests that while training does not affect the likelihood of perpetrators engaging in harassing behavior, it does increase the likelihood that the victim will confront the perpetrator. From an organizational perspective, this is highly desirable. Because sexual harassment is about power, enabling victims to speak up when they have been harassed may serve as a strong deterrent against future harassment.

REFERENCES

Bisom-Rapp, S. (2001). An ounce of prevention is a poor substitute for a pound of cure: Confronting the developing jurisprudence of education and prevention in employment discrimination law. *Berkeley Journal of Employment and Labor Law, 22*, 1–47.

Blakely, G. L., Blakely, E. H., & Moorman, R. H. (1998). The effects of training on perceptions of sexual harassment allegations. *Journal of Applied Social Psychology, 28*, 71–83.

Commerce Clearing House. (1998). *Employers liable for harassment: Training, documentation, new implementation.* (Labor Law Reports No. 621, Issue 1979).

Goldberg, C. (2007). The impact of training and conflict avoidance on responses to sexual harassment. *Psychology of Women Quarterly, 31*, 62–72.

Gutek, B. A. (1985). *Sex and the workplace: Impact of sexual behavior and harassment on women, men, and organizations.* San Francisco, CA: Jossey Bass.

Kraiger, K., Ford, K. J., & Salas, E. (1993). Application of cognitive, skill-based, and affective theories of learning outcomes to new methods of training evaluation. *Journal of Applied Psychology, 78*, 311–329.

Moyer, R. S., & Nath, A. (1998). Some effects of brief training interventions on perceptions of sexual harassment. *Journal of Applied Social Psychology, 28*, 333–356.

Noe, R. A. (2002). *Employee training and development* (2nd ed.). New York: McGraw-Hill.

Perry, E., Kulik, C., & Field, M. (2009). Sexual harassment training: Recommendations to address gaps between the practitioner and research literatures. *Human Resource Management, 48*, 817–837.

Perry, E. L., Kulik, C. T., & Schmidtke, J. M. (1998). Propensity to sexual harass: An exploration of gender differences. *Sex Roles, 38*, 443–460.

Tracey, J. B., Hinkin, T. R., Tannenbaum, S., & Mathieu, J. E. (2001). The influence of individual characteristics and the work environment on varying levels of training outcomes. *Human Resource Development Quarterly, 12*, 5–23.

York, K. M., Barclay, L. A., & Zajack, A. B. (1997). Preventing sexual harassment: The effect of multiple training methods. *Employee Responsibilities and Rights Journal, 10*, 277–289.

7

"Broken Windows Theory" Applied to Workplace Discrimination: The Importance of Adding Workplace Violence Training to Equal Employment Opportunity Management Programs

Michele A. Paludi, Jennie D'Aiuto, and Carmen A. Paludi, Jr.

INTRODUCTION

The Occupational Safety and Health Administration (OSHA, 2004) noted that each year 2 million employees are victims of workplace violence. Homicide is the leading cause of occupational death for women; it is the second leading cause of occupational death for men (Meleis, 2001; Paludi, Nydegger, & Paludi, 2006). The Society for Human Resource Management has indicated that the incidence of workplace violence has increased steadily (Esen, 2004). In addition, they found that 48 percent of employees surveyed reported experiencing a violent incident in their workplace in the previous two years, including the following: verbal threats (39 percent), pushing and shoving (22 percent), and fist fights (14 percent) (SHRM, 2000).

Behavioral examples of workplace violence include, but are not limited to, the following: verbal threats, nonverbal threats, pushing, shoving, hitting, assault, stalking, and murder. All employees are at risk for workplace violence (Baron & Neumann, 1996; Kelloway, Barling, & Hurrell,

2006). However, some employees are at greater risk, however, including those who exchange money with the public; deliver goods, services, or passengers; work during late or early morning shifts; work alone; work in health care or social services; and work in retail (Chappell & DeMartino, 1998; VandenBos & Bulatao, 1996).

Research on workplace violence has documented the impact of workplace violence on several areas of functioning, including the following: emotional and psychological, physiological or health related, career and work, social, and self-perception (Bowie, Fisher, & Cooper, 2005; Kelloway, Barling, & Hurrell, 2006). Most victims experience severe distress associated with the violence, including the following: withdrawal from social settings, depression, fear, anger, anxiety, substance abuse, sleep disturbances, eating disorders, changes in work habits, absenteeism, lack of trust, changes in social network patterns, and relationship difficulties.

Research has documented the impact of workplace violence on the organization, including the following: decreased morale, increased absenteeism, decreased productivity, increased turnover, reduced team cohesion and performance, and reduced job satisfaction.

Preincident indicators have been identified by co-workers of employees who committed an act of workplace violence: increased mood swings, unstable emotional responses, increased use of alcohol and other drugs, unexplained increase in absenteeism, comments indicating suicidal tendencies, decrease in attention paid to hygiene and appearance, depression and withdrawal, preoccupation with violent movies and acts, planning to "solve all the problems" at the workplace (Einarsen, Hoel, Zapf, & Cooper, 2003). Employees failed to recognize these symptom as indicators of potentially violent behavior.

Many of these early symptoms of workplace violence illustrate incivility and harassment or discrimination of employees. Incivility in the workplace has been defined as discourteous or rude behavior that violates norms for respect for co-workers and supervisors (Andersson & Pearson, 1999). Examples of incivility include verbal abuse, supervisors and employees dismissing clerical staff by virtue of their status, name calling, supervisors yelling at employees, pushing employees, shoving employees, inappropriate e-mails, and taking credit for work completed by another employee (Andersson & Pearson, 1999; Cortina, Magley, Williams, & Langout, 2001; also see Nadal's discussion of microaggressions in chapter 3 of this volume).

Readers should consult volume 1 of this book set to review the various types of harassment and discrimination. For example, sexual harassment is a form of sex discrimination that is defined legally by the Equal Employment Opportunity Commission (2009) as follows:

> unwelcome sexual advances, requests for sexual favors, and other verbal or physical conduct of a sexual nature when any one of the following criteria is met:
>
> - Submission to such conduct is made either explicitly or implicitly a term or condition of the individual's employment;
> - Submission to or rejection of such conduct by an individual is used as the basis for employment decisions affecting the individual;
> - Such conduct has the purpose or effect of unreasonably interfering with an individual's work performance or creating an intimidating, hostile or offensive work environment.

Sexual harassment is defined psychologically as unwanted, sexually offensive behavior that threatens individuals' psychological health and well-being (Levy & Paludi, 2002). Examples of workplace conduct that creates an intimidating, hostile, or offensive work environment include, but are not limited to, the following: unwelcome sexual advances; obscene or insulting sounds; pinching, pushing, and brushing up against another's body; and offensive e-mails, pictures, or posters displayed in the work area.

Empirical research on workplace violence has reported a significant relationship among incivility, discrimination or harassment, and violence in the workplace (Andersson & Pearson, 1999; Atkinson, 2000; Lim & Cortina, 2005; Nydegger, Paludi, DeSouza, & Paludi, 2006; Reio & Ghosh, 2009) to what Andersson and Pearson (1999) referred to as a "spiraling effect" of incivility.

For example, Lim and Cortina (2005) found that gender harassment is correlated with incivility. Examples of gender harassment (Fitzgerald et al., 1988) include unwanted sexual attention expressed through crude words, acts and gestures that convey hostile, and misogynist attitudes. Thus, incivility, harassment or discrimination, and workplace violence do not occur in a vacuum; they occur in a climate of disrespect.

The impact of workplace incivility and sexual harassment on employees is identical to those symptoms listed above with respect to workplace violence (Cortina & Wasti, 2005; Dansky & Kilpatrick, 1997; Lundberg-Love &

Marmion, 2003). Furthermore, the explanations for all three types of workplace mistreatment involve abuse of power (Lim & Cortina, 2005; Paludi & Paludi, 2003).

Thus, we recommend including training on workplace violence in an organization's equal employment opportunity management program; to discuss multiple forms of interpersonal mistreatment simultaneously rather than independently. In Table 7.1 we have outlined a sample training program that discusses workplace violence in two major sections: (1) an overview of the definition, behavioral examples, incidence, and impact of workplace violence; and (2) the organization's policy and procedures for preventing and dealing with complaints of workplace violence. In this training program, we recommend discussing a continuum of workplace violence with incivility on one end and workplace violence, including homicide, at the other. In between these two endpoints is harassment or discrimination of an employee because he or she is a member of a federal- or

Table 7.1
Sample Outline of a Training Program for Employees on Workplace Violence

---

Goals of the Training Program

Provide all members of the workplace with a clear understanding of their rights and responsibilities with respect to workplace violence.

Enable employees to identify workplace violence.

Provide employees with information concerning the organization's policy statement and procedures against workplace violence.

Discuss the emotional and physical reactions to being a victim of workplace violence.

Dispel myths about workplace violence.

Explore responsible behavior in dealing with employees who engage in workplace violence.

Discuss the employer's central role in preventing workplace violence.

Create an environment free of workplace violence and fear of retaliation for speaking out about workplace violence.

At the Conclusion of This Training Program, Employees Will Achieve the Following

Assess their own perceptions of the definition, incidence, and psychological dimensions of workplace violence.

Discuss the continuum beginning with incivility, and progressing to harassment, and workplace violence.

Label behavior as indicative of workplace violence.

(Continued)

Table 7.1 (*continued*)

Identify the organization's policy and procedures for reporting workplace violence.
Identify their rights and responsibilities under the organization's policy and
   procedures on workplace violence.

Topics for Presentation and Discussion

Part I: Welcome, Introductions, and Review of Goals of Training Program

Trainers welcome employees to the training program.
Trainers introduce themselves, their qualifications and background.
Trainers summarize goals of the training program.
Trainers ask employees to state their own goals for the training.
Trainers present responses to all employees.

Part II: Myths vs. Realities about Workplace Violence

Trainers ask employees to provide examples of behaviors they believe illustrate
   workplace violence.
Trainers discuss each contributed response with all trainees.
Trainers provide an overview of the training program, noting where each issue
   raised by trainees is addressed.

Part III: Definition and Incidence of Workplace Violence: At-Risk Employees

Trainers present definition of workplace violence:
   Violent occurrences involving co-workers and/or managers and supervisors
   Violent acts committed by employees, clients, and/or vendors
   Violent acts committed by individuals who have no legitimate right to be on
      the work premises
Trainers provide employees with behavioral examples of workplace violence:
   Verbal threats
   Nonverbal threats
   Pushing
   Shoving
   Hitting
   Assault
   Stalking
   Murder
Trainers present recent data on incidence of workplace violence.
Trainers cite Occupational Safety and Health Administration (OSHA) findings
   that 2 million employees per year are victims of workplace violence.
Trainers discuss at-risk employees:
   Exchange money with public
   Deliver passengers, goods, and/or services
   Work alone
   Work during early morning or late night shifts

(Continued)

Table 7.1 (*continued*)

Have extensive contact with the public
Health care workers
Social services workers
Retail workers
Taxi drivers
Trainers note that workplace violence can occur in any organization.
Trainers make summary comments from this unit.

Part IV: Preincident Indicators

Trainers discuss research findings about preincident behaviors:
    Increased use of drugs
    Unexplained increase in absenteeism from work
    Withdrawal and depression
    Inattention to physical appearance and hygiene
    Threats made to co-workers or supervisors
    Suicidal statements
    Mood swings
    Preoccupation with violence
    Plan to "solve" all the problems in the workplace
    Unstable emotional responses
    Empathy with individuals who have committed violent acts
    Escalation of domestic problems
Trainers make summary comments from this unit.

*Part V: Workplace Violence: Impact on Employees
and Workplace*

Trainers discuss psychological symptoms, including the following:
    Depression
    Anger
    Shame
    Denial
    Fear
    Depression
    Frustration
    Shock
    Anxiety
    Isolation
    Helplessness
Trainers discuss physical symptoms, including the following:
    Headaches
    Tiredness
    Eating disorders

(*Continued*)

Table 7.1 (*continued*)

Sleep problems
Lethargy
Drug abuse
Gastrointestinal disorders
Trainers discuss career effects:
  Changes in work habits
  Absenteeism
  Changes in career goals
Trainers discuss interpersonal effects:
  Fear of new people
  Lack of trust
  Change in social network
  Relationship problems
  Withdrawal from co-workers
Trainers discuss impact on self-concept:
  Poor self concept
  Powerlessness
  Isolation
Trainers discuss the impact of workplace violence on the workplace:
  Decreased morale
  Increased absenteeism
  Increased turnover
  Decreased productivity
Trainers make summary comments from this unit.

Part VI: Intimate Partner Violence as a Workplace Concern

Trainers discuss intimate partner violence (domestic violence).
Trainers note that women who are victims of violence perpetrated by their
  mates account for one-quarter of women who are murdered in a given year.
Trainers note that homicide is the leading cause of occupational deaths of women.
Trainers note that abusers interfere with women's employment before, during,
  and after work.
Trainers note examples of prework abuse that prevents more than 50 percent of
  women from going to work:
  Physically restrained
  Beaten
  Having clothing cut up
Trainers discuss how abusers interfere with employees during work:
  Harassing calls
  Harassment in person
  Stalking

(*Continued*)

Table 7.1 (*continued*)

Trainers discuss women's responses to intimate partner violence that spills over
    into the workplace:
    Fear losing their job
    Ashamed of appearance
    Ashamed of being battered
    Frightened
Trainers make summary comments from this unit.

*Part VII: Continuum of Incivility, Harassment and Discrimination, and
Workplace Violence*

Trainers present definition and examples of incivility.
Trainers review organization's equal employment opportunity policies and
    procedures.
Trainers note similarity in responses of employees to incivility, harassment and
    discrimination, and workplace violence.
Trainers discuss organization's commitment to creating a climate in which civility
    is valued.
Trainers make summary comments from this unit.

*Part VIII: Organization's Policies on Workplace Violence and Intimate
Partner Violence as a Workplace Issue*

Trainers ask participants to refer to organization's policies.
Trainers discuss the organization's policy statements and procedures.
Discuss organization's policy and procedures for filing a complaint of workplace
    violence:
    Written and/or oral complaints
    Confidentiality
    Prompt investigations
    Impartiality
    Retaliation
    Determining credibility
    Role of witnesses
    Sanctions and corrective action offered
    False complaints
Discuss policy on intimate partner violence, noting the following:
    Personalized safety plans
    When employee has an order of protection
Trainers introduce individual(s) responsible for investigating complaints of
    workplace violence.
Trainers discuss security measures the organization has in place, for example:
    Weapons policy
    Employee identification badges

(Continued)

Table 7.1 (*continued*)

On-site guard services
Coded card keys for access
Video surveillance
Increased lighting
Alarm systems
Escort and buddy systems
Trainers make summary comments from this unit.

Part IX: Conclusion

Trainers use case studies to provide examples of behavior to participants. The participant are asked about their perceptions of the behavior illustrated in the case studies and how their organization would address such behavior.

Trainers lead a guided discussion about workplace violence.

Trainers refer to participants' goals outlined at the beginning of the training to determine whether goals were met.

Trainers discuss definitions of workplace violence generated at the beginning of the training.

Trainers distribute acknowledgment forms for employees to sign and date attesting they were in attendance at the training. A copy of the acknowledgment form is provided to the employee; human resources maintains a copy.

Trainers lead a general discussion and question-and-answer period.

Trainers provide post-training evaluations.

Trainers remain to discuss issues with employees privately.

---

state-protected class, for example, sex, race/color, national origin, sexual orientation, age, or disability (see volume 1 of this book set).

We note that more severe forms of workplace mistreatment are likely to occur when smaller problems are left to fester. This is the basic tenet of the "broken windows" theory—when broken windows are left unfixed and minor crimes unpunished, criminal behavior is perceived as being encouraged (Kelling & Coles, 1996). As Nydegger et al. (2006) noted: "the broken windows theory can be applied to workplaces trying to prevent and deal with workplace violence. . . . If what is perceived by the organization to be trivial isn't handled immediately, more severe forms of workplace violence may result" (p. 53). In our consulting work, we have found this approach in training on workplace violence to be beneficial for changing corporate culture with respect to discrimination and workplace violence. If management does not intervene at the beginning of this continuum of workplace abuse (incivility), employees are likely to infer that the employer does not offer assistance if and when the incivility spirals into harassment and discrimination or workplace violence.

In addition to the training program on workplace violence, employers should enforce an anti–workplace violence policy statement and investigatory procedures. We refer the reader to sample workplace violence policies, including intimate partner violence as a workplace issue, in Nydegger et al. (2006). Sample policy statements on workplace violence and intimate partner violence are presented in appendix B. We also recommend using needs assessments and post-training evaluations to facilitate optimal training programs (see volume 1, chapter 14).

Furthermore, we recommend organizations work with their Employees Assistance Programs (EAPs) on workplace violence in the following ways: (1) providing short-term counseling to managers and employees; (2) providing referrals for counseling within the employee's community; (3) consulting with a Threat Assessment Team; (4) training managers to deal with employee victims of workplace violence without diagnosing the employee; (5) providing referrals for domestic violence shelters in the community for victims of intimate partner violence that has spilled over to the workplace; and (6) advising managers on how to identify preincident indicators of workplace violence (Paludi, Wilmot, & Speach, in press; Smith & Mazin, 2004).

Finally, organizations should conduct annual anonymous organizational climate surveys (Parker et al., 2003) to determine whether employees perceive their work environment to be tolerant of incivility and other forms of interpersonal mistreatment or free from mistreatment. Climate surveys also help employers establish a benchmark for evaluating modifications in their workplace violence management program, including incivility and harassment or discrimination prevention (Reio & Ghosh, 2009).

REFERENCES

Andersson, L., & Pearson, C. (1999). Tit for tat? The spiraling effect of incivility in the workplace. *Academy of Management Review, 24,* 452–471.
Atkinson, W. (2000). The everyday face of workplace violence. *Risk Management, 47,* 12.
Baron, R., & Neumann, J. (1996). Workplace violence and workplace aggression: Evidence on their relative frequency and potential causes. *Aggressive Behavior, 22,* 161–173.

Bowie, V., Fisher, B., & Cooper, C. (Eds.). (2005). *Workplace violence: Issues, trends, and strategies.* New York: Willan.

Chapel, D., & DeMartino, V. (1998). *Violence at work.* Geneva: International Labour Office.

Cortina, L., Magley, V., Willilams, J., & Langout, R. (2001). Incivility in the workplace: Incidence and impact. *Journal of Occupational Health Psychology, 6,* 64–80.

Cortina, L., & Wasti, S. (2005). Profiles in coping: Responses to sexual harassment across persons, organizations, and cultures. *Journal of Applied Psychology, 90,* 182–192.

Dansky, B., & Kilpatrick, D. (1997). Effects of sexual harassment. In W. O'Donohue (Ed.), *Sexual harassment: Theory, research, and practice* (pp. 152–174). Boston: Allyn & Bacon.

Einarsen, S., Hoel, H., Zapf, D., & Cooper, C. (2003). *Bullying and emotional abuse in the workplace: International perspectives in research and practice.* New York: Taylor & Francis.

Esen, E. (2004). *SHRM workplace violence survey.* Alexandria, VA: Society for Human Resource Management.

Fitzgerald, L. F., Shullman, S., Bailey, N., Richards, M., Swecker, J., Gold, Y., et al. (1988). The incidence and dimensions of sexual harassment in academia and the workplace. *Journal of Vocational Behavior, 32,* 152–175.

Kelling, G., & Coles, C. (Eds.). (1996). *Fixing broken windows: Restoring order and reducing crime in our communities.* New York: Free Press.

Kelloway, E., Barling, J., & Hurrell, J. (2006). *Handbook of workplace violence.* New York: Sage.

Levy, A., & Paludi, M. (2002). *Workplace sexual harassment.* Upper Saddle River, NJ: Prentice Hall.

Lim, S., & Cortina, L. (2005). Interpersonal mistreatment in the workplace: The interface and impact of general incivility and sexual harassment. *Journal of Applied Psychology, 90,* 483–496.

Lundberg-Love, P., & Marmion, S. (2003). Sexual harassment in the private sector. In M. Paludi, & C. Paludi (Eds.), *Academic and workplace sexual harassment: A handbook of cultural, social science, management, and legal perspectives* (pp. 78–101). Westport, CT: Praeger.

Meleis, A. (Ed.). (2001). *Women's work, health, and quality of life.* New York: Haworth.

Nydegger, R., Paludi, M., DeSouza, E., & Paludi, C. (2006). Incivility, sexual harassment, and violence in the workplace. In M. Karsten (Ed.), *Gender, race, and ethnicity in the workplace* (pp. 51–81). Westport, CT: Praeger.

OHSA (Occupational Health and Safety Administration). (2004). *Guidelines for preventing workplace violence for health care and social service workers.* Retrieved October 25, 2009, from http://www.osha.gov/Publications/osha3148.pdf.

Paludi, M., Nydegger, R., & Paludi, C. (2006). *Understanding workplace violence: A guide for managers and employees.* Westport, CT: Praeger.

Paludi, M., & Paludi, C. (Eds.). (2003). *Academic and workplace sexual harass-ment.* Westport, CT: Praeger.

Paludi, M., Wilmot, J., & Speach, L. (in press). Intimate partner violence as a workplace concern: Impact on women's emotional and physical well-being and careers. In M. Paludi (Ed.), *Feminism and women's rights worldwide.* Westport, CT: Praeger.

Parker, C., Baltes, B., Young, S., Huff, J., Altmann, R., LaCost, H., & Roberts, J. (2003). Relationships between psychological climate perceptions and work outcomes: A meta-analytic review. *Journal of Organizational Behavior, 24,* 389–416.

Reio, T., & Ghosh, R. (2009). Antecedents and outcomes of workplace incivil-ity: Implications for human resource development research and practice. *Human Resource Development Quarterly, 20*, 237–264.

SHRM (Society for Human Resource Management). (2000). Retrieved May 11, 2010, from http://www.shrm.org.

Smith, S., & Mazin, R. (2004). *The HR answer book.* New York: AMACOM.

VandenBos, G., & Bulatao, E. (Eds.). (1996). *Violence on the job: Identifying risks and developing solutions.* Washington, DC: American Psychological Association.

8

Emerging Evidence on Diversity Training Programs

Eden B. King, Lisa M. V. Gulick, and David A. Kravitz

Increasing diversity in the global workplace, coupled with evidence of challenges that can arise when diverse individuals interact, has generated a variety of diversity management efforts. One of the most commonly espoused (Cox & Blake, 1991) and implemented (Esen, 2005) strategies is diversity training. Diversity training refers to formal educational programs designed to address cultural awareness and intercultural behaviors, and encompasses programs with a wide variety of labels, including racial awareness, antidiscrimination, and sexual harassment prevention training. Historically, such efforts grew out of civil rights legislation and focused on compliance, evolving over time into awareness initiatives, and more recently, into complex and interactive sessions (Herring, 2009) that focus on behavior capabilities and improving individual's diversity management competency. Diversity management competency refers to "an individual's level of awareness and knowledge of how culture and other aspects of one's group identity are crucial to an informed professional understanding of human behavior in and outside of work and the interpersonal skills necessary to effectively work with and manage demographically diverse individuals, groups, and organizations" (Avery & Thomas, 2004, p. 382). This chapter briefly describes the status of diversity training initiatives and summarizes emerging empirical evidence on diversity training. Possessing a comprehensive understanding of what occurs in both practice and research is essential for integrating knowledge, informing the way forward, and promoting the utilization of effective best practices.

STATUS OF DIVERSITY TRAINING

The current status of diversity training programs is informed by practitioner reports. The prevalence of diversity training has increased markedly in recent years. Surveys of the Society for Human Resource Management (SHRM) membership revealed an increase from 32 percent (Rynes & Rosen, 1995) to 67 percent (Esen, 2005) in a single decade. In structured interviews, diversity training providers (Bendick, Egan, & Lofhjelm, 2001) indicated that their programs consist of about 25 trainees with one or two instructors, lasting 10 hours, with frequent use of activities that would stimulate active learning. The content of training included discrimination, stereotypes, and the business case for diversity. The most commonly cited goals of training were to change workplace behavior, promote organizational change, and increase awareness. Trainers reported a small but positive effect of their training, particularly with regard to awareness outcomes. Based on these results, Bendick et al. (2001) suggest that effective diversity training will (1) have strong support from top management, (2) be tailored to each organization, (3) link diversity to central operating goals, (4) be taught by managerial or organization development professionals, (5) enroll employees of all levels, (6) involve discussion of discrimination as a general process, (7) explicitly address individual behavior, (8) be complemented by changes in human resources practices, and (9) affect the corporate culture. Taken together, it is likely that diversity training adhering to these guidelines will benefit organizations.

EMERGING DIVERSITY TRAINING EVIDENCE

In line with contemporary preferences for evidence-based management, empirical evidence on the effectiveness of approaches to diversity training is emerging. A recent review of the diversity training literature (Kulik & Roberson, 2008) determined that diversity training has been linked with positive short-term outcomes, but has mixed effects in the long term. In the following section, we briefly summarize existing evidence according to phases of general training programs: needs analysis, antecedent conditions, training design, and evaluation.

Needs Analysis

First and foremost, it is of critical importance to consider the training needs, goals of a diversity training program, and the environment in which the program will be implemented. Best practice dictates that any training intervention begin with an analysis of individual and organizational needs before implementing actual training (Salas & Cannon-Bowers, 2001). Additionally, organizational theorists suggest that companies may be operating in different developmental stages and that training must be designed in line with these stages (Agars & Kattke, 2004). Furthermore, person-level analyses are needed to determine trainees' level of trust in the trainer, how well the trainee knows other participants, and whether they have received previous diversity training (Roberson, Kulik, & Pepper, 2003). If, for example, individual trainees or the organization as a whole are resistant to diversity training, the program may need to begin with an "unfreezing" process (Allen & Montgomery, 2001), aimed at reducing resistance or backlash before delving into the training program. Unfortunately, such a detailed needs analysis may be impractical, particularly for smaller organizations with limited resources (Hite & McDonald, 2006) and at the individual level when many employees are to be trained.

ANTECEDENT CONDITIONS

Trainees' experiences during training are affected by what they bring to the work environment with them. This includes aspects of their personality and experience that may be explored in the needs analysis process, as well as the organizational conditions that lead up to the training (Salas & Cannon-Bowers, 2001). Researchers have begun to study the efficacy of framing of diversity training and pretraining interventions.

A frame is "a psychological devise that offers a perspective and manipulates salience in order to influence subsequent judgments" (Holladay, Knight, Paige, & Quiñones, 2003, p. 246). A comparison of the effectiveness of training that was framed as either remedial or developmental, labeled as either "Diversity Training" or "Building Human Relations," yielded a complex pattern of results. Although the findings do not definitively point to a particular strategy as being more effective than another, they suggest that some trainees benefit more from training when it is framed broadly as a developmental opportunity to learn about building human relations rather than remedial and focused narrowly on racial awareness. Unfortunately, more work is needed to clarify what type of framing should be implemented in practice.

In addition to the framing of diversity training, research has considered the effectiveness of brief interventions before training. In one study of students in a diversity training program, half of the trainees set specific, challenging, and attainable personal goals related to diversity, whereas the other half did not set any goals related to diversity (Madera, King, & Hebl, 2009). Over the course of six months, those individuals who set such goals were more likely to report engaging in diversity-supportive behaviors than individuals who did not set goals. In another experimental study, before engaging in either diversity training or wine-tasting training, half of the participants learned about a perceptual bias called the "bias blindspot" which reflects a tendency for individuals to think that others are more biased than they are personally biased (Gulick, King, Kravitz, Peddie, & Jose, 2009). The results of this study suggest that such pretreatment can encourage diversity-supportive behaviors over time. If confirmed, this finding is of value to diversity practitioners.

Training Design

The specific components of effective diversity training programs have rarely been studied by organizational researchers. Roberson et al. (2003) summarized the most common questions of contention among diversity training researchers: (1) what is the best type of training? (awareness, skill, combination); (2) how should diversity be defined? (narrow versus broad); (3) should confrontational approaches be used? (directly discuss an individual's opinions on diversity); (4) what should the group composition look like? (heterogeneous or homogenous groups); and (5) do the demographics of the trainer matter? (trainer-trainees are similar or different). The answer to each of these questions seems to be "it depends." For example, Roberson, Kulik, and Pepper (2001) studied the implications of group composition and prior experience with diversity training in a sample of teaching assistants. With regard to knowledge and behavioral criteria, homogeneous groups led to higher performance for trainees with more experience, but group type had no effect for trainees with less experience.

Much more research is needed. Individuals responsible for designing diversity training programs should consider the results of needs analyses to determine what the goals of training are in the context in which it is given and in light of the trainees' backgrounds, beliefs, and experiences.

Evaluation

When considering training evaluation, it is important to consider both *what* should be measured and *how* it should be assessed. Outcomes of training can include general reactions to the training, learning (including knowledge, attitudes, and behaviors), transfer of training content to the job, and organizational-level outcomes. With regard to diversity training, the primary focus of most evaluations has been on the immediate reactions of trainees to the training (see Kulik & Roberson, 2008), which generally seem to be positive. Less well understood but much more important, however, are the implications of diversity training for behaviors that occur on the job. Indeed, according to a survey of human resources professionals, practitioners, and diversity experts, one of the major concerns in the field of diversity is the predominant focus on awareness rather than action (Esen, 2005).

It is imperative that training evaluation is aligned with training goals. Because the most common goal cited by diversity trainers (Bendick et al., 2001) is to change workplace behavior of trainees, this is where measurement should focus. How, then, can we assess these behaviors? Self-report methods are subject to socially desirable responding and thus may be problematic. An alternative method would be to engage trainees' workgroups in the evaluation process and initiate a 360-degree appraisal of the employee's diversity-related behaviors (Sanchez & Medkik, 2004). A less costly alternative might be to assess the behavioral judgments of trainees using a situational judgment test (Gulik et al., 2009; Roberson et al., 2001) that requires trainees to indicate what they would do in a relevant workplace situation. Ultimately, organizations may be interested in assessing organizational outcomes such as an organization's climate for diversity turnover, and productivity over time to determine the effectiveness of diversity management programs.

CONCLUSION

Overall, diversity training research has begun to address meaningful questions about how to implement effective education programs related to diversity. It has been stated that, "now more than ever, organizations must rely on workplace learning and continuous improvement in order to remain competitive" (Salas & Cannon-Bowers, 2001, p. 471). Given population shifts and findings that diversity can engender conflict, the need for training seems particularly strong with regard to diversity training. Thus, more research is needed to ensure that learners develop diversity management competency successfully.

REFERENCES

Agars, M. D., & Kattke, J. L. (2004). Models and practices of diversity management: A historical review and presentation of a new integration theory. In M. S. Stockdale, & F. Crosby (Eds.), *The psychology and management of workplace diversity* (pp. 55–77). Oxford: Blackwell.

Allen, R. S., & Montgomery, K. A. (2001). Applying an organizational development approach to creating diversity. *Organizational Dynamics, 30*(2), 149–161.

Avery, D. R., & Thomas, K. M. (2004). Blending content and contact: The roles of diversity curriculum and campus heterogeneity in fostering diversity management competency. *Academy of Management Learning and Education, 3*, 380–396.

Bendick, M., Jr., Egan, M. L., & Lofhjelm, S. M. (2001). Workforce diversity training: From anti-discrimination compliance to organizational development. *Human Resource Planning, 24*(2), 10–25.

Cox, T. H., & Blake, S. (1991). Managing cultural diversity: Implications for organizational competitiveness. *Academy of Management Executives, 5*(3), 45–56.

Esen, E. (2005). *2005 workplace diversity practices survey report.* Alexandria, VA: Society for Human Resource Management.

Gulick, L. M. V., King, E. B., Kravitz, D. A., Peddie, C., & Jose, I. (2009). Enhancing diversity training outcomes: Recognizing bias about bias. Unpublished manuscript, George Mason University, Fairfax, VA.

Herring, C. (2009). Does diversity pay? Race, gender, and the business case for diversity. *American Sociological Review, 74*, 208–224.

Hite, L. M., & McDonald, K. S. (2006). Diversity training pitfalls and possibilities: An exploration of small and mid-sized U.S. organizations. *Human Resource Development International, 9*(3), 365–377.

Holladay, C. L., Knight, J. L., Paige, D. L., & Quiñones, M. A. (2003). The influence of framing on attitudes toward diversity training. *Human Resource Development Quarterly, 14*(3), 245–263.

Kulik, C. T., & Roberson, L. (2008). Diversity initiative effectiveness: What organizations can (and cannot) expect from diversity recruitment, diversity training, and formal diversity mentoring programs. In A. P. Brief (Ed.), *Diversity at work* (pp. 265–317). Cambridge: Cambridge University Press.

Madera, J., King, E. B., & Hebl, M. R. (2009). Enhancing the effects of diversity training: How setting goals and mentor support can improve trainees' attitudes and behaviors. Unpublished manuscript, University of Houston, Houston, TX.

Roberson, L., Kulik, C. T., & Pepper, M. B. (2001). Designing effective diversity training: Influence of group composition and trainee experience. *Journal of Organizational Behavior, 22*(8), 871–885.

Roberson, L., Kulik, C.T., & Pepper, M. B. (2003). Using needs assessment to resolve controversies in diversity training design. *Group & Organization Management, 28*(1), 148–174.

Rynes, S., & Rosen, B. (1995). A field survey of factors affecting the adoption and perceived success of diversity training. *Personnel Psychology, 48*, 247–270.

Salas, E., & Cannon-Bowers, J. A. (2001). The science of training: A decade of progress. *Annual Review of Psychology, 52*, 471–499.

Sanchez, J. I., & Medkik, N. (2004). The effects of diversity awareness training on differential treatment. *Group and Organization Management, 29*, 517–536.

III

Meeting Emerging
Strategic Challenges

9

On Diversity and Competitive Advantage

Kenneth W. Moore

In today's global and hypercompetitive world, most managers recognize that the new game of business requires speed, flexibility, and continual self-reinvention. Executives understand that skilled and motivated people from diverse backgrounds and experiences can lead to a significant competitive advantage over other organizations.

Diversity, in one form or another, has been an operating and integral part of our professional and personal lives since the founding of this country. As a modern philosophy, it is difficult to argue with Martin Luther King's desire to see his children judged on the content of their character rather than on the color of their skin. Yet philosophical agreements do not necessarily mean that actions will happen and that changes will result. There has to be a compelling reason for change. For individuals, that compelling reason is, more often than not, enlightened self-interest. For organizations, diversity generates competitive advantage. How do we develop our leaders to take advantage of the opportunities presented by a diverse culture?

RETHINKING TRAINING STRATEGY

Many well-constructed leadership programs tend to focus on the theoretical and academic thinking of past scholars. Organizational development concepts like Maslow's Hierarchy of Needs and McGregor's Theory X vs. Theory Y are useful background tools, but they do not lead to tangible competitive advantage. Our current world is vastly different from the world in which Maslow and McGregor based their research.

In the 21st-century knowledge economy, for example, hierarchical structures have been replaced by networks at Google. Bureaucratic systems at General Electric have been transformed into flexible processes, and control-based authority has evolved into relationships that focus on empowerment, coaching and the delivery of results that enhance the mission of the company.

It is evident that the accumulated wisdom and knowledge of senior management cannot be effectively distributed to selected individuals and departments down the line to generate temporary advantages or to solve short-term problems. Wisdom and knowledge have always existed in the heads of all individuals where value added concepts and practices are nurtured.

THE MEANING OF DIVERSITY

It can be argued that diversity in the U.S. traces its philosophical roots to racial, ethnic, and gender characterizations, of which much has been written. In the 21st century's digitally interconnected and global marketplace, however, these characterizations are rapidly being augmented by additional forces that are just as compelling. Diversity in race, ethnicity, and gender are just three elements that are being reconsidered to answer a primary question: "Will my company's approach to diversity add to, or subtract from, our ability to achieve our business plan?"

These additional concepts of diversity include, but are not limited to, generational differences, religious and political differences, demographic shifts to other regions of the country, and socio-cultural issues represented by lifestyles, values, and belief systems. Thus, diversity is an accumulation of related concepts that must be integrated into the basic cultural DNA of the company.

THE FOCUS ON HUMAN CAPITAL

Human beings, not machines or processes, create competitive advantage. Each employee comes to the company with a fundamental set of knowledge, skills, and abilities (KSAs). They also come with a unique set of experiences, biases, and expectations. Leadership's job is to capitalize on these unique KSAs and build upon their strengths.

HOW DOES ONE DO THIS?

With tight budgets, managers will spend money on subjects that will justify a return on their investment. Thus, the development training focus is no longer based on theoretical history. It is based on subjects that center on desired outcomes as viewed by the employee, the customer, and the owners—outcomes that cause customers to continue buying our products or services at a premium price. More explicitly, it is based on the execution of the business plan, not just on philosophical desires.

The training mind-set is not specifically directed at diversity as a desirable philosophical state of existence. That's a given. Rather, it is directed at generating value from the complexities of business and tapping into the distinct KSAs of the people who work with you. Consider these examples:

Diversity and the Search for Talent

Many businesses long ago realized that their ability to tap into the skills and insights of their employees such as language and cross-cultural skills provided them with an advantage over other organizations. A city like New York has a huge immigrant population, many of whom do not speak English. Organizations that employ multilingual people who speak English and Portuguese, Russian, Spanish, or Arabic are able to work effectively and productively with those communities.

Today's so-called Generation Y (those born between 1985–2000) have much different views of work and play than their parents or grandparents. Practically from the day they were born, they have been wired into the 24/7 mind-set that runs counter to the 8:00 A.M. to 5:00 P.M., 40-hour workweek mind-set of current employment practices and the law. They insist on a work-life balance, because their loyalty to their employer is not reciprocated. They want to work for a socially progressive company that advances corporate social responsibilities in the communities in which they do business. And, they are nomadic—willing to go to where they are appreciated and valued.

Understanding generational issues is a key ingredient in attracting and retaining high caliber employees as well as managing current employees. Leaders need to understand and act on the issues affecting the four generations of human capital: age discrimination, pensions and health care, shifting demographics, child and elder care, digitization of work, outsourcing to secure lower costs, professional and social network development, and movement of industrial sectors to geographies that provide cheaper labor, lower energy cost, and a political climate that is pro-business.

Diversity as a Key Element of Business Strategy

Progressive-thinking organizations recognize that diversity has a direct impact on whether the company survives and prospers or goes out of business. Because wisdom and knowledge cannot be effectively delegated in the 21st century's fast-moving economy, execution of the business plan depends on the skills, ideas, experiences, and talent of local employees. These are the people who produce and deliver their products and services to customers. They are the ones who identify internal and external opportunities that generate new business prospects and solutions that benefit the customers, the stakeholder, and the employees.

For example, Madame C. J. Walker (1867–1919) was an African American laundress who identified a need for beauty and hair care products for black women. She identified a large market need and helped satisfy that need with her products. Walker's beauty products complemented her belief that one of the ways black women could gain access to business careers and financial power was by looking more acceptable to members of the dominant mainstream white society. She became the first American female to become a millionaire on her own achievements—and an active proponent of women's rights and racial integration.

During World War II, U.S. Marines in the Pacific used Native American Navaho code talkers to send and receive classified messages to the battlefield commanders. The complexities of the Navaho language, and the absolute lack of any Japanese Navaho speakers, became a significant factor in the Marines' ultimate success on Iwo Jima, Guadalcanal, and Tarawa.

Diversity and Core Competence

An organization's core competence—that which it does better than anyone else and is valued by the customer—is in a state of constant change. Each company identifies its core competency: Nordstrom's focus is on exemplary customer service, Black and Decker's expertise is on electric motors, and Sony's is on its miniaturization skills. A company's core competency provides a direct benefit to its customers, is not easily replicated by competitors, and can be leveraged into multiple units of an organization.

In the 21st century, core competencies can be found within the employees themselves. The ability to capitalize on the creativity of its employees is a key ingredient to sustainability in the fast-changing world. There is a trust and respect that the organization has for its employees. It demonstrates this trust and respect by directing problem solving and opportunity development downward to those people who actually build and deliver the product or service and interact with the customer.

Consider the ubiquitous Egg McMuffin. It was not invented by McDonalds' corporate research and development team. Instead, it was created by a single franchise owner in California who experimented with various breakfast items. At that time (1972), McDonalds was only serving lunch and dinner. From that creative spirit of one individual, McDonalds was able to take this unique idea and parlay it into an entire breakfast menu—and business segment—focused around the Egg McMuffin.

Diversity and National Cultures

Each nation generates its own culture based on its history and experiences. While difficult to describe, they exist and are powerful forces that must be understood. Concepts such as equal opportunity for all regardless of race, creed, gender, and ethnicity are ingrained into the American psyche. These concepts are nonstarters in other countries that are governed by strict authority or theology. Life, liberty, and the pursuit of happiness are constitutional guarantees in the United States; however, they are not found anywhere in Iran, Sudan, or Cuba.

Furthermore, the United States generally is considered an individual-oriented society in which the individual is celebrated and praised. Where individual praise for a job well done in the United States would be seen as a positive motivator or reward, individual celebration and praise in China causes discomfort with most managers and employees because their society embraces collectivism or teamwork.

Concurrently, the U.S. generally adheres to a short-term orientation in which results that are not generated immediately are viewed as less valuable than results that are achieved immediately, or within the next fiscal quarter. It is neither right nor wrong—it is just normal. As such, sharp executives accept a nation's time-line horizon for what it is and modify their operations accordingly.

CONCLUSION

Concepts of diversity, as seen through the lens of the American experiences, embrace pluralism. Pluralism, for example, allows for all religions to coexist. It allows leaders to tap into the wisdom, experience, and strengths of a community's environment and culture and extract from it substances that benefits everyone.

In the United States, we are blessed to have developed our awareness and appreciation of the strengths that ethnic, racial, gender, generational, and other communities bring to the social and professional fabric of society. Resolving business and social issues is dependent on an open and constructive sharing of diverse points of view. Yet, as we become more enmeshed in the global community, we also must be aware that other nations might not see the issues from the same perspective as us. While the American baby boomers were experiencing Woodstock, Vietnam, and the civil and women's rights movements during the 1960s, our counterparts in China were experiencing Mao's Cultural Revolution. Our perspectives are vastly different. We must continue to develop our awareness and appreciation for the diversity contained in our world, embrace the positive aspects of such diversity, and establish a common ground upon which safe, stable, and prosperous societies can coexist. This is the basis for U.S. competitive advantage.

10

Reducing Stigma about Employees with HIV/AIDS: Workplace Responses

Laura G. Barron, Mikki Hebl, and Michele A. Paludi

> The test of courage comes when we are in the minority. The test of tolerance comes when we are in the majority.
>
> —Ralph W. Sockman, senior pastor of Christ
> Church of New York City

In 2006, the Equal Employment Opportunity Commission (EEOC) filed a Human Immunodeficiency Virus (HIV)–related disability discrimination lawsuit against Chesapeake Academy in Arnold, Maryland. The suit alleged that Chauncey Stevenson, a second-grade teacher was fired when the school learned of his HIV positive status. The EEOC claimed the school's headmaster told Mr. Stevenson that the parents and others in the school community would not want him to teach. Consequently, the school did not renew Mr. Stevenson's academic contract for the following year (2006–2007). A ruling stated that in addition to offering monetary relief in the form of a $79,750 settlement, Chesapeake Academy had to make retributions by (1) adding a notice indicating its commitment to maintaining an environment free of disability discrimination and retaliation, and (2) providing training to all managers in an attempt to make them aware of disability discrimination. Chesapeake did not admit liability in the consent decree.

More recently, the EEOC also filed a lawsuit in September 2009 in the U.S. District Court for the District of Maryland, alleging that Innershore Enterprises, Inc., doing business as Marlow 6 Theatre, violated federal law when it fired a concession manager because she was HIV positive. Once Marlow 6 became aware of this employee's HIV status, she was reassigned to the less desirable position as theater "greeter" and placed on a different work shift. The theater owner and president reportedly stated that "I can do what I want" in reference to altering the manager's position. This suit was still actively being pursued at the time this chapter was written.

FROM STIGMA TO DISCRIMINATION

A stigma refers to a characteristic that devalues a person, and designates a person as flawed, or somehow less than fully human in the eyes of other society members (Deacon, 2006; Scheid, 2005). As the cases at the beginning of this chapter illustrate, more than 25 years after AIDS was first reported, the stigma of HIV/AIDS continues to exist in the U.S. workplace. First, U.S. employers are still making consequential personnel decisions (for example, termination, demotion) on the basis of employee HIV/AIDS status. Second, stereotypes and attitudes of prejudice toward employees with HIV/AIDS status are so entrenched that employers continue to "justify" such personnel actions as necessary to satisfy the prejudices of the larger community (for example, "HIV status would not be well received").

Fortunately, the cases at the beginning of this chapter also illustrate that workplace discrimination on the basis of HIV/AIDS status is not only consequential for the employees with HIV/AIDS. Rather, employers can expect to face legal penalty for their discriminatory actions. EEOC Action Regional Attorney Debra Lawrence noted that "[a]s long as employers continue to make employment decisions based on uninformed prejudices and irrational fears, we will continue to bring lawsuits like this" (EEOC, 2009a). Indeed, even given that only a small percentage of individuals who experience workplace discrimination file with the EEOC (see D'Aiuto, Smith, & Paludi, appendix A in volume 1), in 2008 alone, the EEOC received 19,453 complaints of disability discrimination including 185 related to HIV discrimination and harassment (EEOC, 2009b; also see Paludi, DeSouza, & Dodd, chapter 2 in volume 1).

In this chapter, we briefly review legal protection from HIV/AIDS employment discrimination and harassment under the Americans with Disabilities Act (ADA), and requirements of "reasonable accommodation" for HIV/AIDS. We then focus on the additional ADA requirement of "reasonable care" that employers must take in preventing and responding to HIV/AIDS discrimination and harassment.

LEGAL RESPONSIBILITIES

In organizations with 15 or more employees, the federal ADA legally protects all applicants and employees who have HIV and AIDS. Although not all individuals with medical conditions can prove that they are "disabled" under the law, the 2008 ADA amendment specifies that major impairments to immune system functioning, such as that resulting from HIV or AIDS, are covered. Even employees who are wrongly perceived or regarded as having HIV or AIDS (for example, because they are gay or because they have multiple partners) are covered by the ADA. Importantly, employees who are stigmatized because of their relationship or association with someone who has HIV or AIDS (for example, a friend, a family member) also are covered by the ADA.

The ADA provides protection not only from discrimination toward employees with HIV/AIDS in formal personnel decisions (hiring, termination, demotion, compensation, training), but also from harassment based on HIV/AIDS status, such as ridicule, social isolation, or bullying (Fishbein, 2002; Herek, 1998; Vest, Tarnoff, Carr, Vest, & O'Brien, 2003; Whetten, Reif, Whetten, & Murphy-McMillan, 2008).

According to the ADA guidelines, being HIV positive or having AIDS does not prevent employees or applicants from performing the "essential functions" of the position. Although the ADA does contain an exception for situations in which a disability would pose a direct threat to the health and safety of others, this is interpreted narrowly based on individual assessment. While a surgeon with HIV who performs invasive manual procedures may not be able to perform the essential functions of her position under the ADA (EEOC, 2009c) under most situations, such an exception would not apply. For instance, ADA guidelines specify that HIV would not prevent an employee from food handling, as HIV is not a disease transmissible through food supply according to lists maintained by the Centers for Disease Control and Prevention (CDC) or the Food and Drug Administration (FDA).

Workplaces must provide reasonable accommodations for employees who are HIV positive or have AIDS (see volume 1, chapter 2 for a detailed description of reasonable accommodations). Such accommodations that may be most relevant to employees with HIV/AIDS include, but are not limited to, the following: adjustments to work schedules, or offering flexible employment for medical appointments, counseling, and medical treatment (for example, telecommuting, time off or career break, job sharing, as long as it is not offered to avoid in-person contact with employees) (Blanck, Andersen, Wallach, & Tenney, 1994; EEOC, 2009c; Foote, 2000).

In addition to providing reasonable accommodations, organizations must exercise "reasonable care" (see volume 1, chapter 14) in preventing and dealing with HIV/AIDS discrimination and harassment. This reasonable care includes at a minimum: (1) an effective and enforced policy, (2) effective and enforced complaint procedures, and (3) training programs for all members of the organization. Note that such steps as providing official company antidiscrimination policies and diversity training programs have been found to relate to decreased perceptions of discrimination toward other stigmatized groups (see Button, 2001; Griffith & Hebl, 2002; Ragins & Cornwell, 2001).

A sample policy concerning HIV/AIDS awareness in general and the organization's responsibilities in providing reasonable accommodation and reasonable care is presented in appendix B. Employers should include HIV/AIDS policy and procedures separate from the ADA policy statement, with cross-references to both policies. A sample ADA policy is also present in appendix B.

The third component of reasonable care is for organizations to facilitate training programs on HIV/AIDS for managers and nonmanagerial employees. The goal of HIV/AIDS training (as well as the policy statement) is to (1) assist the organization in de-stigmatizing the disease; (2) encourage safe behavior at the workplace (for example, Occupational Safety and Health Administration [OSHA] Bloodborne Pathogens Standards) as well as in the community; (3) improve understanding of the workplace's HIV/AIDS policy and complaint procedures; and (4) improve understanding of HIV and AIDS and available treatment options. Myths versus stereotypes about HIV/AIDS may be addressed in the training—for example, HIV may be spread through casual contact with an HIV infected co-worker, HIV and AIDS are the same disease, people with AIDS look a certain way (they are easily recognizable), or all gay individuals have AIDS.

A sample training program is presented in Table 10.1. This training program is designed for managers and may be easily adjusted for employees. We encourage the reader to consult with sources on needs assessment and post-training evaluations to develop and facilitate effective training programs (Barbazette, 2006; Blanchard, Thacker, & Blanchard, 2003; Brown, 2002; see Paludi et al., chapter 13 in volume 1).

In addition to these elements of reasonable care, organizations should include the following in their HIV/AIDS management program: posters, signs, ribbons, and articles in company newsletters. All of these educational programs will assist in endorsing the organization's commitment with respect to HIV/AIDS as well as de-stigmatize the diseases.

Table 10.1
Sample Training Program for Managers on HIV/AIDS Discrimination and Harassment

---

Goals of the Training Program

Provide managers with a clear understanding of their rights and responsibilities with respect to HIV/AIDS discrimination and harassment.

Provide managers with information concerning the organization's policy statement and procedures against HIV/AIDS discrimination and harassment.

Provide managers with information about reasonable accommodations for employees.

Discuss the emotional and physical reactions to being a victim of HIV/AIDS harassment and discrimination.

Dispel myths about HIV/AIDS.

Discuss responsible safety behavior in the workplace.

Discuss central role for the employer and managers in preventing HIV/AIDS discrimination and harassment.

At the Conclusion of This Training Program, Managers Will Achieve the Following

Assess their own perceptions of the definition, incidence, and psychological dimensions of HIV/AIDS discrimination and harassment.

Identify the organization's policy and procedures for reporting HIV/AIDS discrimination and harassment.

Identify their rights and responsibilities under the organization's HIV/AIDS policy and procedures.

Topics for Presentation and Discussion
Part I: Welcome, Introductions, and Review of Goals of Training Program

Trainers welcome managers to the training program.

Trainers introduce themselves, their qualifications and background.

Trainers summarize goals of the training program.

Trainers ask managers to state their own goals for the training.

Trainers present responses to all managers.

Table 10.1 (*continued*)

Part II: Myths vs. Realities about Workplace Violence

Trainers ask managers to provide examples of behaviors they believe illustrate
  HIV/AIDS discrimination or harassment.
Trainers discuss each response, then present them to the group.
Trainers provide an overview of the training program, noting where in the
  training each issue raised by managers will be discussed.

Part III: Definition and Incidence of HIV/AIDS

Trainers present definition of HIV.
Trainers present definition of AIDS.
Trainers cite current statistics on the incidence of HIV and AIDS among
  employees.
Trainers discuss the Americans with Disabilities Act (the organization's policy
  statement and that HIV/AIDS is considered a disability by the ADA).
Trainers summarize this unit.

Part IV: Myths vs. Realities

Trainers identify myths associated with HIV/AIDS.
Trainers counter myths with realities about HIV/AIDS.
Trainers discuss relationship among stereotypes or stigma, prejudice, and
  discrimination and harassment of employees.
Trainers discuss stigma associated with sexual orientation.
Trainers summarize this unit.

***Part V: HIV/AIDS Discrimination and Harassment: Impact on Employees
and Workplace***

Trainers discuss psychological symptoms, including the following:

  Depression
  Anger
  Shame
  Denial
  Fear
  Frustration
  Shock
  Anxiety
  Isolation
  Helplessness

Trainers discuss physical symptoms, including the following:

  Headaches
  Tiredness

(Continued)

Table 10.1 (*continued*)

Eating disorders
Sleep problems
Lethargy
Drug abuse
Gastrointestinal disorders

Trainers discuss career effects:

Changes in work habits
Absenteeism
Changes in career goals

Trainers discuss interpersonal effects:

Fear of new people
Lack of trust
Change in social network
Relationship problems
Withdrawal from co-workers

Trainers discuss impact on self-concept:

Poor self concept
Powerlessness
Isolation

Trainers discuss the impact of HIV/AIDS discrimination/harassment on the
workplace:

Decreased morale
Increased absenteeism
Increased turnover
Decreased productivity
Decreased job satisfaction
Reduced team cohesion and performance

Trainers summarize this unit.

*Part VI: Organization's Policies on Americans with Disabilities Act and
HIV/AIDS*

Trainers ask participants to refer to organization's policies.
Trainers discuss the organization's policy and procedures for filing a complaint
of HIV/AIDS discrimination or harassment:

Written and/or oral complaints

(Continued)

Table 10.1 (*continued*)

Confidentiality
Prompt investigations
Impartiality
Retaliation
Determining credibility
Role of witnesses
Sanctions and corrective action offered
False complaints

Trainers introduce individual(s) responsible for investigating complaints of
   HIV/AIDS discrimination and harassment.
Trainers discuss procedures related to employees informing the workplace about
   their HIV or AIDS status:

Confidentiality
Separate filing system for documents
Reasonable accommodations requests
Confidentiality of medical insurance information

Trainers summarize this unit.

Part VII: Conclusion

Trainers use case studies to ask participants their perceptions of specific
   examples of behavior and how their organization would address this
   behavior.
Trainers lead a guided discussion about HIV/AIDS as a workplace concern.
Trainers refer to participants' goals outlined at the beginning of the training to
   determine whether goals were met.
Trainers discuss myths vs. realities of HIV/AIDS generated at the beginning of
   the training.
Trainers distribute acknowledgment forms for managers to sign and date
   indicating they attended the training. A copy of the acknowledgment form is
   provided to the manager; human resources maintains a copy.
Trainers lead a general discussion and question-and-answer period.
Trainers provide post-training evaluations.
Trainers remain to discuss issues with managers privately.

We also recommend that the Employees Assistance Program (EAP) facilitate noon-time seminars on HIV/AIDS to encourage a dialogue among
managers and employees. When possible, employers should extend EAP
services to employees' families. Including a trained HIV/AIDS counselor
as a peer educator may be part of the program. EAPs also may provide

pre-test and post-test counseling for applicants and employees taking an HIV/AIDS test.

Finally, organizations should continuously monitor the effectiveness of their HIV/AIDS management program, using metrics to determine employees' understanding of the disease and the organization's policy and procedures (for example, strengths-weaknesses-opportunities-threats [SWOT] analysis, audit, and barrier analysis; see DeFour & Paludi, chapter 5 in volume 1). Employers should conduct organizational cultural climate surveys to assess the efficacy of current training programs, policies, and procedures and to ensure continuous improvement in the organization's reasonable care to prevent HIV/AIDS harassment and discrimination.

REFERENCES

Barbazette, J. (2006). *Training needs assessment: Methods, tools, and techniques.* New York: John Wiley & Sons.

Blanchard, N., Thacker, J., & Blanchard, P. (2003). *Effective training: Systems strategies and practices.* Upper Saddle River, NJ: Prentice Hall.

Blanck, P., Andersen, J., Wallach, E., & Tenney, J. (1994). Implementing reasonable accommodation using ADR under the ADA: The case of a white-collar employee with bipolar mental illness. *Mental and Physical Disability Law Reporter, 18,* 458–464.

Brown, J. (2002). Training needs assessment: A must for developing an effective training program. *Public Personnel Management, 31,* 569–578.

Button, S. B. (2001). Organizational efforts to affirm sexual diversity: A cross-level examination. *Journal of Applied Psychology, 86,* 17–28.

Deacon, H. (2006). Towards a sustainable theory of health-related stigma: Lessons from the HIV/AIDS literature. *Journal of Community and Applied Social Psychology, 16,* 418–425.

EEOC (Equal Employment Opportunity Commission). (2009a). *Chesapeake academy to pay $79,750 for disability discrimination.* Retrieved November 8, 2009, from http://www.eeoc.gov/eeoc/newsroom/release/archive/9-24-09e.html.

EEOC (Equal Employment Opportunity Commission). (2009b). *Marlow 6 theatre sued by EEOC for disability bias.* Retrieved November 8, 2009, from http://www.eeoc.gov/eeoc/newsroom/release/archive/9-23-09c.html.

EEOC (Equal Employment Opportunity Commission). (2009c). *Disability discrimination.* Retrieved November 1, 2009, from http://www.eeoc.gov/laws/types/disability.cfm.

Fishbein, H. (2002). *Peer prejudice and discrimination: The origins of prejudice.* Mahwah, NJ: Erlbaum.

Foote, W. E. (2000). A model for psychological consultation in cases involving the Americans with Disabilities Act. *Professional Psychology: Research and Practice, 31*(2), 190–196.

Griffith, K., & Hebl, M. (2002). Acknowledgment of sexual orientation in the workplace. *Journal of Applied Psychology, 87,* 1191–1199.

Herek, G. (1998). *Stigma and sexual orientation: Understanding prejudice against lesbians, gay men, and bisexuals.* New York: Sage

Ragins, B. R., & Cornwell, J. M. (2001). Pink triangles: Antecedents and consequences of perceived workplace discrimination against gay and lesbian employees. *Journal of Applied Psychology, 86,* 1244–1261.

Scheid, T. (2005). Stigma as a barrier to employment: Mental disability and the Americans with Disabilities Act. *International Journal of Law and Psychiatry, 28,* 670–690.

Vest, M. J., Tarnoff, K., Carr, J. C., Vest, J., & O'Brien, F. (2003). Factors influencing a manager's decision to discipline employees for refusal to work with an HIV/AIDS infected coworker. *Employee Responsibilities and Rights Journal, 15*(1), 31–43.

Whetten, K., Reif, S., Whetten, R., & Murphy-McMillan, L. (2008). Trauma, mental health, distrust, and stigma among HIV-positive persons: Implications for effective care. *Journal of Psychosomatic Medicine, 70,* 531–538.

11

The Destructive Consequences of Discrimination

Timothy R. Stacey and Paula K. Lundberg-Love

INTRODUCTION

When working with individuals suffering from psychological distress such as depression and anxiety, it is important to understand what factors play a role in the development of such disorders. One such factor is discrimination. Discrimination is the treatment or consideration of—or making a distinction in favor of or against—a person or thing based on the group, class, or category to which that person or thing belongs rather than on individual merit. Discrimination affects various populations and can occur in different ways. Therefore, understanding the link between discrimination and distress is critical. Although psychological distress can underlie symptoms such as anxiety and depression, it also can give rise to poor self-esteem and substance abuse.

TYPES OF DISCRIMINATION

Because individuals are discriminated against for a variety of reasons, discrimination will be experienced differently by different groups in different cultures. Kessler, Mickleson, and Williams (1999) found that ethnicity, gender, age, and aspects of appearance are the most common reasons for discrimination, while religion, socioeconomic status, sexual orientation, and physical or mental disabilities also are common. While the reasons for discrimination transcend culture, the manifestations of discrimination vary drastically among different cultures. For example, one study found that African American youth experience discrimination in the form of being perceived as dangerous, untrustworthy, or unable to succeed in school (Sellers, Copeland-Linder, Martin, & Lewis, 2006). In the same American culture, however, Chinese Americans experience discrimination based on stereotypes portraying them as perpetually foreign, or unable to acculturate, and lacking in social competence, where the latter is defined as the perception of an individual as unable to interact appropriately in social situations (Cheryan & Monin, 2005). Additionally, individuals can suffer the impact of discrimination simply through the fear of discrimination (Jackson et al., 1996) The fear or expectation of discrimination can increase for various minority groups based on the current events within their cultures. The National Survey of Latinos (2006) found that more than one-half of a nationally representative sample expected an increase in discrimination based on current U.S. policy debates on immigration. Similarly, the Arab American community saw an increase in discrimination after September 11, 2001, when the American Arab Anti-Discrimination Committee reported four times the physical and psychological attacks on Arab Americans in the United States (Moradi & Hasan, 2004).

PSYCHOLOGICAL EFFECTS OF DISCRIMINATION

While manifestations of discrimination can vary greatly, the psychological effects of discrimination are similar. Research has shown that discrimination is linked to poor mental and physical health (Yip, Gee, & Takeuchi, 2008). Discrimination even can lead to higher rates of depression, anxiety, and substance abuse in individuals. Links between lifetime discrimination and mental health disorders across nationally representative samples of individuals have shown increased rates of major depression and generalized anxiety disorder. The effects of discrimination bear a resemblance to those of other types of traumatic experiences. The link between the lifetime prevalence of discrimination and its resultant depression and anxiety are comparable to those associated with sexual assault and exposure to combat (Kessler, Davis, & Kendler, 1997). Discrimination has been linked to higher rates of substance abuse. Studies of the African American population have shown that discrimination leads to higher rates of cigarette smoking (Singleton, Harrell, & Kelly, 1986), alcohol usage (Brown & Tooley, 1989), and other types of substance abuse (Wright, 2001).

EFFECTS OF DISCRIMINATION THROUGH HATE CRIMES

The psychological effects of discrimination discussed in the previous section can be exacerbated by events that are in themselves traumatic. McDevitt (1999) contrasted the effects of biased assaults (that is, assaults that occur based on a negative stereotype the offender holds against the victim) and nonbiased assaults (that is, assaults not directly resulting from an act of discrimination or prejudice) and found that victims of biased assaults reported higher rates of nervousness, anger, intrusion, or personal invasion, than victims of nonbiased assaults. Various theories have been presented with respect to why victims of hate or biased crimes may experience more psychological distress, for longer periods of times as opposed to victims of nonhate crimes.

One such theory by Janoff-Bulman (1979) attempted to explain the effects of hate crimes via the differences between behavioral self-blame and characterological self-blame. This theory explains that psychological distress is experienced by crime victims because the safe world in which they lived has been shattered. After this event, the victim attempts to gain a sense of self-control through behavioral self-blame. In effect, the victim tries to attribute the cause of the event in some way to a behavior executed by the victim. In this way, if the victim believes that he or she is partially to blame, then that means the victim can take measures to prevent being victimized in the future. In characterological self-blame, the victim attributes the events of the crime to some characterological flaw. In this situation, the victim is unable to regain any sense of control over his or her ability to prevent future victimization. Instead, because the victimization occurred due to a specific characteristic that the victim is unable to control, the victim believes that she or he is unable to prevent her or his future victimization. Because the illusion of control or the ability to prevent future victimization is not present in the case of characterological self-blame, higher rates of depression are reported in individuals who adopt this postvictimization view of the world (Janoff-Bulman, 1979).

FACTORS INVOLVED IN THE LINK BETWEEN PSYCHOLOGICAL DISTRESS AND DISCRIMINATION

Although many studies have found a link between discrimination and psychological distress, it is important to study the mediating variables between these links to understand which individuals within a population may be at higher risks to suffer the psychological effects of discrimination.

One factor that has been investigated in the link between discrimination and distress is the loss of a sense of personal control. Reductions in the levels of one's sense of control play a role between discrimination and the experience of psychological distress (Branscombe & Ellemers, 1998). This study linked discrimination to lower levels of perceived control over one's life. This lower sense of control over one's life is associated with lower self-esteem and greater psychological distress among Arab American individuals (Moradi & Hasan, 2004).

Self-esteem plays a role in the discrimination-distress link. A study by Sanchez and Vilain (2009) looked at collective self-esteem, which is the way in which an individual evaluates his or her social group, in male to female transsexuals and its effects on psychological distress. The study examined how collective self-esteem helped an individual cope with discrimination. The authors found that positive identification correlated inversely to levels of psychological distress. In the study, the more positive an individual felt about the transgender community, the less psychological distress they reported. Conversely, the more fear a participant expressed about the possible effects their transgender identity may have, the more psychological distress was reported. This study suggests that the internalization of one's feelings regarding one's transsexual identity may negatively influence one's mental health (Sanchez & Vilain, 2009). These results were consistent with those from other studies that investigated the impact of discrimination on self-esteem among different minority groups. A study by Liang and Grossman (2008) reported that among a sample of college students, Asian Americans had negative feelings about being Asian American. Additionally, the results indicated that negative feelings regarding being Asian American lowered one's personal self-esteem and that such individuals tended to have more interpersonal problems (Liang & Grossman, 2008). Similarly, Fischer and Holz (2007) found that women who held a negative view of women as a social group had more symptoms of depression than women who had a positive view of women as a social group. These findings are consistent with the minority stress theory, which suggests that "people who are more fearful of discrimination report more symptoms of depression and anxiety than do those who are less fearful" (Frost & Meyer, 2009).

Additional studies have examined collective self-esteem and a sense of coherence, which is the confidence that the stimuli in one's internal and external environment are structured, predictable, and explicable, and that an individual has the resources to meet the demands posed by the stimuli. A study by Lam (2007) examined the ways that collective self-esteem and a sense of coherence relate to the psychological distress caused by discrimination. The results of this study suggest that individuals who possess a strong sense of coherence and strong collective self-esteem will experience less psychological distress in response to discrimination. In another study by Ying, Akutsu, Zhang, and Huang (1997) found that a strong sense of coherence is negatively associated with depression and anxiety. The results of this study indicated that those who had a diminished sense of coherence were more susceptible to a heightened perception of discrimination, which put them at a higher risk for anxiety and depression (Lam, 2007).

Another mediator that links discrimination to distress is explained by the stress process theory (Ong, Fuller-Rowell, & Burrow, 2009). This theory posits that psychological distress is related to the individual differences with respect to the manner in which an individual is exposed to and reacts to the chronic and day-to-day stress brought on by discrimination. For example, African Americans who are chronically exposed to racial discrimination are more likely to report greater numbers of stressful life events (Harrell, 2000), appraise stressful situations as threats rather than challenges and engage in maladaptive coping behaviors, which increase the probability of negative affective responses (Martin, Tuch, & Roman, 2003). While chronic exposure to discrimination can increase ones psychological distress, discrimination also influences one's well-being as a daily stressor. Repeated encounters with everyday racial problems increase the probability that African American adults will experience psychological distress (Sellers & Shelton, 2003). Solorzano, Ceja, and Yosso (2000) found that daily racial discrimination results in emotions of discouragement, self-doubt, and isolation for African American students.

Stress proliferation, the tendency for stressors to multiply and create other stressors, is another means by which stress affects one's psychological health. This theory accounts for two types of stressors, including primary stressors, the initial events that cause stress for an individual, and secondary stressors, the stress caused by the numerous consequences of the primary stressor. In the context of the discrimination-distress link, chronic exposure to racial discrimination, a primary stressor, may lead to an accumulation or bundling of daily negative events across multiple life domains, or secondary stressors. Chronic exposure to discrimination plays a negative role in the way in which one deals with the other stressors in his or her life. Furthermore, it was found that daily discrimination and negative events mediated the association between chronic discrimination and depression (Ong et al., 2009).

Additionally, cultural competence has been examined in the discrimination-distress link. When rates of depression were examined among Latino immigrants living in the United States, individuals who had lived in the United States for longer than 13 years reported more depressive symptoms than those who had just arrived in the country (Vega et al., 1998). This research suggests that assimilation into the United States is associated with a significant risk of mental disorders, such as depression (U.S. Department of Health and Human Services, 2001). Cultural competence refers to a set of functional skills that facilitate the performance of culturally specific activities or societal roles (Ogbu, 1981). When one looks at the correlation between cultural competence and depression, individuals with higher level of competence experience less depressive symptoms than individuals with low levels of competence (Torres, 2009).

CONCLUSION

Discrimination can have a variety of negative psychological effects on individuals, including depression, anxiety, and even substance abuse. These effects are mediated through a number of different variables. Higher rates of psychological distress are related to decreased self-esteem, a lack of a sense of personal control, and lower levels of competence. Treatment for individuals suffering the negative psychological effects of discrimination can be more effective if one can identify the mediating factors causing the distress. While the link between distress and discrimination has been demonstrated, understanding the mediating factors involved gives an individual aspects of her or his life that she or he can improve to relieve the distress. Although individuals are unable to control people who discriminate unjustly, through an understanding of the mediating variables related to the distress caused by discrimination, an individual may be able to reduce the amount of distress that is perceived. While the link between discrimination and its resultant negative psychological effects has been outlined, it is only through the modification of mediating variables that an individual has the ability to change the effects of discrimination. Although eradicating discrimination may be impossible, by understanding the mediating variables, such as self-esteem and a sense of control, people may be able to lessen the effects of discrimination on a personal level because the power to change is returned to the individual, who can change his or her life, and perhaps lessen the destructive consequences of discrimination.

REFERENCES

Branscombe, N. R., & Ellemers, N. (1998). Coping with group-based discrimination: Individualistic versus group-level strategies. In J. K. Swim, & C. Stangor (Eds.), *Prejudice: The target's perspective* (pp. 243–265). San Diego, CA: Academic Press.

Brown, F., & Tooley, J. (1989). Alcoholism in the black community. In G. W. Lawson, & A. W. Lawson (Eds.), *Alcoholism and substance use in special populations* (pp. 115–130). Rockville, MD: Aspen Publishers.

Cheryan, S., & Monin, B. (2005). Where are you really from? Asian Americans and identity denial. *Journal of Personality and Social Psychology, 89*(5), 717–730.

Fisher, A. R., & Holz, K. B. (2007). Perceived discrimination and women's psychological distress: The roles of collective and personal self-esteem. *Journal of Counseling Psychology, 54*, 154–164.

Frost, D. M., and Meyer, I. H. (2009). Internalized homophobia and relationship quality among lesbians, gay men, and bisexuals. *Journal of Counseling Psychology, 56*, 97–109.

Harrell, S. P. (2000). A multidimensional conceptualization of racism-related stress: Implications for the well-being of people of color. *American Journal of Orthopsychiatry, 70*, 42–57.

Jackson, J. S., Brown, T. N., Williams, D. R., Torres, M., Sellers, S. L., & Brown, K. (1996). Racism and the physical and mental health status of African Americans. *Ethnic Disparities, 6*, 32–47.

Janoff-Bulman, R. (1979). Characterological versus behavioral self-blame: Inquiries into depression and rape. *Journal of Personality and Social Psychology, 37*, 1798–1809.

Kessler, R. C., Davis, C. G., & Kendler, K. S. (1997). Childhood adversity and adult psychiatric disorder in the U.S. National Comorbidity Survey. *Psychological Medicine, 27*, 1101–1119.

Kessler, R. C., Mickelson, K. D., & Williams, D. R. (1999). The prevalence, distribution, and mental health correlates of perceived discrimination in the United States. *Journal of Health and Social Behavior, 40*, 208–230.

Lam, B. T. (2007). Impact of perceived racial discrimination and collective self-esteem on psychological distress among Vietnamese-American college students' sense of coherence as mediator. *American Journal of Orthopsychiatry, 77*, 370–376.

Liang, B., & Grossman, J. (2008). Discrimination distress among Chinese American adolescents. *Journal of Youth and Adolescence, 37*, 1–11.

Martin, J. K., Tuch, S. A., & Roman, P. M. (2003). Problem drinking patterns among African Americans: The impacts of reports of discrimination, perceptions of prejudice, and "risky" coping strategies. *Journal of Health and Social Behavior, 44*, 408–425.

McDevitt, J. (1999, October). Plenary keynote address. *Paper presented at the meeting of Hate Crimes: Research, Policy and Action.* Los Angeles, CA.

Moradi, B., & Hasan, N. T. (2004). Arab American persons' reported experience of discrimination and mental health: The mediating role of personal control. *Journal of Counseling Psychology, 51*, 418–428.

National Survey of Latinos. (2006). *National Survey of Latinos: The immigration debate.* Washington, DC: Pew Hispanic Center; Menlo Park, CA: Henry J. Kaiser Family Foundation.

Ogbu, J. U. (1981). Origins of human competence: A cultural-ecological perspective. *Child Development, 52*, 413–429.

Ong, A. D., Fuller-Rowell, T., & Burrow, A. L. (2009). Racial discrimination and the stress process. *Journal of Personality and Social Psychology, 96*, 1259–1271.

Sanchez, F., & Vilain, E. (2009). Collective self-esteem as a coping resource for male-to-female transsexuals. *Journal of Counseling Psychology, 56*, 202–209.

Sellers, R. M., Copeland-Linder, N., Martin, P., & Lewis, R. (2006). Racial identity matters: The relationship between racial discrimination and psychological functioning in African American adolescents. *Journal of Research on Adolescence, 16*, 187–216.

Sellers, R. M., & Shelton, J. N. (2003). The role of racial identity in perceived racial discrimination. *Journal of Personality and Social Psychology, 84*, 1079–1092.

Singleton, E. G., Harrell, J. P., & Kelly, L. M. (1986). Racial differentials in the impact of maternal cigarette smoking during pregnancy on fetal development and mortality: Concerns for black psychologists. *Journal of Black Psychology, 12*, 71–83.

Solorzano, D. G., Ceja, M., & Yosso, T. (2000). Critical race theory, racial microaggressions, and campus racial climate: The experience of African American college students. *Journal of Negro Education, 69*, 60–73.

Torres, L. (2009). Attributions to discrimination and depression among Latino/as: The mediating role of competence. *American Journal of Orthopsychiatry, 79*, 118–124.

U.S. Department of Health and Human Services. (2001). *Mental health: Culture, race, and ethnicity—a supplement to Mental health: A report of the Surgeon General.* Rockville, MD: U.S. Department of Health and Human Services.

Vega, W. A., Kolody, B., Aguilar-Gaxiola, S., Alderete, E., Catalano, R., & Caraveo-Anduaga, J. (1998). Lifetime prevalence of DSM-III-R psychiatric disorders among urban and rural Mexican Americans in California. *Archives of General Psychiatry, 55*, 771–782.

Wright, E. M. (2001). Substance abuse in African American communities. In S. L. A. Straussner (Ed.), *Ethnocultural factors in substance abuse treatment* (pp. 31–51). New York: Guilford Press.

Ying, Y. W., Akutsu, P., Zhang, X., & Huang, L. (1997). Psychological dysfunction in Southeast Asian refugees as mediated by sense of coherence. *American Journal of Community Psychology, 25*, 839–859.

Yip, T., Gee, G., & Takeuchi, D. (2008). Racial discrimination and psychological distress: The impact of ethnic identity and age among immigrant and United States–born Asian adults. *Developmental Psychology, 44*, 787–400.

12

Organizational Efforts to Support Diversity

María del Carmen Triana and María Fernanda Garcia

In 2008, the Equal Employment Opportunity Commission (EEOC, 2009) received more than 95,000 discrimination claims, most of which were related to race and sex discrimination. Although approximately two-thirds of these claims may be dismissed (Goldman, Gutek, Stein, & Lewis, 2006), the number of claims filed indicates that discrimination is not a thing of the past. Whether it is warranted or unwarranted, perceptions of discrimination exist in the 21st-century workplace. Importantly, these perceptions harm not only the individual employee (that is, the victim of the discrimination) but also the organizations in which these employees work as well as the societies in which these organizations operate. Perceptions of discrimination harm individual employees in multiple ways: psychologically, physiologically, and socially (Clark, Anderson, Clark, & Williams, 1999; Dipboye & Colella, 2005). Perceptions of discrimination harm the organizations in which these employees work in terms of job dissatisfaction and higher turnover (Dipboye & Colella, 2005). Perceptions of discrimination harm societies overall because these perceptions affect individuals and institutions beyond the organization in which a discriminatory event occurs. For example, think about the hundreds of millions of dollars spent on costly lawsuits such as the racial discrimination suit against Coca-Cola settled for $192.5 million or the one against Texaco settled for $176.1 million (King &

Spruell, 2001) and the tarnished public images of these companies as a result of these events (Pruitt & Nethercutt, 2002; Wentling & Palma-Rivas, 1997). Clearly, perceptions of discrimination lead to unwanted consequences for any and all parties involved and should be managed to prevent further harm to employees, employers, and societies at large.

The focus of this short chapter is to examine the latest research focused on mitigating the harmful effects of perceived discrimination in the workplace. What can organizations do to mitigate the harmful effects of perceived discrimination? It is this challenging question that we sought to investigate in our recent article published in the *Journal of Organizational Behavior* (Triana & Garcia, 2009). In that article, we examined the nature of the relationship between employees' perceived racial discrimination, defined as being treated differently than others on the basis of one's group membership (Allport, 1954), and procedural justice, which refers to the fairness of the procedures used in the organization to arrive at one's work outcomes (Thibaut & Walker, 1975). We studied how that relationship was affected by organizational efforts to support diversity, defined as employees' perceptions that the practices of the organization indicate that valuing and promoting diversity is a priority in the organization.

To test the effect of organizational efforts to support diversity on the relationship between perceived discrimination and procedural justice, we drew a sample from a predominantly Hispanic community in a city along the U.S.-Mexican border. We found a negative relationship between perceived racial discrimination and procedural justice, as prior research has shown for other forms of discrimination (for age discrimination, see Bibby, 2008; for gender discrimination, see Blau, Tatum, Ward-Cook, Dobria, & McCoy, 2005; Foley, Hang-Yue, & Wong, 2005). Most important, and consistent with the group-value model of procedural justice (Tyler & Lind, 1992), which states that people look at the procedures that those in authority put in place to assess their standing and worth within the group, we also found that perceived organizational efforts to support diversity mitigate the harmful effects of perceived racial discrimination on procedural justice. Furthermore, this effect had an indirect impact on both affective commitment, which refers to one's emotional attachment to the employer (Allen & Mayer, 1990), and organizational citizenship behavior, defined as discretionary actions an employee willingly engages in outside of their normal duties to help the organization (Organ, 1988).

Taking into consideration that our sample had low levels of reported perceived racial discrimination (probably due to the fact that our participants were mainly Hispanics in a majority Hispanic community), our findings have strong implications for management. Our findings suggest that if the organization appears to be implementing practices that indicate the organization values and supports diversity, employees who have experienced discriminatory acts from certain individuals at work feel as though their treatment has been more procedurally fair than employees who experience racial discrimination but do not perceive that their organizations value and support diversity. This has important practical implications for organizations. As long as the employees believe that the organization's top decision makers and policies are supportive of diversity, if employees perceive that they are the targets of racial discrimination from certain individuals with whom they interact at work, the negative feelings that result from perceived discrimination need not necessarily spread to the employees' views about the entire organization.

In addition to the finding that organizational efforts to support diversity are important, the ideal situation is for the organization to implement diversity management practices along with a zero-tolerance policy for discriminatory acts of any kind. The best policy against discrimination in the workplace is to stop it from happening in the first place (Dipboye & Colella, 2005). Therefore, it is critical for organizations to have a zero-tolerance policy against all forms of discrimination and to make this policy known to employees through training and other reminders, such as posters or articles posted on company intranets. Because organizations cannot control all the individual-to-individual actions in the workplace that may be perceived as being discriminatory, it is also important to demonstrate organizational efforts to support diversity by sincerely embracing diversity management.

Following are some practical examples of common ways in which organizations can demonstrate organizational efforts to support diversity through their actions. According to a recent diversity benchmarking report by Catalyst (2006), the most frequently used diversity management practices target diversity on the basis of sex, race, sexual orientation, working parent status, disability status, part-time working status, and age or generational issues, as well as issues pertaining to nationality and religion. Diversity management practices utilized to target these particular groups of people include events like engaging in diversity recruiting, observing religious and cultural holidays, implementing employee engagement surveys, organizing community outreach and cultural events, and conducting bias avoidance and stereotype training (Catalyst, 2006). Some diversity management practices, however, have produced mixed results (Kalev, Dobbin, & Kelly, 2006; Kravitz, 2007). The somewhat-limited research on the efficacy of diversity management practices indicates that the most effective programs are those that are supported by top management and those for which people are held accountable for the results (Kalev et al., 2006; Kravitz, 2007). Programs such as diversity councils, affirmative action programs, targeted recruiting, work-life balance programs, and the inclusion of minorities in top management have been shown to be effective, particularly when top management has been assigned responsibility for the success of these programs (Kalev et al., 2006; Kravitz, 2007). Along with a zero-tolerance policy toward discrimination at work, companies on the leading edge of diversity management have implemented these practices to mitigate the damaging effects of perceived discrimination at work.

REFERENCES

Allen, N. J., & Meyer, J. P. (1990). The measurement and antecedents of affective, continuance, and normative commitment to the organization. *Journal of Occupational Psychology, 63*, 1–18.

Allport, G. (1954). *The nature of prejudice.* Boston, MA: Beacon Press.

Bibby, C. L. (2008). Should I stay or should I leave? Perceptions of age discrimination, organizational justice, and employee attitudes on intentions to leave. *Journal of Applied Management and Entrepreneurship, 13*, 63–86.

Blau, G., Tatum, D. S., Ward-Cook, K., Dobria, L., & McCoy, K. (2005). Testing for time-based correlates of perceived gender discrimination. *Journal of Allied Health, 34*, 130–137.

Catalyst. (2006). *2006 Catalyst Member Benchmarking Report.* New York: Author.

Clark, R., Anderson, N. B., Clark, V. R., & Williams, D. R. 1999. Racism as a stressor for African Americans: A biopsychosocial model. *American Psychologist, 54*, 805–816.

Dipboye, R. L., & Colella, A. (2005). *Discrimination at work: The psychological and organizational bases.* Mahwah, NJ: Erlbaum.

EEOC (Equal Employment Opportunity Commission). (2009). *Charge statistics FY 1997 through FY 2008.* Retrieved May 11, 2010, from http://www.eeoc.gov/stats/charges.html.

Foley, S., Hang-Yue, N., & Wong, A. (2005). Perceptions of discrimination and justice: Are there gender differences in outcomes? *Group & Organization Management, 30*, 421–450.

Goldman, B., Gutek, B., Stein, J. H., & Lewis, K. (2006). Employment discrimination in organizations: Antecedents and consequences. *Journal of Management, 32*, 786–830.

Kalev, A., Dobbin, F., & Kelly, E. (2006). Best practices or best guesses? Assessing the efficacy of corporate affirmative action and diversity policies. *American Sociological Review, 71*, 589–617.

King, A. G., & Spruell, S. P. (2001). Coca-Cola takes the high road. *Black Enterprise, 31*(7), 29.

Kravitz, D. A. (2007). Can we take the guesswork out of diversity practice selection? *Academy of Management Perspectives, 21*, 80–81.

Organ, D. W. (1988). *Organizational citizenship behavior: The good soldier syndrome*. Lexington, MA: Lexington Books.

Pruitt, S. W., & Nethercutt, L. L. (2002). The Texaco racial discrimination case and shareholder wealth. *Journal of Labor Research, 13*, 685–693.

Thibaut, J., & Walker, L. (1975). *Procedural justice: A psychological analysis*. Hillsdale, NJ: Erlbaum.

Triana, M., & García, M. F. (2009) Valuing diversity: A group-value approach to understanding the importance of organizational efforts to support diversity. *Journal of Organizational Behavior, 30*, 941–962.

Tyler, T. R., & Lind, E. A. (1992). A relational model of authority in groups. *Advances in Experimental Social Psychology, 25*, 115–191.

Wentling, R. M., & Palma-Rivas, N. (1997). *Diversity in the workforce: A literature review (MDS-934)*. Berkeley, CA: National Center for Research in Vocational Education.

13

Stereotyping of Veterans and Baby Boomers in the Workplace: Implications for Age Discrimination Prevention

Jennifer L. Martin, Marie Fuda, and Michele A. Paludi

GENERATIONAL COMPARISONS: VALUES ABOUT THE MEANING OF WORK AND THE WORKPLACE

For the first time in U.S. history four generations are working side by side in organizations (Howe & Strauss, 2000): veterans (born between 1922 and 1945), baby boomers (born between 1946 and 1964), generation X (born between 1965 and 1979), and millennials (born between 1980 and 2000; see Dziech, chapter 14 in this volume). Each generation has been described as having unique experiences and values that influence them in their critical life stages of development (Chambers, 2005). For example, veterans grew up during the aftermath of the economic depression and experienced World War II as a major event. Baby boomers share the following life events: first landing on the moon, the British music invasion, the reemergence of the women's liberation movement and the civil rights movement. Gen Xers share growing up with massive job layoffs of their parents and the highest divorce rates in this country. Millennials experienced terrorist attacks, being connected globally 24/7, and having parents who planned all aspects of their lives for them.

Chambers (2005) and Zemke, Raines, and Filipczak (2000) noted that, as a consequence of these significant life events, veterans want to build a legacy and are resistant to change. In addition, baby boomers value competition, recognition, money, and job title. For gen Xers, the important values include global awareness, cyber literacy, and personal safety. Millennials value diversity, multiculturalism, team building, patriotism, meaningful employment, children and family, and globalism (Zemke et al., 2000).

Human resource and management literatures stress how these different values associated with the four generations influence their work ethic, work expectations, and work behavior (Brady & Bradley, 2008; Twenge & Campbell, 2008; Wong, Gardiner, Lang, & Coulon, 2008). Smola and Sutton (2002) noted that gen Xers report less loyalty to their organization, want to be promoted more quickly, and are more "me-oriented" than are baby boomers.

Veterans and baby boomers often criticize gen Xers and millennials for not sharing their same work ethic—for example, being physically present at work for eight hours a day, five days a week. Gen Xers and millennials are described as working hard while integrating their family with work roles—for example, working at home and placing value on getting the work accomplished rather than on "face time" (Guss & Miller, 2008).

Considerable attention in recent years has been devoted to managing employees (Dowing, 2006; Loughlin & Barling, 2001) to avoid intergenerational conflict in the workplace (see Dziech, chapter 14 in this volume). The focus has been on easing the entry of the youngest generation in the workforce and helping them to become engaged employees, much to the neglect of the older generations who are perceived as near retirement.

As Chamberlain (2009) recently noted, however, we may be "overgeneralizing the generations." Unlike the human resource literature, social science research has alerted us to the similarities among the generations, not differences in their work behavior and work ethic. Focusing on generational differences ignores within-group variability. The overemphasis on differences by employers provides confirmation of the stereotype that veterans and millennials are "opposite," that one's own generational values are normative, and that other generations are a deviation from the norm.

Research at the Sloan Center on Aging and Work (discussed by Chamberlain, 2009) reported that baby boomers and veterans are similar in what they want from their employer—for example, flexible work schedules to accommodate families, opportunities to participate in training programs, an understanding and supportive manager, and fairness in promotions. In addition, Wong et al. (2008) reported few statistical differences among the generations; when differences were obtained, they were due to age, not generation. Deal's (2007) study of approximately 3,000 organization leaders found that the top three values of all generations were family, love, and integrity. What differed was how individuals of each generation exhibited these values in their personal lives and at work. In addition, Deal (2007) reported that no matter what one's generation, employees value achievement, work-life balance, responsibility, and trustworthy leadership.

FROM STEREOTYPES AND PREJUDICE TO DISCRIMINATION: INTERGENERATIONAL CONFLICT FROM AGEISM

The perceptions held by employees and managers that meaningful differences exist among the generations are a great challenge facing 21st-century organizations. Empirical research has indicated that these perceptions contribute to conflict or dysfunction in organizations and contribute to the expression of stereotypic comments and behavior, often leading to age discrimination toward employees in the veterans' and baby-boomers' generations (Brady & Bradley, 2008; SHRM, 2009).

Stereotypes refer to individuals' thoughts and cognitions that typically do not correspond with reality. Stereotypes occur when individuals are classified by others as having something in common because they are members of a particular group or category of people (for example, veterans, the elderly, millennials). Psychological research has identified the following characteristics of stereotypes (Fiske, 1993):

1. Groups that are targeted for stereotypes are easily identified and relatively powerless.
2. There is little agreement between the composite picture of the group and the actual characteristics of that group.
3. This misperception is difficult to modify even though individuals who hold stereotypes have interacted with individuals of the group who disconfirm the stereotypes.
4. This misperception is the product of a bias in individuals' information-processing mechanisms.

Characteristics such as generation are salient features that individuals use to categorize an individual (Fiske, 1998). Individuals activate stereotypical traits about these characteristics (Wigboldus, Dijksterhuis, & van Knippenberg,

2003). Thus, knowing or assuming an individual is a baby boomer or veteran, an employer may think they "live to work," are "forgetful," are a "technophobe," and are "unable to multitask."

Psychologists have identified an emotional component to stereotypic cognitions—that is, the prejudicial as well as behavioral component to individuals' cognitions (discrimination and harassment). Thus, individuals' statements and nonverbal gestures directed toward employees in the baby-boomer and veterans generations (for example, "She must be having a Senior moment," "You can't teach an old dog new tricks," "More workplace accidents are caused by baby boomers and veterans") provide insight into those individuals' structured sets of beliefs about age and generation. Butler noted that "[a]geism can be seen as a process of systematic stereotyping of and discrimination against people because they are old, just as racism and sexism accomplish this with skin color and gender" (as cited in Cohen, 2001, p. 576).

Empirical research has suggested that employees in the gen X and millennial generations hold more stereotypes about and stigmatize veterans and baby boomers than do older co-workers (McCann & Giles, 2002; Rupp, Vodanovich, & Crede, 2006). In addition, empirical research has found that older employees receive lower ratings on their performance appraisals than do younger employees when based on subjective manger ratings (Rupp et al., 2006). While younger employees are extended time to improve their performance, older employees are not provided with extra time but rather are characterized by their advanced age (for example, loss of cognitive abilities, reaction time causing poor performance).

Thus, ageist behaviors are found in the expectancies managers and employees hold regarding the capabilities of older employees, which in turn shape employment decisions. This is especially true when managers are gen Xers or millennials. Babcock (2006) has argued that "hidden bias" affects decisions about which individual is hired, promoted, assessed, and paid. However, Babcock and Greenwald (cited in Babcock, 2006) have found that individuals are not aware of their implicit biases, including biases toward older individuals.

The reality is that chronological age has little to do with job performance (Martin, chapter 1 in volume 1; Rupp et al., 2006). Segrave (2001), for example, reported that in an organization consisting of employees all 50 years of age or older, there was 18 percent higher productivity, 16 percent lower turnover of workers, 40 percent decreased absenteeism, and 60 percent decreased inventory loss.

Despite this reality, discrimination against individuals in the baby-boomer and veteran generations still exists in workplaces in the United States. In March 2009, the Equal Employment Opportunity Commission (EEOC) published its report dealing with the number of charges of workplace discrimination filed with this agency in 2008. The EEOC identified 24,582 complaints of age discrimination in this period (see Martin, chapter 1 in volume 1), up 29 percent from the previous year.

The American Association of Retired Persons (AARP, 2003) reported that 67 percent of employees reported age discrimination. In addition, the AARP survey indicated that 9 percent of respondents reported being passed up for a promotion (the "gray ceiling") and 5 percent stated they did not get a salary increase because of their age.

According to social science research (Fiske, 1993), stereotyping in the workplace is likely to be elicited (that is, discriminatory statements and behavior occurs) under the following conditions: (1) rarity (one or a few members of a particular generation present in a particular occupation); (2) priming (ageist comments, nonverbal gestures, pictures, posters, e-mails present in the workplace); (3) participation in the discriminatory behavior by supervisors; and (4) inadequate, ineffective, and unenforced policies, procedures, and training programs on age discrimination.

GOALS OF THE PRESENT CHAPTER

We recommend that organizations must adapt human resource management functions to the shifting generation demographics of the workplace to optimize generational diversity of their employees and reduce age discrimination (also see Martin, chapter 1 in volume 1). In this chapter, we provide recommendations to accomplish this goal, specifically (1) offering suggestions for conducting a human resource audit for managing age and generational diversity and (2) presenting an outline for a training program content and pedagogy on generational differences and age discrimination in the workplace.

Human resource responses to intergenerational conflict and age discrimination must be geared toward the accomplishment of organizational goals and based on key performance indicators. Failure to demonstrate that the audit and training are tied to the organization's mission, values, and strategic plan ignores the importance of human resource functions in the prevention and intervention of misconduct. This, in turn, diminishes productivity and morale, increases absenteeism and turnover, ruins reputations, and thereby negatively affects the bottom line. Chapters 2, 5, and 8 in volume 1 of this book set provide an overview of human resource audits for the following forms of workplace discrimination: disability, national origin, and religion. See these chapters for additional recommendations on conducting an audit as part of an antidiscrimination management program.

In addition, chapter 13 in volume 1 of this book set for a complete discussion of conducting needs assessments before the training and post-training evaluations that may be used in conjunction with training programs on generational differences.

HUMAN RESOURCE AUDITS

Human resource audits provide information for administrators on ways employers are preventing and reacting to discrimination complaints in their organization (Smith & Mazin, 2004). Audits consist of policy reviews, training programs, and investigatory procedures as well as interviewing human resources professionals, interviewing managers at different levels of the organization, and interviewing employees. Audits must ensure federal and state antidiscrimination laws are being followed. As Greenberg-Pophal (2008) stated, a human resource audit is "an analysis by which an organization measures where it currently stands and determines what it has to accomplish to improve its human resource function" (in Dessler, 2009, p. 412). Audits are thus discovery tools that outline areas in which improvement needs to be made in the organization.

With respect to generational comparisons and age discrimination, the audit must include the following dimensions, representing the basic functions of human resource management:

- Legal Compliance
- Compensation and Salary Administration
- Employment and Recruiting
- Orientation
- Terminations
- Training and Development
- Employee Relations
- Files, Record Maintenance, and Technology
- Policies and Procedures
- Communications, Including Employee Handbook

The following sample checklist can be used to conduct an audit regarding age discrimination and generational stereotypes in the workplace:

Legal Compliance

1. Is the human resource department following state laws with respect to age discrimination and harassment as well as federal laws?
2. Does the company ensure that sanctions and corrective action are applied evenly throughout the organization when employees violate the organization's age discrimination policy?
3. Does the company follow the EEOC's fundamentals in investigation age discrimination and harassment complaints: promptness, confidentiality, and impartiality?
4. Does the company offer Family and Medical Leave to all employees, regardless of generation or age?

Compensation and Salary Administration

1. Does the company ensure that it establishes salaries based on skill, responsibility, effort, and working conditions?
2. Does the company examine job grades to ensure that *all* employees have equal opportunity for advancement regardless of age?
3. Has the company developed job descriptions and position titles?
4. Does the company post job openings with salary ranges within the workplace?
5. Does the company encourage employees to openly discuss compensation issues with co-workers rather than fostering an organizational culture that intimidates employees by making it taboo to discuss salaries?
6. Does the company offer rewards programs for all employees regardless of generation or age?

Employment and Recruiting

1. Does the company ensure that security requirements are applied to all job applicants and employees without regard to age?
2. Does the company make employment distinctions based on age only when a bona fide occupational qualification makes it reasonably necessary for the organization to function?
3. Does the company write job descriptions to ensure that it is not excluding older applicants because the qualification involves a relatively new field of study?
4. Does the company ensure that all employees wanting to become a manager or supervisor follow the same procedure regardless of age?

5. Does the company ensure that it does not inquire about a job applicant's age on the application form and during an interview?
6. Does the company ensure that its recruitment practices reach the widest array of applicants?
7. Does the company provide information to all interviewers that details the job requirements?
8. Does the company ensure that it conducts interviews with uniformity by interviewers representing the four generations in the workplace?

Orientation

1. Does the company have a new-employee orientation program that includes training on age discrimination policies and procedures?
2. Does the company request new employees to sign and date an acknowledgment form indicating they received the employee handbook and understand the organization's policy and procedures on age discrimination and harassment?

Terminations

1. Does the company ensure that discipline and termination is applied evenly for violations of the equal employment opportunity policies regardless of the age of the employee?
2. Does the company ensure that investigators of complaints of age discrimination and harassment have credibility in this aspect of workplace discrimination?
3. Does the company have a pair of investigators representing different generations in the workforce to conduct investigations of policy violations?

Training and Development

1. Does the company facilitate regular training programs on age discrimination, including the company's policies and procedures?
2. How do employees learn to whom they should report complaints of age discrimination and harassment?
3. Does the company train it managers and supervisors so they understand their role as "agents" of the company with respect to employees informing them of their perceived age discrimination and harassment?
4. Does the company ensure that it offers training and development on new information technology systems to employees regardless of age?

5. Does the company offer training opportunities and career development opportunities to all employees regardless of age?
6. Does the company have trainers of all generations represented in the workforce who are facilitating programs for employees?

Employee Relations

1. What services are available at the company to employees who have experienced age discrimination and harassment?
2. Does the company ensure that investigators of complaints of age discrimination and harassment are sensitive to collective bargaining agreements?
3. Does the company inform all employees, regardless of generation or age, of the Employees Assistance Programs and Wellness Programs our organization provides?

Files, Record Maintenance, and Technology

1. What metrics does the company have in place to measure the success of its age discrimination and harassment management program?
2. Does the company ensure that the content of the case file of an investigation of a complaint of age discrimination and harassment contains the following:
   - Complaint
   - Response to complaint from accused employee
   - Notes from meetings with all parties to the investigation
   - Letters from individuals involved in the investigation
   - Copies of all standard notification letters to all parties to the investigation
   - Documents (copies of e-mails, letters, and cards) supplied by individuals in the investigation procedure
   - Report by investigator to the president of the organization
   - Signed acknowledgment forms regarding confidentiality, retaliation, and request for witnesses
3. Does the company have in its files copies of signed and dated acknowledgement forms for the following:
   - Receipt of the policy concerning age discrimination and harassment
   - Participation in a training program dealing with age discrimination and harassment
4. Does the company provide a summary at the end of each fiscal year that includes the following:
   - Number of complaints of age discrimination and harassment received
   - Number of complaints sustained

- Number of complaints that were false
- Number of complaints for which insufficient information was present to sustain the allegation
  - Sanctions and corrective action provided
5. Does the company have its information technology department routinely check e-mails to ensure no negative comments or jokes about employees' advanced age or generation are present?

Policies and Procedures

1. Does the company have policy statements dealing with age discrimination in employment and age harassment?
2. Do the policies prohibit discrimination/harassment from peers in addition to discrimination and harassment by managers?
3. Do employees know to whom they should report complaints related to age discrimination and harassment?
4. Are remedies clear and commensurate with the level of age discrimination and harassment?
5. Does the company ensure that it does not have a mandatory retirement policy unless age is a bon fide occupational qualification for performing the job?
6. Does the company offer flexible job arrangements for all employees, regardless of age (flex time, job sharing, desk sharing, time off/career break, telecommuting)?

Communications, Including Employee Handbook

1. Does the workplace foster an atmosphere of prevention by sensitizing individuals to the topic of age discrimination and harassment?
2. Does the company conduct anonymous culture climate surveys with employees to determine their perceptions about the effectiveness of the company's age discrimination and harassment management program?
3. Does the company obtain a metric about the alignment between the organization's stated mission with respect to age discrimination and harassment and behaviors of management and employees, effectiveness of training programs, policies, investigations, and corrective action?
4. Is the age discrimination and harassment policy statement well publicized? Are the statements posted on the company's intranet? Are they posted in the human resources office? Are they included in the employee handbook?

5. Does the company ensure that performance appraisals do not contain stereo-typic references to veterans and baby boomers as well as ratings that are based in stereotypes and not reflections of the individual employee?

Following the completion of the audit, the employer must then understand the reasons for the lack of attention to equal employment opportunity and correct the omissions to meet their responsibility for ensuring reasonable care with respect to age discrimination and harassment (see Paludi et al., chapter 13 in volume 1).

In addition to the human resource audit, we recommend conducting a SWOT analysis (strengths-weaknesses-opportunities-threats analysis) (Williamson, Cooke, Jenkins, & Moreton, 2003) or a barrier analysis (Dineen & Bartlett, 2002). The SWOT analysis provides information that is useful in matching the organization's resources and capabilities to the competitive environment in which it operates. The completed SWOT analysis may be used for the organization's goal setting, strategy formulation, and implementation.

A barrier analysis may be utilized when there is an employment issue, for example, a training program policy that limits opportunities for members of the veteran or baby-boomer generation (or other protected category; see DeFour & Paludi, chapter 5 in volume 1). Through the barrier analysis, an investigation of the triggers (e.g., lack of promotion of older employees, high separation rate of employees who are older) found in the employment issue are identified and resolved.

In addition, the Society for Human Resource Management (2005) offers employers a Diversity Management Toolkit that includes recommendations for dealing with all forms of discrimination/harassment, including age discrimination and harassment.

SAMPLE TRAINING PROGRAM ON GENERATIONAL DIFFERENCES AND AGE DISCRIMINATION

In Table 13.1, we present a sample outline of the content for a training program on generational differences and age discrimination. We recommend organizations having at least two trainers facilitate the program, each from a different generation represented in the workplace. A major goal of this training program is to emphasize the importance of managing employees by focusing on individual differences, not relying on generational stereotypes.

Table 13.1
Sample Training Program on Generational Differences and Age Discrimination

Goals of the Training Program

Provide all members of the workplace with a clear understanding of their rights and responsibilities with respect to age discrimination and harassment.

Enable employees to identify behavior that is age discrimination.

Provide employees with information concerning the policy statement and procedures against age discrimination set up by the organization.

Discuss the emotional and physical reactions to being discriminated against because of one's age.

Encourage employees to examine their personal feelings with respect to age discrimination.

Encourage employees to examine their stereotypes about age and generations.

Dispel myths about age discrimination and harassment and victims of age discrimination.

Explore responsible behavior in dealing with employees who engage in age discrimination and harassment.

Empower employees to take control of their behavior.

Discuss the concept of unwelcomeness and how this is communicated verbally and nonverbally.

Discuss the employer's central role in preventing age discrimination and harassment.

Create an environment that is free of age discrimination and fear of retaliation for speaking out about age discrimination and harassment.

At the Conclusion of This Training Program, Individuals Will Achieve the Following

Assess their own perceptions of the definition, incidence, and psychological dimensions of age discrimination and harassment.

Adequately label behaviors as illustrative or not illustrative of age discrimination and harassment.

Assess age-related stereotypes and whether these stereotypes lead to discriminatory behavior.

Identify the organization's policy and procedures for reporting age discrimination and harassment.

Identify rights and responsibilities under the organization's policy and procedures on age discrimination and harassment.

Topics for Presentation and Discussion

Part I: Welcome, Introductions, and Review of Goals of Training Program

Trainers welcome employees to the training program.

Trainers introduce themselves, their qualifications and background.

(Continued)

Table 13.1 (*continued*)

Trainers summarize goals of the training program.

Trainers ask employees to state their own goals for the training.

Trainers write responses for all employees to see.

Trainers provide myths about the four generations and ask employees for their opinions.

Trainers introduce the remainder of the training program.

Part II: The New Workforce: Four Generations in the Workplace

Trainers ask employees how they believe they have been shaped by their values and work ethics.

Trainers review the literature on generations in the workplace:

    Veterans (born 1925–1945)

    Baby boomers (born 1946–1964)

    Generation Xers (born 1965–1980)

    Millennials (born 1980–2002)

Trainers provide general information about background environment, role models, influential people, sense of self, and other common perceptions for each generation.

Trainers present what each generation uniquely contributes to, or values in, the 21st-century workforce.

    Veterans:

        Value building a legacy

        Value logic and discipline

        Resist change

    Baby boomers:

        Question authority

        Value competition

        Value recognition

        Place importance on title and money

    Gen Xers:

        Are globally concerned

        Cyber literate

        Value personal safety

    Millennials:

        Value diversity

        Embrace change

        Value meaningful work

        Focus on children and family

        Value scheduled, structured lives

        Value multiculturalism

        Impact of terrorism

        Impact of viewing heroism

(Continued)

Table 13.1 (*continued*)

Patriotism
Parent advocacy
Globalism
Trainers summarize this unit.

Part III: Goals of Generations with Respect to Work and Careers

Trainers identify generations' goals with respect to their work:
   Veterans: "build a legacy"
   Baby boomers: "build a stellar career"
   Gen Xers: "build a portable career"
   Millennials: "build parallel careers"
Trainers identify each generation's attitude toward workplace and authority:
   Veterans: loyalty
   Baby boomers: deserve to change
   Gen Xers: suspicion
   Millennials: judge each by its own merit
Trainers identify each generation's attitude regarding rewards and
   compensation:
   Veterans: satisfaction of job well done
   Baby boomers: want money, recognition, and title
   Gen Xers: freedom
   Millennials: meaning
Trainers identify each generation's values regarding performance appraisals:
   Veterans: only hear from supervisors when there is a problem
   Baby boomers: performance appraisals held once a year
   Gen Xers: frequently request, "How am I doing?"
   Millennials: virtual daily coaching
Trainers identify similar preferences among the generations:
   Flexible hours
   Telecommuting
   Compensation
   Professional development
   Temporary work assignments
   Rewards programs
Trainers identify similarities among the generations with respect to work ethics.
Trainers summarize this unit.

Part IV: Principles of Managing Generations

Trainers discuss the following:
   Meaning of balance
   Reward for work results

(*Continued*)

Table 13.1 (*continued*)

Dealing with flexibility and creativity
Attaching feedback directly to performance objectives
Learning preferences
Trainers summarize this unit.

Part V: When Generations Collide: Conflict Management and Conflict Resolution

Trainers discuss ways intergenerational conflict occurs in the workforce.
Trainers provide sample conflict management skills.
Trainers ask participants to identify ways to bridge the generation gap at work.
Trainers identify ways to connect among generations.
Trainers discuss transcending generational labels and categories to view individuals as individuals instead of members of certain groups.
Trainers summarize this unit.

Part VI: Intergenerational Conflict and Age Discrimination

Trainers quiz participants about myths and realities about veterans, baby boomers, gen Xers, and millennials.
Trainers discuss the relationship between intergenerational conflict and age discrimination:
    Myths vs. realities about generations
    Stereotypes, prejudice, and discrimination
    Legal definition of age discrimination and harassment
    Examples of age discrimination and harassment behavior
    Distinguishing compliments and flattery from harassment
Trainers provide research data regarding the impact of age discrimination and harassment on individuals and the workplace.
Trainers summarize from this unit.

Part VI: Organization's Policy

Trainers refer participants to the organization's policy.
Trainers discuss the organization's policy and procedures for filing a complaint of age discrimination:
    Written and/or oral complaints
    Confidentiality
    Prompt investigations
    Impartiality
    Determining credibility
    Role of witnesses
    Sanctions and corrective action offered
Trainers discuss the work/role of Equal Employment Opportunity Commission and Human Rights Commission.

(Continued)

Table 13.1 (*continued*)

Trainers introduce individual(s) responsible for investigating complaints of age discrimination/harassment.

Trainers summarize this unit.

Part VII: Conclusion

Trainers use case studies to provide examples of behavior, and ask participants about their perceptions of that behavior and how their organization would address it.

Trainers discuss intergenerational conflict and age discrimination and harassment.

Trainers refer to participants' goals outlined at the beginning of the training to determine whether goals were met

Trainers distribute acknowledgment forms for employees to sign and date indicating they attended the training. A copy of the acknowledgment form is provided to the employee; human resources maintains a copy.

Trainers lead a general discussion and question-and-answer period.

Trainers distribute a "reaction" evaluation to the participants.

Trainers remain to discuss issues with employees privately.

Pedagogical Techniques to Facilitate Training Program

Several pedagogical methods are available for training employees about generational differences and age discrimination, including the following: lectures, videos and films, simulation exercises, behavioral rehearsal, and Web-based training (DeCenzo & Robbins, 2007; Dessler, 2009; Smith & Mazin, 2004; see Paludi et al., chapter 13 in volume 1). Research has identified benefits and weaknesses of each of these pedagogical methods for training programs on discrimination and harassment in the workplace (Callahan, Kiker, Montgomery, & Cross, 2003; Goldstein & Ford, 2002; Stockdale & Crosby, 2004; Wentling & Palma-Rivas, 2002).

For example, lectures work well for disseminating information about generational differences as well as similarities, legal issues in age discrimination, the organization's policy and procedures, and behavioral examples of age discrimination. It is common, however, for trainees to become bored or impatient and consequently not pay attention to the lecture. This is a serious concern in that employees must understand their rights and responsibilities with respect to age discrimination and their organization's policy.

We recommend the use of case studies and scenarios to encourage trainees to learn through guided discovery to think critically about their stereotypes and hidden biases about the generations and how stereotypes are related to discrimination (Carter, 2002). Case studies, however, do not provide direct practice with issues in understanding generations or age discrimination.

Behavioral rehearsal (role-playing) techniques have been found to be effective for training on communication and interaction skills. One drawback of this pedagogical technique is that it presents opportunities for embarrassment and loss of self-confidence among the trainees. Furthermore, behavioral rehearsal often elicits laughter, which may be perceived negatively by employees who have experienced stereotypic comments about their generation's cognitive and physical abilities.

Blanchard, Thacker, and Blanchard (2003) have recommended the use of videos in training programs, because portions of the video can be repeated or skipped over. The lack of personal contact in video training, however, creates an opportunity for employees to become bored and therefore not receive all of the information they are required to have.

Web-based and PowerPoint training programs have been reported to generate high levels of employees' acquisition and retention of the material presented (Frisbie, 2002) and offers fast-paced learning. Oddsson (2001) has found, however, that this pedagogical technique creates frustration in employees who are not computer literate.

The content we present in Table 13.1 demands in-person training. However, some employees prefer Web-based or PowerPoint training programs. The content presented may be easily adapted for these pedagogical techniques. Information about employees' learning and training preferences may be obtained through a needs assessment (Knowles, Holton, & Swanson, 2005; Paludi et al., chapter 13 in volume 1).

We recommend an interactive pedagogy that encompasses adult learning principles (Knowles et al., 2005; McNamara, 2008), including, for example, the following:

- Practical and problem centered
- Promoting positive self-esteem
- Integrating new ideas with existing knowledge
- Showing respect for the individual learner
- Capitalizing on their individual experience

The major objective of this training program is the facilitation of transference from the training room to the workplace. In addition, a major goal of the training program is to show trainees that the program benefits them pragmatically. Furthermore, trainers should:

- Provide feedback to the participants.
- Model desired behavior throughout the training.
- Use realistic examples, not jargon.
- Allow participants opportunities for practicing information from the training program.
- Encourage trainees to learn from each other.
- Make the content immediately applicable.

Table 13.2
Sample "Reaction" Evaluation Form

Thank you for completing this post-training evaluation form. All of your responses are anonymous and will be kept confidential. Your responses will help us develop and facilitate future training programs.
Please use the following scale in answering the questions on this post-training evaluation:
1: Agree   2: Don't know/Undecided   3: Disagree (circle one)

Part I: About the Trainers

(Trainers' Names) are knowledgeable about the issues.	1	2	3
(Trainers' Names) have effective communication styles.	1	2	3
(Trainers' Names) respected the participants in the session.	1	2	3
(Trainers' Names) answered questions in a respectful manner.	1	2	3
(Trainers' Names) raised my awareness about the issues.	1	2	3

Part II: About the Content

The training program was organized.	1	2	3
The resource material will be helpful to me.	1	2	3
I learned the legal definition of age discrimination.	1	2	3
I learned behavioral examples of age discrimination.	1	2	3
I learned the relationship among stereotypes, prejudice, and discrimination.	1	2	3
I learned about this organization's policy and procedures on age discrimination and harassment.	1	2	3
I learned the realities about comparisons among generations in the workplace.	1	2	3

(Continued)

Table 13.2 (*continued*)

Part III: About the Program in General

The objectives of this training program were clearly identified.	1	2	3
The handouts/power points enhanced the training.	1	2	3
The training increased my awareness of the issues.	1	2	3

Part IV: About Myself

1. I feel that I benefited from participating in this training program.	1	2	3
2. I believe we need more training on these issues.	1	2	3

Part V: Overall Rating of Training Program

Please circle one of the following:
Excellent   Good   Fair   Poor

Part VI: Additional Comments You Wish to Make

_____
_____
_____

Thank You!

ADDITIONAL TRAINING CONSIDERATIONS
Post-Training Evaluations

It is vital to obtain a metric of the effectiveness of a training program in age discrimination and harassment and generational comparisons is vital so that the organization may determine whether the training delivered or failed to deliver the expected organizational benefits (Hoyle, 2006; Morgan & Casper, 2000; Tyler, 2002). Employers should provide trainees with an immediate post-training evaluation asking for their reactions to the training (Kirkpatrick, 1998). We provide a sample evaluation in Table 13.2. This evaluation will determine trainees' opinions about the structure of the training program, location of the program, trainer effectiveness, and so on.

A reaction post-training evaluation is the least valid evaluation technique because it does not obtain information regarding employees' learning, how well they are integrating the new knowledge and skills on their job, whether training has reduced the incidence of age discrimination, or whether there has been increased reporting of discrimination post training (Stockdale & Crosby, 2004). Employers should consider using other evaluation techniques identified by Kirkpatrick (1998) as well, such as learning, behavior, and results.

CONCLUSION

Employees in the baby-boomer and veterans generations often bare the brunt of attribution errors on the part of managers, for example, not being given extra time, as are younger workers, to complete assigned tasks. We recommend establishing networking-mentoring programs to reduce stereotypes and age discrimination. Networking mentoring (Swoboda & Millar, 1986) includes two or more employees fulfilling the roles of mentor and protégé to each other at different times in the relationship. This networking approach is egalitarian rather than hierarchical and is based on a belief in mutual enhancement. An advantage of network mentoring is that it is open to all employees, not only a select few who find an individual to mentor them. Furthermore, network mentoring recognizes and values career breaks—for example, time away from the paid workforce for child rearing or elder care, part time employment, or job-sharing practices. The relationship is based on mutual trust between the protégé and mentor.

Human resources can facilitate, support, and promote network mentoring by providing training for mentors and protégés, by recognizing mentoring activities, rewarding the relationship, and establishing metrics to determine the success of the program.

REFERENCES

AARP (American Association of Retired Persons). (2007). *Perspectives of employers, workers, and policymakers in the G7 countries on the new demographic realities.* Retrieved October 18, 2009, from http://www.aarpinternational.org/usr_doc/intl_older_worker.pdf.

Babcock, P. (2006). Watch out for the minefield of hidden bias. In Society for Human Resource Management (Ed.), *HR Magazine: Guide to managing people* (pp. 44–47). Alexandria, VA: Society for Human Resource Management.

Blanchard, N., Thacker, J., & Blanchard, P. (2003). *Effective training: Systems strategies and practices.* Upper Saddle River, NJ: Prentice Hall.

Brady, E., & Bradley, L. (2008). Generational differences in virtual teams. In *The handbook of high-performance virtual teams: A toolkit for collaborating across boundaries* (pp. 263–271). San Francisco, CA: Jossey-Bass.

Callahan, J., Kiker, D., Montgomery, L., & Cross, T. (2003). Does method matter? A meta-analysis of the effects of training method on older learner training performance. *Journal of Management, 29,* 663–680.

Carter, S. (2002). Matching training methods and factors of cognitive ability: A means to improve training outcomes. *Human Resource Development Quarterly, 13,* 71–87.

Cavanaugh, M., & Walsh, N. (2009, April 22). *How technology is changing our brain* [audio transcript]. Retrieved October 26, 2009, from http://www.kpbs.org/news/2009/apr/22/how-technology-changing-our-brain.

Chamberlain, J. (2009). *Overgeneralizing the generations*. Retrieved October 19, 2009, from http://www.apa.org/monitor/2009/06/workplaces.html.

Chambers, D. (2005). Generations. *Journal of the American College of Dentists, 72*, 27–36.

Cohen, S. (2001). The complex nature of ageism: What is it? Who does it? Who perceives it? *The Gerontologist, 41*(5), 576–577.

Deal, J. (2007). *Retiring the generation gap: How employees young and old can find common ground*. San Francisco, CA: Jossey-Bass.

DeCenzo, D., & Robbins, S. (2007). *Fundamentals of human resource management*. New York: John Wiley & Sons.

Dessler, G. (2009). *Fundamentals of human resource management*. Upper Saddle River, NJ: Prentice Hall.

Dineen, M., & Bartlett, R. (2002). *Six steps to root cause analysis*. Oxford: Consequence.

Downing, K. (2006). Next generation: What leaders need to know about the Millennials. *Leadership in Action, 26*, 3–6.

Fiske, S. (1993). Controlling other people: The impact of power on stereotyping. *American Psychologist, 48*, 621–628.

Fiske, S. (1998). Stereotyping, prejudice, and discrimination. In D. Gilbert, S. Fiske, & G. Lindzey (Eds.), *The handbook of social psychology, vol. 2* (4th ed., pp. 357–411). Boston, MA: McGraw-Hill.

Frisbie, S. (2002). Sexual harassment: A comparison of online vs. traditional training methods. Unpublished doctoral dissertation, Texas Tech University, Lubbock, TX.

Goldstein, I., & Ford, J. (2002). *Training in organizations: Needs assessment, development, and evaluation* (4th ed.). Belmont, CA: Wadsworth.

Guss, E., & Miller, M. (2008, October). *Ethics and generational differences: Interplay between values and ethical business decisions* (SHRM White Paper). Retrieved October 18, 2009, from http://www.shrm.org/Research/Articles/Documents/09-0711_RQ_4_2009_FINAL.pdf.

Howe, N., & Strauss, W. (2000). *Millennials rising: The next great generation*. New York: Random House.

Hoyle, A. (2006). Evaluation of training: A review of the literature. *Public Administration and Development, 4*, 275–282.

Kirkpatrick, D. (1998). *Evaluating training programs: The four levels*. San Francisco, CA: Berrett-Koehler.

Knowles, M., Holton, E., & Swanson, R. (2005). *The adult learner.* New York: Butterworth-Heinemann.

Loughlin, C., & Barling, J. (2001). Young workers' work values, attitudes, and behaviors. *Journal of Occupational and Organizational Psychology, 74*, 543–559.

McCann, R., & Giles, H. (2002). Ageism and the workplace: A communication perspective. In T. Nelson (Ed.), *Ageism* (pp. 163–199). Cambridge, MA: MIT Press.

McNamara, C. (2008). *Effective employee training and development requires some knowledge of adult learning.* Retrieved May 30, 2009, from http://managementhelp.org/trng/dev/basics/adlt.lrn.htm.

Morgan, R., & Casper, W. (2000). Examining the factor structure of participant reactions to training: A multidimensional approach. *Human Resource Development Quarterly, 11,* 301–317.

Oddsson, F. (2001). Computerized training methods: Effects on retention and rate of responding. *Dissertation Abstracts International, 61,* 5546.

Rupp, D. E., Vodanovich, S. J., & Crede, M. (2006). Age bias in the workplace: The impact of ageism and causal attributions. *Journal of Applied Social Psychology, 36*(6), 1337–1364.

Segrave, K. (2001). *Age discrimination by employers.* Jefferson, NC: McFarland & Company.

SHRM (Society for Human Resource Management). (2005). Retrieved September 20, 2009, from http://www.shrm.org.

SHRM (Society for Human Resource Management). (2009). *The multigenerational workforce: Opportunity for competitive success.* Alexandria, VA: SHRM.

Smith, S., & Mazin, R. (2004). *The HR answer book.* New York: AMACOM.

Smola, K., & Sutton, C. (2002). Generational differences: Revisiting generational work values for the new millennium. *Journal of Organizational Behavior, 23,* 363–382.

Stockdale, M. S., & Crosby, F. J. (Eds.). (2004). *The psychology and management of workplace diversity.* Boston, MA: Blackwell.

Swoboda, M., & Millar, S. (1986). Networking mentoring: Career strategy of women in academic administration. *Journal of NAWDAC, 49,* 8–13.

Twenge, J., & Campbell, S. (2008). Generational differences in psychological traits and their impact on the workplace. *Journal of Managerial Psychology, 23,* 862–877.

Tyler, K. (2002). Evaluating evaluations. *HR Magazine, 47,* 85–93.

Wentling, R., & Palma-Rivas, N. (2002). Components of effective diversity training programs. *International Journal of Training and Development, 3,* 215–226.

Wigboldus, D. H. J., Dijksterhuis, A., & van Knippenberg, A. (2003). When stereotypes get in the way: Stereotypes obstruct stereotype-inconsistent trait inferences. *Journal of Personality and Social Psychology, 84,* 470–484.

Williamson, D., Cooke, P., Jenkins, W., & Moreton, K. (2003). *Strategic management and business analysis.* Burlington, MA: Butterworth-Heinemann.

Wong, M., Gardiner, E., Lang, W., & Coulon, L. (2008). Generational differences in personality and motivation: Do they exist and what are the implications for the workplace? *Journal of Managerial Psychology, 23,* 878–890.

Zemke, R., Raines, C., & Filipczak, B. (2000). *Generations at work: Managing the clash of Veterans, Boomers, Xers and Nexters in your workplace.* New York: AMACON.

14

Millennials in the Workplace: Facts, Fiction, and the Unpredictable

Billie Wright Dziech

Writing advice for others is dangerous business. Primarily because of the temptation to assume that what appears true today will also apply to tomorrow. We know, but do not always allow ourselves to admit that "truth" is as elusive a term as "tomorrow"; and that is precisely why any discussion of millennials (or generation Y, as they are also called) in the workplace can border on fiction as well as fact.

Ten years ago in 2000, I stumbled upon Howe and Strauss' widely read book *Millennials Rising*. It was an instant love affair. I used it as a text in an undergraduate composition course and as "food for thought" in literature courses. When the terrorist attacks of September 11 forever changed the world, I was convinced that Howe and Strauss had it right, that the millennial moment had come, that a new generation would soon encounter its "rendezvous with destiny" (Howe & Strauss, 2000, p. 352) and emerge as "America's next great generation" (Howe & Strauss, 2000, p. 3).

It did not happen; and as I began to rethink Howe and Strauss' (2000) work and other simplistic composites of this new age cohort, I realized the foolhardiness of attributing similar characteristics to most members of a generation and of assuming they would remain static over time. Management gurus, the media, pollsters, and even some academics may be comfortable categorizing generation Y and prognosticating about its future, but the truth is millennials are neither as monolithic as most suggest, nor will the vagaries of time allow them to remain unchanged.

In 2002, management expert Claire Raines wrote that millennials were:

> the hottest commodity on the job market since Rosie the Riveter. They're sociable, optimistic, talented, well-educated, collaborative, open-minded, influential, and achievement-oriented. They've always felt sought after, needed, indispensable. They are arriving in the workplace with higher expectations than any generation before them—and they're so well connected that, if an employer doesn't match those expectations, they can tell thousands of their cohorts with one click of a mouse. (Raines, 2002, p. 1)

But at this writing in the summer of 2009, the wide-open job market in which millennials were predicted to begin their careers has disappeared as worldwide recession has dampened the high expectations of the young. Eighteen months ago predictions were that employers and more experienced co-workers would soon need to adjust to millennials' self-assurance, ambition, optimism, and demands for balanced work-life conditions. The good ones were to be courted, rewarded, and carefully trained because generation Y was thought to be the hope of an imminent worker shortage in the United States. The Bureau of Labor Statistics (2008) predicted that by 2010, the nation would lack 10 million skilled workers a concern that was exacerbated by what was then regarded as millennial willingness to change jobs for higher status, better pay, or more attractive working conditions.

That was then. This is now. In the summer of 2009, unemployment in 16 states has reached or exceeded 10 percent, and many of my students who have just graduated from the University of Cincinnati have no jobs and no serious prospects of finding work in areas for which they have been educated at great expense. The outlook is much worse for those who have little or no college experience. If things go as planned by the administration, the situation will change, of course, and our primary worry might once again be hiring, integrating, and retaining enough young people for the current workplace and grooming them for future leadership positions.

Then again, if the economy takes a long time to recover, we might discover that many of the best and brightest members of this new generation, once regarded as optimistic, risk taking, and adaptable to change, have lowered their expectations and opted for government positions, which are rapidly increasing in number and generally are regarded as more safe and secure than jobs in the professions or the marketplace.

There is also the possibility that progressive government spending will eventually plunge the United State into even graver economic straits and millennials' moment will finally arrive. Then they might "emerge from their young-adult collision with history in a way that will make their parents, ancestors, and heirs all extremely proud of them" (Howe & Strauss, 2000, p. 359) as they discover ways to eliminate the federal deficit, balance the budget, decrease dependence on foreign oil, ensure universal health care, or end the trade deficit.

The point is that no one can know. We cannot predict with total accuracy how any generation will fit into the workplace because our "knowledge" rests primarily on theories and assumptions about its characteristics. The reality is that events occur haphazardly, people respond individually and erratically to change, and human values and behaviors alter as personal, workplace, and national and international conditions affect them. For me then, the most accurate approach is to substitute "millennials" for "Russia" in one of Winston Churchill's most famous quotations: "I cannot forecast to you the action(s) of [millennials]. [They are] a riddle wrapped in a mystery inside an enigma." We can say of that riddle only what we know to be true at this moment in time, and much of that truth belies optimistic conjecture. Like every previous generation, millennials will be shaped and changed by unpredictable personal, economic, social, and political circumstances none can foresee, so the wisest course is to avoid generalizations and acknowledge that we are providing only a snapshot in time as we characterize this generation and discuss its inclusion in the workplace.

THE BOOM HEARD ROUND THE WORLD

Discussion of the enigmatic millennials is impossible without a brief look at the generational stereotypes of their parents, who are primarily members of the baby boom generation born between approximately the mid-1940s to the mid-1960s. Although Howe and Strauss (2000) acknowledged that the concept of generational differences is controversial, they argued that a "generational persona" (p. 40) does exist, even though there may be "plenty of individual exceptions" (p. 41) and overlaps that make generations appear "fuzzy at the edges" (p. 41). Generational persona is, they contended, a distinctly human, and variable, creation embodying attitudes about family life, gender roles, institutions, politics, religion, culture, lifestyle, and the future. To identify the persona of a generation, look for three attributes: *perceived membership* in a common generation; *common beliefs and behaviors*; and a *common location in history* (p. 41).

The challenge when applying this definition to baby boomers is remembering that their "common location in history" is quite long. It covers almost a 20-year span between the relatively quiet 1950s and the tumultuous 1960s so that a parent and child could conceivably both have the same label. For this reason, the extent to which so-called baby boomers actually hold or held common beliefs and behaviors is highly debatable because they are an extraordinarily heterogeneous group. What cannot be contested, however, is that they have a perceived membership in a common generation; and that generation has a distinct identity in the public mind.

The end of World War II heralded the birth of what would become for a time the largest generation in American history (http://www.census.gov/popest/national). Elated at the postwar return to normalcy and optimistic about the future, silent generation parents heaped attention, affection, and dreams on their children:

> As children, Boomers experienced post-war optimism and adoring parents groomed to have the perfect family life. As they grew-up, Boomers enjoyed constant attention from a child-obsessed, idealistic America and naturally grew to focus on themselves. At the same time, parents of Boomers amassed sufficient resources to send them to college in record numbers, prolonging the childhood stage and helping to foster the idealistic perspectives that permeated the 60's and 70's. (Ritchie, 2002, p. 29)

At first glance, early boomers' formative years appear uneventful. Many grew up believing, as their parents taught, that hard work and responsibility mattered but also that they were special and entitled to lives of prosperity and happiness. Together parents and children welcomed the arrival of a new phenomenon called television, a technological wonder that few suspected of possessing a power that could ultimately transform American families and values. In the beginning, it seemed to offer nothing more than harmless diversion for young fans of Howdy Doody and the Mouseketeers, as well as a way for families to bond around the television and watch the antics of Lucy Ricardo and Ethel Mertz. But escape was not to be had for long. More and more, television became the instrument of the outside world as news broadcasts and special programming depicted in gruesome detail the catastrophic events of the day.

Children grow up, and over time, budding first-wave boomers found Peyton Place and even the news more compelling than the Mouseketeers. Then suddenly before an older generation knew what had "hit it," the Age of Aquarius and Timothy Leary had dawned; and "flower children" were weathering rain, mud, and sickening sanitary conditions to listen to a new kind of music and experiment with drugs and sex during the "summer of love" at Woodstock. For many, nothing was off limits; if it "felt good," they were perfectly willing to "do it."

Television brought not only sex but also the assassinations of the Kennedys and Martin Luther King and the war in Vietnam into boomers' living rooms. The sight of bombs, blood, and bodies soon led to the "Hell no; I won't go" and "Make love, not war" movement; and families became increasingly fractured by lifestyle and political disagreements. History has yet to provide an unbiased assessment of a generation that was a mixture of so many characteristics—idealism, youth, inclusiveness, progressiveness, destructiveness, self-absorption, immaturity, traditionalism, and judgmentalism. For some, the Vietnam years were a frightening, chaotic nightmare; for others, a long, seemingly never-ending party. But end they did, and when they were over, a new generation would assess the price.

THE LEAST WANTED GENERATION

Born between approximately the early 1960s and late 1970s (once again the exact birth dates are matter of dispute), generation X was in many ways the product of a dying American dream in which happily married couples' children played safely behind white picket fences while smiling daddies went to work and mommies stayed home and cheerfully baked cookies. Looking back, many gen Xers would describe their childhood and adolescence as totally opposite from the experiences of the millennials who followed them. What came to be called "latchkey" and "at-risk" children were offspring of darker interpretations of the American dream, the least wanted of any generation of children in the history of America. Whatever their politics, gen X parents, who were largely boomers, had grown up center stage. When Vietnam ended and the hope of shaping or restoring the world to their expectations failed, many simply changed focus. Howe and Strauss (2000) maintained that "Boomers came of age forging a lifelong reputation for narcissism (and) judgmentalism" (p. 54); their lives were, they said, ultimately shaped more by self-exploration and accumulation than social and political reformation. That too is a generalization, but it is clear that the post–Vietnam era led for many to a reversal of lifestyle and reshaping of values. In what some of their cohorts felt to be a betrayal of their earlier opposition to materialism and tradition, they tended to turn inward and some would say to become more self-absorbed than ever.

Baby boomer Ritchie observed:

The Boomer generation was doted on and placed in the spotlight because it was the first generation born after World War II. Boomers were given many more opportunities than their parents had, which added to their mystique as the "special generation" and has led them to be very concerned with their own self interests. (2002, p. 29)

For those who had become mothers, the women's liberation movement offered an opportunity to cater to self as well as others, and especially the educated among them began leaving cookie dough and kitchens behind as they set out in hopes of breaking the glass ceiling. By 1970, women accounted for 38.1 percent of the labor force, a figure that would continue to grow as years passed. At the same time, men were being told to liberate themselves from work and stereotypes and discover their "feminine sides."

With all the exploration, there was often little time for children. Women were overburdened with jobs, childcare concerns, and household responsibilities. Men, confronted with paradigms for marriage and parenthood that took some getting used to, became increasingly confused about what women wanted, what their own obligations were, and what the demands for change meant to "real men."

Divorce and abortion rates climbed to their highest levels in history, birth rates plummeted, babies and toddlers were exiled to day care centers, and generation X's latchkey kids came home to empty houses that eventually confounded the advice of "experts," who allayed parental fears by maintaining that "quality time" mattered more to children than "quantity." Birth rates that had peaked at 4,027,490 in 1964 plunged to 3,144,198 by 1975 (Centers for Disease Control, 2009). Not everyone was disturbed by the change, of course. To some, the "baby bust" seemed positive. In fact, on March 27, 1972, the Rockefeller Commission on Population Growth and the American Future submitted its final report to then President Richard Nixon. Its conclusions were unequivocal:

Our immediate goal is to modernize demographic behavior in this country: to encourage the American people to make population choices, both in the individual family and society at large, on the basis of greater rationality rather than tradition or custom, ignorance or chance. . . . The time has come to challenge the tradition that population growth is desirable. . . .

In sum, it should be evident that, even if the recent unexpected drop in the birthrate should develop into a sustained trend, there is little cause for complacency. Whether we see it or not—whether we like it or not—we are in for a long period of growth, and we had best prepare for it. . . .

As a Commission, we have formed a definite judgment about the course the nation should make. We have examined the effects that future growth alternatives are likely to have on our economy, society, government, resources, and environment, and we have found no convincing argument for continued national population growth. On the contrary, the plusses seem to be on the side of slowing growth and eventually stopping it altogether. (1972, chapter 8)

Even today many gen Xers will argue that their entire age cohort was affected by the realization that it was, for the most part, unwanted. The result, according to Howe and Strauss, was that "Gen X has the worst reputation of all living generations. . . . [It is viewed as] the most selfish and complaining generation, and the least heroic. Ask for one-word descriptors, and you hear a harsh critique, with terms like *slacker, alienated,* and *punkish*" (2000, p. 54). Those who felt alienation undoubtedly did so because as "the most unsupervised generation of young Americans in . . . history, Xers were left to fend for themselves" (Martin & Tulgan, 2002, p. 7). "A generation that . . . endured childhood independency coupled with intense technological advances" (Brown, Haviland, & Morris, as cited in quoted in Martin and Prince, 2008), they had higher crime, drug abuse, and suicide rates than any before them.

Negative assessments of the cohort were not diminished by the stereotypical gen Xer's insistence on communicating a dark view of life with visual aesthetics—multiple tattoos, body piercings, and t-shirts bearing hostile slogans. Coming home to empty houses, Xers' "cultural" diet might consist of television programs like *South Park* or *Married with Children.* News of violence and drugs was everywhere as the rise of AIDS and the crack epidemic filled the air waves.

But perhaps the threat that had the greatest long-term impact on both early and late gen Xers was the economic instability that many came to regard as normal. A 2008 research study by Jacob S. Hacker and Elisabeth Jacobs found that from 1969 to 2004, instability in family incomes rose sharply. They described the recession of the 1980s as:

the worst economic downturn since the Great Depression. . . . Much of the rise in income volatility occurred prior to 1985. . . . While less educated and poorer Americans have less-stable family incomes than their better-educated and wealthier peers, the increase in family income volatility affects all major demographic and economic groups. . . . A wealth of research in psychology and economics suggests that major income fluctuations create not just financial hardship, but also anxiety and discontent. . . .

Research suggests that a wide range of important outcomes—happiness, child well-being, even, perhaps, obesity—may be worsened by sharp fluctuations in income. (Jacobs & Hacker, 2008, paragraphs 6, 5, 9, 66)

If gen X was scarred by being the least wanted in the nation's history, its plight would be multiplied many times over when it became the first group of Americans to face the probability that it would never enjoy the economic security and prosperity its forebears had known. The last quarter of the 20th century, like the early years of the 21st century, was marked by a series of recessions, layoffs, and downsizing that belied Boomers' assumptions that if they were loyal and hard working, employers would feel obliged to reward their allegiance with lifelong tenure and financial support.

No strangers to job insecurity, gen Xers have thus come to be regarded as more realistic about the workplace. Able to accept diversity and eager to increase their expertise in technology that sometimes threatens their elders, contemporary gen Xers tend to remain distanced and consummate individualists in workplaces still dominated by baby boomers. Management consultants say they are serious, self-reliant, and dependable but retain their early mistrust of institutions and regulations and do not expect lifetime employment.

Work appears to have assumed a different role in their lives from those of their parents. When the American Business Collaboration (ABC) commissioned the Families and Work Institute to prepare a 2002 report on comparisons and contrasts between baby-boomer and generation X workers, researchers discovered that baby boomers are "work centric"—that is, they place a more importance on work than on family. An equally significant finding was that the younger workers were far less likely to express a desire to advance and assume more responsibility in their jobs.

THE ADVENT OF THE TROPHY CHILDREN

The recession of 2009 may change the attitudes of employees and jobless workers, of course; but who can predict with infallibility? There was a time when the Rockefeller Commission must have thought with certainty, for instance, that its report would help to slow the American birth rate; but the 1980s quickly dispelled that notion. A decade after it appeared, a totally unexpected baby boom had once again begun. Population growth not only increased, but also grew at such a rate that, before it ended in approximately 2000, the largest generation in American history would already be making its presence felt. Current estimates are as high as 103 million (Madland & Teixeira, 2009), easily exceeding figures for the boomers and the handful of early gen Xers who are its parents.

Unlike its latchkey predecessors, this new generation was not about to be ignored. For families and businesses, it was destined to be a "special" and "entitled" group. The first to notice that a population shift was occurring were those most likely to profit from it, and so proof of the existence of this unexpected and increasingly powerful force was to be found in, of all places, the local mall. Shoppers had once been forced to search for limited choices of teddy bears and cribs, but suddenly they discovered entire stores devoted to babies' and toddlers' needs. As the years rolled by, marketers' attention turned equally enthusiastically to post-toddler millennials, so much so that Howe and Strauss described the generation as "a consumer behemoth, riding atop a new youth economy of astounding scale and extravagance" (2000, p. 265). In 2007, William Blair & Company, an internationally known global investment and research provider organization, estimated the consumer power of generation Y at an astounding $2 trillion annually.

Actually, the economic explosion began with the earliest millennials, babies and toddlers who set the pace for those that followed. In 1976, for example, a woman named Joan Barnes realized there were not many facilities where parents could take their children to participate in "directed parent-child developmental play programs" (Faber, 1984, p. 1), so she convinced her husband to invest in a business that would fulfill this need. At the time, they probably did not foresee they were on the cusp of a movement that would make them millionaires many times over. Barnes believed families would be attracted to places where the "goal is not physical fitness. It's self-esteem. These children are mastering skills at their own pace with the love and support of their parents. Everyone wants a confident child" (Faber, 1984, p. 1).

The perfect facilities for demonstrating parental love and support turned out to be a series of Barnes-owned locations called "Gymboree Play and Music." In 1986, Barnes experienced another epiphany: Parents who were willing to pay for not only development of play and music skills probably also wanted the best-dressed child. And with that goal in mind, a multimillion dollar clothing empire was born.

Gymboree was one example in hundreds or even thousands of attempts to cater to the new generation. Seemingly out of nowhere babies and children were "in" once more; and as the 1980s and 1990s progressed, it became increasingly clear that a child-centered culture was emerging.

Tots through teens could boast not only their own designer fashion lines but also clothing, toy, and entertainment stores devoted exclusively to them. Babies and toddlers, "kids," and teens were suddenly everywhere—on the covers of magazines and on television and movie screens. As time passed, producers discovered the monetary magic of not only films marketed to adolescent audiences but also of "family" movies like *Three Men and a Baby* and *Sleepless in Seattle*. Studios like Walt Disney revived what had seemed to be a moribund animation market with soon-to-be classics like *The Lion King* and *The Little Mermaid,* and a television industry for toddlers gradually emerged.

There was more to this new culture than toys and entertainment, of course. Parents who were willing to pay unheard of sums for designer children's clothes were even more intent on ensuring that young millennials be as physically perfect as possible. Boomers "bought into" the media obsession with body image and the theory that women, as well as men, should strive to "have it all"—beauty, brains, talent, and success. The result was that at the turn of the century when the first millennials arrived on college campuses, a significant number looked visibly different from their generational predecessors. By far more attractive and more expensively dressed than earlier generations, they were fixated on appearance.

In her book, *The Body Project,* Joan Brumberg compares the New Years' resolution of a young Victorian girl with that of a contemporary female:

Resolved, not to talk about myself or feelings. To think before speaking, to work seriously, to be self-restrained in conversations and actions. Not to let my thoughts wander. To be dignified. Interest myself more in others. (Brumberg, 1997, p. xxi)

The contrast between this pledge and that of a quotation from a present-day adolescent is revealing:

I will try to make myself better in any way I possibly can with the help of my budget and baby-sitting money. I will lose weight, get new lenses, already got new haircut, good makeup, new clothes and accessories. (Brumberg, 1997, p. xxi)

New Year's resolutions aside, any assumption that the millennium heralded a more comely race of human beings would be a colossal misinterpretation.

Parental affection, orthodontia, dermatology, and plastic surgery rather than lucky genetic evolution account for the near perfect skin, teeth, and noses that have become commonplace among generation Y. "Commonplace" is a crucial term here because these kinds of procedures are no longer available only to the wealthy. Most are by now routine across all but the lowest economic bracket; and "baby-sitting" money of millennials in the latter group is far more likely to be spent on efforts to improve appearance than anything else.

If millennial children were to have the high self-esteem and confidence Joan Barnes assumed necessary, they needed to be groomed for the future in every possible way. So harried boomers, many of whom already worked long hours, added gymnastics, dancing, cheerleading, music, football, soccer, basketball, tennis, golf, hockey, and lacrosse lessons—plus assorted camps—to their already frenzied lives. Leisurely Saturdays and Sundays gradually disappeared as lessons, recitals, and organized youth sports gained momentum.

Most of the latter required money for the purchase of equipment and ultimately far greater investment for space in which to transport clothing, racquets, balls, clubs, and sticks. Enter the Dodge Caravan (1983), the Plymouth Voyager (1984), and the Toyota Van (1984), vehicles that began decades of "gas guzzling," not with the intention of polluting the environment but rather to meet the demands of families with children whose accumulation of possessions began in infancy and did not cease at college graduation.

Extracurricular activities demanded many children's and parents' time and energy, but schoolwork also required equal or more investment. Frustrated with what they considered the apathy of generation X, parents and teachers determined that change was in order. "Zero tolerance" became the governing phrase of the millennial era, as the young rapidly learned that inattention to academics would not be accepted. Homework and testing increased so significantly that doctors began expressing concern about the physical dangers of toting heavy book bags, and child psychologists like David Elkind pleaded with adults to recognize the grave dangers of "hurrying" children into "growing up too fast too soon" (Elkind, 1981, book subtitle).

Zero tolerance also focused on inappropriate behavior; and the results were, in some respects, successful. Teen drug and alcohol abuse began to decline in the late 1990s, but millennials, age 18–25, currently have the highest rates of illicit drug abuse (19.7 percent) of all age cohorts. This is also true of alcohol abuse; 43.6 percent report binge drinking, and 17.2 percent say they are heavy drinkers. Millennials also indicate a slight increase (4.1 percent in 2002 to 4.6 percent in 2007) in use of prescription drug pain relievers (Substance Abuse & Mental Health Services Administration, 2007). Millennial boosters like Howe and Strauss (2000) and authors of 1990s articles in such magazines as *Newsweek, The New York Times,* and *Vogue* touted the arrival of a millennial sexual counterrevolution and a growing commitment to virginity among the young.

Like their predecessors, millennials share with gen X awareness of living in an extraordinarily chaotic and dangerous time almost devoid of genuine heroes. A 1999 survey of the Class of 2000 lists the "events that made the greatest impression (on them) as (1) Columbine, (2) the War in Kosovo, (3) the Oklahoma City bombing, (4) Princess Di's death, (5) the Clinton impeachment trial, (6) the O. J. Simpson trial, (7) the Rodney King riots, (8) the Lewinsky scandal, (9) the Fall of Berlin, and (10) the McGwire-Sosa homer derby" (as cited in Howe & Strauss, 2000, p. 19).

As the first of the new generation made its way to college campuses, the horrors of September 11 and the Virginia Tech murders, as well as controversy over the war in Iraq, contributed to an almost eerie sense of anxiety; and college personnel began to complain of interference from "helicopter" parents who were "hovering" over their children and not allowing them to grow up. Parents, on the other hand, were not thrilled with the party atmosphere and frequent danger on campuses that were no longer willing to act *in loco parentis* but were all too eager to exact exorbitant amounts in tuitions and room and board.

DESPERATELY SEEKING THE REAL MILLENNIALS

Like Howe and Strauss, many others have exaggerated either the virtues or the limitations of this new group that is poised to enter the workplace. *Millennials Rising: the Next Great Generation,* the title of the Howe and Strauss (2000) work, demonstrates the extremes to which some have gone in their adulation. Although the authors insisted the future holds no certainty, their overall discussion leaves little doubt that they believe millennials to be headed toward greatness. They argued at one point:

> [After all], the decade is the Oh-Ohs [2000s]. The generation is the Millennials. When the two come together, the young people of America will dazzle the nation much as the Boomers did in the 60s, though to a very different effect. (2000, p. 364)

Millennial Makeover: My Space, YouTube, and the Future of American Politics, in essence, presented generation Y as the nation's greatest hope for a revolution by the idealistic, civic-minded young (Winograd & Hais, 2008). In an online review of a 2008 book about the millennials, Muhammad Yunus, co-winner of the 2006 Nobel Peace Prize, echoed such sentiments when he stated:

> In my travels around the world, I have been very impressed by today's young people. They are smart, caring, creative, and generous. I share the hope . . . that this new generation will help re-orient our planet and conquer the problems of poverty, war, and pollution that currently plague it. (as cited in Greenberg & Weber, 2008)

How any age cohort can rationally be expected to end war, poverty, and pollution and to "reorient" (the) planet against evils that have plagued earth since the beginning of time remains to be seen, of course.

A therapist interviewed by *The Dallas Evening News* recognized the hyperbole in imagining generation Y a probable world savior:

> [This group has] been overparented, overindulged and overprotected. They haven't experienced that much failure, frustration, pain. We were so obsessed with protecting and promoting their self-esteem that they crumble like cookies when they discover the world doesn't revolve around them. They get into the real world and they're shocked. You have to be very careful in how you talk to them because they take everything as criticism. (as cited in Hall, 2008)

Tulgan (2009) also disputed the notion of an emerging Millennial "great generation":

> Throughout their childhood, Gen Yers were told over and over, "Whatever you think, say, or do, that's okay. Your feelings are true. Don't worry about how other kids play. That's their style. Their style is valid *and* your style is valid."
>
> This is what child psychologists called "positive tolerance," and it was only one small step to the damaging cultural lies that somehow "we are all winners and everyone gets a trophy." In fact, as children, most Gen Yers simply showed up and participated—and actually *did* get a trophy.
>
> Every step of the way, Gen Yers' parents have guided, directed, supported, coached and protected them. Gen Yers have been respected, nurtured, scheduled, measured, discussed, diagnosed, medicated, programmed, accommodated, included, awarded, and rewarded as long as they can remember. Their parents, determined to create a generation of superchildren, perhaps accelerated their childhood. . . . Many psychologists have observed that Gen Yers act like highly precocious late adolescents well into adulthood. (2009, pp. 7–8)

So where does truth lie? Probably between the extremes and within the lists of so-called millennial characteristics that have been proposed over time. Hundreds of books, articles, and Web postings have attempted to describe them. Almost everyone agrees that, like their parents, they are a wanted, sheltered generation; but some feel that, as in the case of the boomers, all the attention has resulted in overprotected, indulged young people who unjustifiably perceive themselves to be special and entitled. At the same time, millennials are widely praised for their philanthropic, civic-minded natures. Employers are advised that they are cooperative, responsive to authority and rules, eager to learn, and more conventional and conservative in appearance and behavior than generation X and the baby boomers. They are also told that millennials are self-reliant, confident, achievement and future oriented, optimistic, and adaptable to and energized by change. Finally, there is universal agreement that they are the most technologically advanced, diverse and inclusive, globally oriented, and environmentally conscious of all generations preceding them.

As we have observed, the problem with such lists is that members of generations are never completely homogenous and that even the most stereotypical can be transformed by life events. An additional challenge when discussing generation Y, however, is that often the characteristics attributed to this group conflict with one another and with highly respected studies, self-reports, and observable behaviors of the group. Because it is risky to use aggregate contemporaneous views of the emerging generational workforce to provide information to employers, the most reliable approach probably is to explain how their current and past behaviors conflict with abstract theories and how stereotypes of the group are at odds with one another. An attempt to moderate overly positive views of millennials, however, is not meant to present a negative view of them. It is simply to warn against excessive expectations and to establish that like all generations, they are a complex and imperfect group that requires training and support as it attempts to meet the demands of an equally complicated and imperfect workplace.

DISHONESTY: EPIDEMIC

It would be a great mistake for employers to take on face value one of the most widespread mischaracterizations of millennials as totally "good kids" responsive to rules and authority. The problem is that this view simply does not comport with reality. In 1992, the Josephson Institute, an internationally known training and consulting nonprofit began biennial surveys of the ethics of American youth. The results of its 2008 sample of 29,760 of private and public high school students revealed that lying, cheating, and stealing were rampant and "paint a troubling picture of our future politicians and parents, cops and corporate executives, and journalists and generals" (Josephson Institute, 2008).

The research found that 64 percent of students indicated they had cheated on at least one test in the past year, and 38 percent admitted to doing so two or more times. Stealing was as bad; 23 percent said they stole from a parent or relative in the past year, and 20 percent revealed that they stole from a friend. They also lied in significant numbers: 49 percent of males and 36 percent of females admitted they sometimes lie to save money. Ironically, 26 percent said they were not truthful on one or two questions on the survey (Josephson Institute, 2008).

Even more disturbing was the researchers' observation that the statistics are probably underreported and that the reports of dishonesty have increased 60 percent for males and 35 percent for females since the last survey in 2006. To make matters worse, many of the young respondents did not appear to comprehend the seriousness of their own and their friends' lapses in ethics. Given an item asking whether they considered themselves better than most people when required to do right, 77 percent said that they were superior to others; and an amazing 93 percent declared they were satisfied with their personal ethics and character (Josephson Institute, 2008).

Additional studies are prolific and produce similar or even more shocking findings. Among these is the "Academic Cheating Fact Sheet" produced by The Educational Testing Service (ETS), which reported:

In the past it was the struggling student who was more likely to cheat just to get by. Today it is also the above-average college bound students who are cheating . . . 73% of all test takers, including prospective graduate students and teachers agree that most students do cheat at some point. 86% of high school students agreed. Cheating no longer carries the stigma that it used to. Less social disapproval coupled with increased competition for admission into universities and graduate schools has made students more willing to do whatever it takes to get an A. . . . While about 20% of college students admitted to cheating in high school during the 1940s; today between 75% and 98% of college students surveyed each year report having cheated in high school.

Students who cheat often feel justified in what they're doing. They cheat because they see others cheat and they think they will be unfairly disadvantaged. The research on college cheating is just as disturbing.

Rutgers professor, Don McCabe, studied academic misconduct for years and helped found the Center for Academic Integrity at Duke University. In a four-year survey of 62,000 undergraduates on 96 campuses, he found that two-thirds admitted to cheating at one time or another (as cited in Glater, 2006). Gregory Cizak, author of *Cheating on Tests: How to Do It, Detect It, and Prevent It* (1999), reported that 75 percent of collegians admitted they had cheated at least once and 84 percent said cheating is necessary to get ahead. He analyzed numerous surveys to conclude:

> College cheating also works its way into the business marketplace. Students don't just say, "OK. I cheated in school, but now I'm in the workplace and it ends here." They are forming bad habits that carry over into the market. . . . Employers eager to hire graduates with prestigious degrees and excellent grades may be in for an unpleasant surprise when their new hires don't live up to expectations. (Knowledge@W. P. Carey, 2008, p. 1)

Rising rates of academic dishonesty are indisputable, as are the number of rationalizations young people give for misbehavior. If students begin to cut corners as early as grade school and feel justified in doing so, once they reach the workplace and the stakes are even higher, the impulse to cheat under pressure or to achieve a career goal could obviously cause some to compromise their integrity.

On the other hand, numerous studies have shown that higher expectations and more intense competition have contributed to exceptionally high stress among gen Y college students (mtvU, 2006). Perhaps the solution to concerns about millennial honesty should lead not to excessive caution and oversight in the workplace where the youngest age cohort, in all probability, is no more ethical or unethical than any other generation. A better solution would be for employers to disregard immoderate projections of millennials' abilities and collaborate with them and other employees to eliminate excessive stress that tempts workers to behave inappropriately.

MONEY: IT MATTERS

Contemporary data indicate that early predictions about millennials being less materialistic than their predecessors were woefully false. In 2000, Howe and Strauss predicted:

> Parents are of two minds about the impact of commerce on today's America. When they reflect on their own lives—especially on their own various

quests for individuality and fulfillment, most of which happened in an earlier and simpler era—they see the positive side. Commerce gives them all the choices they want when they want them. What can be bad about that? Yet when they reflect on what could be best for their children, most of them see the negative side.

On the whole, Millennials give Boomers high marks for managing a prosperous economy and for including kids in their earning and spending priorities. At the same time, Millennials seem willing to heed their parents' message about excessive commercialism. (2000, p. 286)

Between publication of *Millennials Rising* and 2010, things obviously changed. Sharon Jayson began a 2007 *USA Today* article, "Ask young people about their generation's top life goals and the answer is clear and resounding: They want to be rich and famous" (2007, p. 1). She cited comments from young people like a 22-year-old who summarized the culture of her generation:

When you open a celebrity magazine, it's all about the money and being rich and famous. . . . The TV shows we watch—anything from *The Apprentice* where the intro to the show is the "money song"—to *Us Weekly* magazine where you see all the celebrities and their $6 million homes. We see reality TV shows with Jessica and Nick living the life. We see Britney and Paris. The people we relate to outside our friends are those people. (2007, p. 1)

A 2007 Pew Research Poll confirmed this perception when it reported that 81 percent of 18- to 25-year-old millennials said their first or second most significant life goal is getting rich and their second goal is achieving fame (51 percent) (as cited in Jayson, 2007).

In 2009, the young face serious hurdles because of a recession that will have long-term effects. Fewer jobs are available, and older employees who have lost retirement funds are working longer. College graduates often leave school with enormous debt at a time when the federal deficit has reached a crisis point. It appears that the economy will improve slowly; and when and if that happens, employers will confront a generation of young people who have been reared to feel themselves entitled and suddenly find the world of work less hospitable then they anticipated. Unlike more cynical generation Xers, who have endured the vagaries of the marketplace all their lives, millennials, as a group, may be less prepared to face career obstacles and financial deprivation. That will be the moment when employers—and they—will discover who they really are: overindulged trophy children whose acquisitiveness leads to greater calamity or genuine heirs of a work ethic and values that have made America great.

SEX: TROUBLE AHEAD

Sexual conduct is another area in which reality clashes with rosy assessments of generation Y. Howe and Strauss emphasized millennials' improved behavior and celebrated the Center for Disease Control and Prevention's finding that the number of high school students having intercourse decreased from 1988 to 1995 (2000, p. 197). Although the 2007 percentage remained lower than in 1991, the latest figure is higher than the measurement taken in 2005. Far more important is that the most recent survey indicates that among millennials 47.8 percent of high school students said they had had intercourse at least once, and 14.9 percent responded that they had done so with four or more partners (National Center for Chronic Disease Prevention & Health Promotions, 2007).

But college-age millennials are the ones who have captured most of the headlines, thanks to authors like *Rollingstone's* Janet Reitman, whose article "Sex and Scandal at Duke" (2006) explained that at one of America's most highly regarded institutions traditional intercourse is common, and oral sex nearly ubiquitous, regarded as sort of a form of elaborate kissing that really does not mean very much. Whatever sex goes on, the girls say, is done in the context of the "hookup," which describes anything from making out to full-on intercourse. As one male student describes it, it "exists in a whirlwind of drunkenness and horniness that lacks definition—which is what everyone likes about it (because) it's just an environment of craziness and you don't have to worry about it until the next morning" (as quoted in Reitman, 2006).

Hookups, which are one-time encounters, often involving alcohol, can be only roughly defined because they may include a wide range of behaviors from kissing to oral sex to intercourse between strangers, acquaintances, or even friends who have no expectations of a further intimate or romantic relationship. In the hookup, no strings are attached, only sex for enjoyment by young people who contend they are too busy to become involved in a relationship or so stressed they "need" the physical release sex can provide.

Collegians in dormitories across America immediately understood the argument a friend of the heroine in Tom Wolfe's novel *I Am Charlotte Simmons*, made when she told Charlotte not to be upset by hookup culture:

> College is like this four-year period when you can try anything—and everything—and if it goes wrong, there's no consequences. . . . College is

the only time your life, or your adult life anyway, when you can really *experiment*, and at a certain point, when you leave, when you graduate or whatever, everybody's memory like evaporates. You tried this and this and this and this, and you learned a lot about how things are, but nobody's gonna remember it. It's like amnesia, totally, and there's no record and you leave college exactly the way you came in, pure as rainwater. (Wolfe, 2004, p. 168)

Since the late 1990s, perhaps hundreds, perhaps thousands, of research studies, articles books, and media accounts have dealt with the hookup culture, which some say was common in the 1970s and 1980s, as well as in the following years. There are scattered small surveys but no large scale empirical evidence of its prevalence; authors usually contend that "the majority of" or "most" millennials engage in the behavior. Some, like sociologist Kathleen A. Bogle (2008) maintained that "after college there is a discernable shift to more formal dating" (as quoted in Guess, 2008), but there is only anecdotal proof that this is the case, and Bogle herself acknowledged,

> It is really difficult to measure how hooking up affects people psychologically as they age and move into post-college relationships. . . . The transition to the post-college dating scene [is] not necessarily an easy one. Many of the 20-something-year-old men and women I spoke with were confused over how to act in certain scenarios after college, not knowing if they were on a date or just "hanging out and hooking up." Some of the people I interviewed had never been on a formal date until after college, so figuring out the rules for the "new" system was a big adjustment for them. (2008, p. 16)

That confusion poses an extraordinary challenge in the workplace, where managers and workers have only recently come to grips with the fact that sexual harassment is an issue that is here to stay. Books and Internet sites offer endless advice about managing generation Y, but few or none attempt to address the thorny issue of how to deal with young people accustomed to the concept of recreational sex. Not all millennials practice or approve of hookup culture, but it is for everyone a constant and everyday fact of life, very dissimilar to even the most sexually charged workplaces; and none of the experts appear ready to tackle the daunting issue of how co-workers and managers themselves will and should react to employees with this value system.

Ironically, the task of discouraging sexual harassment was easier years ago when laws were first evolving. Then the basic challenge was explaining the sexual harassment dynamic to male audiences that were often in denial about the damage that sexual comments, gestures, and propositions could inflict. Women were primarily the targets of unacceptable behavior; so most, if not all, sympathized with efforts to control libido running wild in workplaces and classrooms.

But times have changed. Millennials live amid the most highly sexualized culture in American history. Their clothing alone tells the story. They have fewer tattoos and piercings than gen Xers wore; but once the snow melts in the spring, they discard sweatshirts and jeans for clothing markedly different from their predecessors. Baby boomers remember being sent home from school if their "short" skirts did not touch the floor when they kneeled. Millennial females are lucky if their skirts cover their thongs and their breasts stay put in halter tops. Male students' shorts seem to grow briefer every year, while the decorative holes that adorn them creep ever closer to the most worrisome locations. Young and attractive, they are a generation responding to the only culture they have ever known. Sex sells the clothes millennials wear, the hair styles they chose, the magazines they buy, the music they dance to, and the films they see. It has been in every nook and cranny of their lives since their earliest memories; and like it or not, there is no reason to believe that society will ever turn back the clock. Who knows when or why so much changed? Maybe it happened with one snap of a Washington intern's thong or with the zealous political response that somehow legitimized sex any where, any time, with anyone. Maybe a lot of women finally decided casual sex with all too eager young men was one more glass ceilings to be broken. Maybe a steady diet of films and Hollywood idols' lifestyles altered the meaning of "relationships" for millennials too busy preparing for careers to work at romance. Maybe massive hooking up between strangers had been going on all along, and no one admitted it. More than likely, a mixture of forces that we will never completely understand occurred.

Exactly what will happen when this new generation enters the workplace is impossible to foresee, but some things are certain. Educators say they have schooled teens and collegians well about appropriate dress, language, and physical interaction between individuals; but the truth is they have devoted only cursory, and in some cases no, attention to the behaviors that will demand a "wake-up call" from students once they leave the classroom. A rude awakening also will occur in workplaces in which training has been inadequate. There is no place in offices, factories, and malls for crude humor, propositions, or hookups, and that is a lesson everyone will be forced to digest instantaneously. Sexual harassment laws are not about to disappear, and a major task for employers and managers must be to educate themselves and both new and seasoned workers about the enormity of the challenge they face.

COLLABORATION AND PHILANTHROPY: ANYONE'S GUESS

Besides the joy of watching them learn and the sheer pleasure of their company, one of the most interesting parts of spending time with this group of young people is having the opportunity to measure their experiences against the generational myths by which they have been characterized. Two of the least disputed characterizations of generation Y are that they prefer to work in teams and are exceptionally civic minded and community oriented. Anyone who knows millennials well and has their trust can attest to the fact that these are either slight misconceptions or in some cases serious exaggerations by so-called experts who have not examined the complexities underlying their assumptions.

Take, for example, the theory about millennial preferences for collaboration. In the 1970s, as the women's movement was gaining power, some educators began advocating for "open classrooms," where students would have the opportunity to interact and express their feelings about subjects rather than sitting woodenly listening to teachers spout facts in what was essentially a linear teaching-learning mode. Much of this innovation was based on the realization that stereotypic males and females absorbed knowledge in different ways and that the prevailing classroom model catered to males' linear learning styles rather than females more subjective ways of acquiring information. In response, many academics converted straight lines of desks into circles, designed assignments requiring students to work together, and, when applicable, encouraged them to talk about their feelings. The intent was to be more inclusive and move beyond the "hidden curriculum" (Snyder, 1973) that taught passivity and acquiescence.

In general, the change worked well for females. Maybe not so well for males, although controversy still exists around that point. Instructional styles are not, of course, the focal point here. What does matter is that the concept of group work rapidly gained not simply a foothold but a grip on the environment of many classrooms. Once rejected as "touchy-feely" or "cop-out" teaching methods became ingrained in typical millennial classrooms. For instance, English instruction now involves endless hours of peer review in which students analyze and critique one another's papers. Majors in a variety of college disciplines collaborate on projects because they are told, often truthfully, that this is the way the workplace characteristically functions.

Although this assertion is generally accurate, the assumption that millennials clamor for collaboration and group activity is simply false. Ask a bright young person who has endured the boredom and humiliation of having a C student criticize her "A" history paper, and you might reconsider. Encourage a weak student to admit his anxiety about being evaluated by peers as well as his professor, and you might recognize the error in the collaboration assumption. Inquire of two honors students how they felt about having to collaborate with disinterested peers on an assignment, and you will understand that the millennial-as-work-groupie is more wishful thinking than reality.

What millennials do bring to the workplace is *training* in cooperative activity. They know how to negotiate group projects because educators have so often required and in a few cases taught collaboration. But that does not necessarily mean that all or even the majority prefer to work with others most of the time. Many people are more productive when they work individually; and while management gurus frequently overlook that point and offer oversimplified portraits of generation Y, managers should recognize that, like other generations, millennials have diverse work styles. The individual hire has to be fitted to the tasks a job requires, so it is never safe to assume that birth date predicts the ways in which workers will be most efficient and satisfied.

As educators began moving desks around and requiring peers to interact, they also encouraged "hands-on" or experiential learning. Eventually they became enthusiastic about extending students' experience beyond the classroom. Parochial schools often used this model, but its popularity became especially widespread once Congress created the Community Service Act of 1990. It included a program called Serve America that was renamed Learn and Serve America when Congress enacted the Corporation for National and Community Service Trust Act in 1993. Learn and Serve America provides various forms of funding, but most high schools and higher education institutions maintain and, when necessary, finance service learning or community service programs on their own.

The difference between service learning and community service is that community service typically involves having students perform activities that benefit the larger community or some smaller entity within it. Service learning, on the other hand, is ideally more structured and connects specific service projects to well-defined learning goals. For almost two decades, both types of service have been all the rage on college campuses and have greatly benefited individuals and communities. In addition, they have taught students the value of civic engagement, which is often required or preferred by employees in work settings.

Howe and Strauss argued that the new millennial "communitarianism" (2000, p. 237) means that:

> millions of diverse kids will manage to crowd together into a newly positive definition of youth. . . . Free-market incentives, individualism, and the search for innate fulfillment are all the rage for many boomer adults, but less so for their kids—who are constantly told that *they* need selfless values. Rather than resist this message, kids seem to accept it. On the whole, they're not as eager to grow up putting self ahead of community the way their parents did. (2000, p. 237)

On the surface, the authors were right. I cannot recall a single millennial graduation ceremony when someone did not recite an impressive list of service projects performed by graduates, and without a doubt, students should be encouraged to contribute to their communities and to care for those less fortunate. That being said, it is a significant leap from reading a list of graduates' service to assuming all or even most will continue serious commitments to service, and that is a crucial point for every community-minded business or other type of work organization to recognize.

Like group projects, community service has seldom been a choice for generation Y. Faculty members are often encouraged and sometimes rewarded for implementing creative and newsworthy projects. Depending on their majors, college students may have service requirements in several classes during a given quarter or semester. Many, if not most, entail leaving the campus for another location, a demand that poses special burdens on those who have long labs or studios throughout the school week. In addition, many institutions require that students perform a specific number of service hours before they can earn a diploma.

The approach works well for some and not so well for others who emerge from the experience less enthusiastic then their peers. The complaints of the latter are numerous. They resent having to juggle different projects in separate classes at one time or being forced to take time from school work to travel excessive distances to perform service. They complain of being assigned "busy work" unconnected to the discipline in which the service is required. One of my students tells of having to spend the weekend sleeping in a cardboard box to "learn about poverty"; another of being assigned to pick up dead butterflies at a local exhibit as children ripped off their wings. Still another insists he did not become more civic minded as a result of spending five hours picking up highway garbage.

Obviously, some service projects are ill-conceived and some students misunderstand the purpose of valid assignments, so it is unfair to criticize the concept on the basis of isolated examples. No disputing statistics shows volunteerism has risen among the young, but it is important to distinguish when service is performed out of choice and when it is merely a requirement. Beyond the fact that education institutions need to be more cautious in designing service activities, this is important information for an employer deeply involved in the community and expecting similar commitment from employees. Champions of the millennials imply that everyone born after 1980 will chose to spend life doing good works, but that is simply a theory, and hiring a gen Yer on the assumption that it will happen is not a smart decision. There are no guarantees that a millennial will be any more eager to participate in community activities than a baby boomer. In fact, just the opposite might occasionally be the case, since the more cynical will admit, as one of my own students recently did, that they are "overdosed on the community stuff."

THE DOUBLE-EDGED SWORD OF TECHNOLOGY

A point no one disputes is that generation Y is extraordinarily adept with digital technology. Why shouldn't it be? With few exceptions, it has been a significant part of millennials' lives from their earliest memories; and employers have long been eager to take advantage of their expertise. Ever-changing technological advancements mean that they are poised to make long-term contributions, and their skills at handling digital tools will always be in demand.

And yet a recent book by college professor Mark Bauerlein (2008) made an unsettling point. In *The Dumbest Generation: How the Digital Age Stupifies Young Americans and Jeopardizes Our Future*, he discussed "only the intellect of under-30-year-olds" (p. 7) to argue that the digital age has resulted in troubling "knowledge deficits" (p. 11) among America's youth. Bauerlein contended that millennials spend inordinate time on "digital diversions" (2008, p. xi) like computers, television, and video games. This finding is hardly a new revelation, but his "attempt to consolidate the best and broadest research" (2008, p. 7) like the National Assessment of Educational Progress, the National Survey of Students Engagement, the American Time Use Survey, the Kaiser Family Foundation Program for the Study of American Media and Health, the Survey of

Public Participation in the Arts, National Endowment for the Arts, and Nielson's "How Users Read on the Web" was impressive.

Noting popular and academic assumptions that millennials' digital proficiency is somehow linked to learning, he posed the question of why, if this is the case, knowledge and skills levels have not increased and test scores have, in fact, declined among the young. Bauerlein (2008) then described "a certain kind of intelligence, (p. 95), which he called "screen literacy" (p. 95). He maintained:

> It improves [young people's] visual acuity, their mental readiness for rushing images and updated information. At the same time, however, screen intelligence doesn't transfer well to non-screen experiences, especially the kinds that build knowledge and verbal skills. It conditions minds against quiet, concerted study, against imagination unassisted by visuals, against linear, sequential analysis of texts, against an idle afternoon with a detective story and nothing else (p. 95)

Millennials use their digital tools, he said, primarily for recreational and social purposes so that they are seldom exposed to any culture but their own. Coupled with contemporary emphasis on encouraging self-esteem among the young, this increases their self-absorption, and according to Bauerlein (2008), has had (and will continue to have) devastating effects.

> Yes, young Americans are energetic, ambitious, enterprising, and good, but their talents and interests and money thrust them not into books and ideas and history and civics but into a whole other realm and other consciousness. A different social life and a different mental life have formed among them. Technology has bred it, but the result doesn't tally with the fulsome descriptions of digital empowerment, global awareness, and virtual communities. Instead of opening young American minds to the stores of civilization and science and politics, technology has contracted their horizon to themselves, to the social scene around them. Young people have never been so intensely mindful of and present to one another, so enabled of adolescent contact. Teen images and songs, hot gossip and games, and youth-to-youth communications no longer limited by time or space wrap them up in a generational cocoon. . . .
>
> They have all the advantages of modernity and democracy, but when the gifts of life lead to social joys, not intellectual labor, the minds of the young plateau at age 18. . . . The fonts of knowledge are everywhere, but the rising generation is camped in the desert, passing stories, pictures, tunes, and texts back and forth, living off the thrill of peer attention. Meanwhile, their

intellects refuse the cultural and civic inheritance that has made us what we are up to now.

[Millennials] are latter-day Rip Van Winkles, sleeping through the movements of culture and events of history. . . . From their ranks will emerge few minds knowledgeable and interested enough to study, explain, and dispute the place and meaning of our nation. . . . Adolescence is always going to be more or less anti-intellectual, of course, and learning has ever struggled against immaturity, but the battle has never proven so uphill. (2008, pp. 10, 234)

A BETTER PLACE TO WORK

Depending on your experience and point of view, millennials might compose either the "dumbest" or the next "greatest" generation, but no one can deny that they can bring a lot to the workplace. One of their greatest strengths is that they are, without dispute, the most inclusive and adaptable of working age cohorts. It is not oversimplification to say that more than any generation before them, they understand and respect differences in others. Tulgan (2009) put it this way:

The power of diversity has finally kicked over the melting pot. Generation Y is the most diverse generation in history in terms of ethnic heritage, geographical origins, ability/disability, age, language, lifestyle preference, sexual orientation, color, size, and every other way of categorizing people. But this doesn't make Gen Yers feel alienated and threatened. Rather, they take the concept of diversity to a whole new level. . . . To Gen Yers, every single person, with his or her own combination of background, traits, and characteristics, is his or her own unique diversity story. . . . For Generation Y, difference is cool. (p. 8)

Their respect for diversity is a product of deliberate efforts by adults who understood the need to change a culture in which children's stories like *Little Black Sambo* were routine. By and large, the attempts worked, and generation Y has grown up with books and television programs like the *Clifford the Big Red Dog* series that routinely features a little girl in a wheel chair. Full inclusion is a reality in classrooms across the country, where millennials have been sensitized to the ways in which human beings are, despite their differences, linked by common needs and emotions. Some might waiver in their enthusiasm for community service; but this other, more fundamental virtue can have longer lasting benefits in places where co-workers are less inclined to appreciate or tolerate diversity.

Their open-mindedness is directly related to their consciousness of themselves as citizens of not just the United States but the world in general.

Strange as it may seem to some, they cannot remember a time the latest news or communication with someone on the other side of the continent or even the globe was not at their fingertips. Their ability to transcend space, their greater global consciousness has affected their sense of time and made them more adaptable to change than other more insulated generations. Bauerlein (2008) would probably say they are incapable of understanding change, but clearly they know how to live with it as many others do not, and that adaptability bodes well for the workplace.

The truth is that at this point in time most of what we can say of the millennials is conjecture, as Tulgan (2009) pointed out:

> Trying to figure out who Gen Yers are deep inside is the wrong tactic. How can you possibly figure out what their mind and spirit really are like? How can you figure out what their inner motivations really are? You are not qualified to do so. And I would argue that it's really none of your business anyway. . . . You cannot—and should not—teach them what to believe, but you can certainly teach them how to behave. It's not really your place to teach them values. But it is certainly your place to teach them how to be good citizens within your organization. (pp. 114–115)

In many ways, millennials are no different from any other generation (see Martin, Fuda, & Paludi, chapter 13 in this volume) and the eagerness to paint a definitive portrait of them has often been a disservice. They are neither "dumb" nor "great." Like others before them, they will bring youth and energy to workplaces that are always in need of rejuvenation; and barring a cataclysmic event like a world war, most probably will make their contributions to the nation in separate and private ways. They are, after all, "a riddle wrapped in a mystery inside an enigma" (as cited in Brainy Quotes); and only time will tell how history will remember them.

REFERENCES

Bauerlein, M. (2008). *The dumbest generation: How the digital age stupefies young Americans and jeopardizes our future.* New York: Penguin.

Bogle, K. (2008). *Hooking up: Sex, dating, and relationships on campus.* New York: New York University Press.

Brumberg, J. (1997). *The body project.* New York: Random House.

Bureau of Labor Statistics (2008). Retrieved May 12, 2010, from http://www.bls.gov.

Cizak, G. (1999). *Cheating on tests: How to do it, to detect it, and prevent it.* Mahwah, NJ: Erlbaum.

Elkind, D. (1981). *The hurried child: Growing up too fast too soon*. Reading, MA: Addison-Wesley.

Faber, N. (1984, September 24). Move over, Romper Room: All the best babies come to boogie at Joan Barnes' Gymboree. *People Magazine, 22*(13), 118–120. Retrieved May 12, 2010, from http://www.people.com/people/archive/issue/07566840924.00.html.

Glater, J. (2006, May 18). Colleges chase as cheats shift to higher tech. *New York Times*. Retrieved May 12, 2010, from www.nytimes.com/2006/05/18/education/18cheating.html.

Greenberg, E., & Weber, K. (2008). *Generation we: How Millennial youth are taking over America and changing our world forever.* Emeryville, CA: Pachatusan.

Guess, A. (2008, January 29). The sociology of hooking up. *Inside Higher Ed.* Retrieved May 12, 2010, from www.insidehighered.com/news/2008/01/29/hookups.

Hall, C. (2008, February 24). Millennials need to get real about work world. *Dallas Morning News*. Retrieved May 12, 2010, from http://www.dallasnews.com/sharedcontent/dws/bus/columnists/chall/stories.

Howe, N., & Strauss, W. (2000). *Millennials rising: The next great generation*. New York: Vintage Press.

Jacobs, E., & Hacker, J. S. (2008, May 29). *The rising instability of American family incomes, 1969–2004: Evidence from the panel study on income dynamics economic* (EPI Briefing Paper No. 213). Retrieved May 12, 2010, from www.epi.org/content.cfm/bp213.

Jayson, S. (2007, January 10). Generation Y's goal? Wealth and fame. *USA Today.* Retrieved May 12, 2010, from http://www.usatoday.com/news/nation/2007-01-09-gen-y-cover_x.htm.

Josephson Institute. (2008). *The ethics of American youth: 2008 summary.* Retrieved May 12, 2010, from http://www.charactercounts.org/programs/reportcard/index.html.

Knowledge@W. P. Carey. (2008). *Are millennials prone to cheating to get ahead?* Retrieved May 12, 2010, from http://www.knowledge.wpcarey.asu.edu/article.cfm?articleid=1590.

Madland, D., & Teixeira, R. (2009). *New progressive America: The millennial generation*. Retrieved May 12, 2010, from www.americanprogress.org/issues/2009/05/millennial_generation.html.

Martin, C., & Tulgan, B. (2002). *Managing the generation mix: From collision to collaboration.* Amherst, MA: HRD Press.

Martin, N. M., & Prince, D. (2008, December). Factoring for X: An empirical study of Generation X's materialistic attributes. *Journal of Management and Marketing Research, 1*, 65–78.

mtvU. (2006). *College mental health study: Stress, depression, stigma, and students.* Retrieved May 12, 2010, from http://www.halfofus.com/_media/_pr/mtvUCollegeMentalHealthStudy2006.pdf.

National Center for Chronic Disease Prevention and Health Promotions. (2007). *Sexual risk behaviors*. Retrieved May 12, 2010, from http://www.cdc.gov/HealthyYouth/sexualbehaviors.

Raines, C. (2002). *Managing millennials*. Retrieved May 12, 2010, from http://www.generationsatwork.com/articles/millenials.htm.

Reitman, J. (2006, June 1). Sex and scandal at Duke. *Rolling Stone*. Retrieved May 12, 2010, from http://www.rollingstone.com/news/story/1046/sex_scandal_at_duke.

Ritchie, K. (2002). *Marketing to Generation X*. New York: Free Press.

Rockefeller Commission (1972). *Population and the American future*. Retrieved May 12, 2010, from http://www.population-security.org/rockefeller/001_population_growth_and_the_american_future.htm.

Snyder, B. (1973). *The hidden curriculum*. Cambridge, MA: MIT Press.

Substance Abuse and Mental Health Services Administration. (2007). *National survey on drug use and health*. Retrieved May 12, 2010, from http://www.cdc.gov/HealthyYouth/yrbs/index.htm.

Tulgan, B. (2009). *Not everyone gets a trophy: How to manage Generation Y*. San Francisco, CA: Jossey-Bass.

Winograd, M., & Hais, M. (2008). *Millenial makeover*. New Brunswick, NJ: Rutgers University Press.

Wolfe, T. (2004). *I am Charlotte Simmons*. New York: Farrar, Straus & Giroux.

15

Processes and Struggles with Racial Microaggressions from the White American Perspective: Recommendations for Workplace Settings

Kevin Leo Yabut Nadal, Katie E. Griffin, Vivian M. Vargas, Marie-Anne Issa, Oliver B. Lyons, and Michael Tobio

Blatant racism has been pervasive throughout the history of the United States, ranging from the genocide of Native Americans to the centuries of slavery of African Americans to the internment of Japanese Americans during World War II. The civil rights movement made strides to promote equality in the United States, resulting in many laws and acts that have attempted to prevent overt and assaultive racial discrimination in our country. With the election of President Barack Obama in 2008, as well as the decrease in race-based hate crimes over the past 30 years, many believe that racism no longer exists in American society. This misconception may be due to the notion that explicit racism may not manifest in individuals' everyday lives and because the United States has become more politically correct. It is no longer acceptable for systems, groups, or individuals to be overtly racist, but racism may manifest in more covert forms. On a societal level, this has been labeled as aversive racism (Dovidio, Gaertner, Kawakami, & Hodson, 2002), modern racism (McConahay, 1986), and symbolic racism (Sears, 1988). More recently, a surge of literature has emerged in psychology and other fields and has conceptualized subtle interpersonal racism as racial microaggressions (see Sue, Capodilupo, et al., 2007).

Racial microaggressions are defined as "brief and subtle vocal, behavioral, or environmental cues that, intentionally or unintentionally, communicate a negative or derogatory message to members of another race" (Sue, Capodilupo, et al., 2007, p. 271; see Nadal, chapter 3 in this volume). One of the main differences between racial microaggressions and the aforementioned forms of racism is that it focuses on the interpersonal interactions between whites and people of color, whereas aversive racism, modern racism, and symbolic racism predominantly describe racism on systemic or institutional levels. Racial microaggressions are so insidious because they occur on a daily basis and are so subtle that the victim must decide whether or not the instance qualified as an insult, if the insult was race-related, or both. Empirical studies have found that the process of dealing with microaggressions can be psychically draining for people of color, can lead to an array of negative emotions, and potentially may lead to mental health problems (Rivera, Forquer, & Rangel, in press; Sue, Bucceri, Lin, Nadal, & Torino, 2007; Sue, Capodilupo, & Holder, 2008; Sue, Nadal, et al., 2008; Watkins, LaBarrie, & Appio, in press).

Three forms of racial microaggressions have been identified (Sue, Capodilupo, et al., 2007). First, *microassaults* are the most related to the overt or "old-fashioned" racism of the past and include explicit negative actions or remarks that are meant to hurt the intended victim. For example, when someone uses a racial slur to insult another individual during an argument, they may not be physically assaultive but intentionally may choose hurtful words. Second, *microinsults* are actions or vocalizations that communicate insensitivity to those of another race and are often done without the knowledge of those engaging in them. For example, when a black individual is told by a white person that she or he is "articulate," the person of color may feel slighted because the white individual did not expect her or him to be intelligent. Meanwhile, the white individual may be well-intentioned and may not be aware of the racial implications of her or his statement. Finally, *microinvalidations* are communications that communicate that one's worldviews, thoughts, emotions, or experiences with race are not true, real, or rational. This can occur if a person of color attempts to explain to a white individual that they have been the target of racism, only to be told not to be so sensitive or that racism no longer exists (Sue, Bucceri, et al., 2007). Because dominant society defines what is considered normal in a given culture (for example, through media, education systems, government), persons of color may experience these microinvalidations and have white individuals routinely question their racial realities (Sue, Capodilupo, & Holder, 2008).

A taxonomy of racial microaggressions was proposed in the *American Psychologist* in 2007 and outlined the various types of microaggressions that may be directed toward people of color (see Sue, Capodilupo, et al., 2007). To be "*alien in one's own land*" refers to feelings that people of color are perpetual foreigners and are "outsiders" even in their own country. For example, when an Asian American is told that she or he "speaks good English" a negative message is sent that she or he was assumed to be an immigrant. This can be especially frustrating to an Asian American who was born in the United States and whose first language is English. "*Assumption of criminality*" describes instances in which people of color are assumed to be dangerous, violent, or prone to crime. For instance, when a Latino or African American individual is followed around by a storeowner or worker while shopping, a negative message is conveyed that the person of color would steal or vandalize. Finally, an individual is made to feel as though he or she is a "*second-class citizen*" when that individual receives substandard treatment than that of a white person. For example, when a person of color is seated in the back of the restaurant when plenty of room in the front is notable, the person of color may perceive an indirect message that whites receive superior treatment and that people of color need to be hidden or segregated from the rest of the restaurant.

Empirical studies have been conducted to explore the issue of racial microaggressions from the perspective of the victim. These studies have included experiences of Latino Americans (Rivera et al., in press), Asian Americans (Sue, Bucceri, et. al. 2007), and African Americans (Sue, Capodilupo, & Holder, 2008; Sue, Nadal, et al., 2008; Watkins, LaBarrie, & Appio, in press). These qualitative studies have supported that taxonomy of racial microaggression categories do exist and that the various types of microaggressions (microassaults, microinsults, and microinvalidations) are normative in the lives of people of color. Another study reported that people of color feel uncomfortable in classroom settings in which their peers and their teachers demonstrate microaggressions on a regular basis (Sue, Lin, Torino, Capodilupo, & Rivera, 2009). Additionally, other studies have found that microaggressions also affect other members of target groups, including women (Capodilupo et al., in press), lesbian, gay, and bisexual persons (Nadal, Issa, et al., in progress); and persons with disabilities (Keller, Galgay, Robinson, & Moscoso, in press).

Examining racial microaggressions (and other forms of microaggressions) from the perspectives of minority group members has been beneficial in understanding the negative impacts of microaggressions on the "victims" or "recipients" of such incidents. No known empirical studies, however, have explored the experiences of the dominant group (whites, men, heterosexuals) who may be the "perpetrators" or "enactors" of microaggressions. Instead, the aforementioned microaggression literature (theoretical, anecdotal, and empirical) has examined the target groups' perceptions of dominant groups' reactions to microaggressions when they are confronted. As a result, the actual perceptions, processes, or struggles of the dominant group members who witness or engage in microaggressions are unknown.

For example, when an Asian American man and an African American woman were asked to move to the back of an airplane when other white passengers were not, the man of color verbally challenged a white flight attendant on the potential racial implications of the incident (see Sue, Capodilupo, et al., 2007). His observation of the white woman was that she was defensive when she was confronted, that she was horrified to be accused of being a racist, and that she could not understand his perception, worldview, or racial reality. But what were the actual cognitive and emotional processes of the white woman in this case? Was she really defensive, horrified, and unable to understand his perspective? Did the incident have an impact on her life and her perceptions of race? If she was never confronted by the Asian American man (or other persons of color in subsequent situations), would she ever recognize the potential microaggressions that she may enact onto others? And finally, what were the reactions of the other white individuals who witnessed or observed the incident, and what impact did it have on their lives?

Given the dearth of research on the reactions, processes, and perspectives of dominant group members with regard to microaggressions, the purpose of this study is to examine how whites understand and experience racial microaggressions—as perpetrators or enactors of such behaviors, observers or witnesses to racial microaggressions enacted by others, or even as victims or recipients of microaggressions themselves. Because of the exploratory nature of this study, it presents no hypotheses. Rather, the following research questions are utilized to examine the perspectives of this population:

1. Do whites recognize racial microaggressions when they occur?
2. How do whites react to racial microaggressions when they occur, when they are confronted, or both?
3. What are the cognitive and emotional reactions that whites have to racial microaggressions?
4. What impacts do racial microaggressions have on whites' mental health?

METHOD

The current phenomenological study used a qualitative method to understand the experiences of white persons as recipients and enactors of microaggressions. Focus groups were utilized since such methods have been demonstrated to be useful in eliciting new information, generating new hypotheses, and better explaining the range and depth of the beliefs and attitudes of a defined population (Seal, Bogart, & Ehrhardt, 1998). A consensual qualitative research (CQR) method was employed in all stages of the study—conceptualization, methods, and data analysis (see Hill, Thompson, & Williams, 1997; Hill et al., 2005). The CQR uses (1) open-ended questions to get a more in-depth investigation of the experiences, (2) multiple judges to get different perspectives, (3) consensus among the judges to find meaning in the data, (4) at least one auditor to check the team's work, and (5) domains, core ideas, and their cross-analyses to analyze the data (Hill et al., 2005).

PARTICIPANTS

Four focus groups were conducted, with a range of three to five members in each group and an average number of about four participants each. Fifteen people participated, which included nine women and six men. Participants ranged in age from 18 to 33 (Mean = 22.9, Std. Dev. = 4.22). All 15 participants identified as white/Caucasian, with various ethnicities including Russian, Albanian, and Eastern European; only one participant reported immigrating to the United States. The majority of participants identified as heterosexual ($n = 13$) and two identified as bisexual. Nine participants claimed a denomination of Christianity as their religion, while one individual reported being agnostic, another atheist, and four participants who declined to state a religious affiliation. Nine participants were students, and the remaining six participants reported a spectrum of careers, ranging from acting to business.

RESEARCHERS

The research team consisted of six graduate students and a full-time professor at a public college in the Northeast. The graduate students were enrolled in master's programs in psychology or counseling. Researchers included one Asian American male professor, two white American female students, two white American male students, one Latina American female, and one Arab female. Each of the four focus groups conducted was led by a different interviewer or moderator (all four were white), and each group was observed by two members of the research team. Before data collection, the researchers discussed their biases concerning the topic and the research, as well as their expectations of outcomes. For instance, the researchers agreed that they believe that racial microaggressions exist, that white people have difficulty discussing racial issues, and that racial microaggressions have a negative impact on the lives of people of color. All six student researchers worked on coding, and the professor served as the auditor (which will be discussed further in the analysis section). Power dynamics were also discussed to allow students to communicate openly and effectively with the professor.

MEASURES

A semistructured interview was developed by the research team, who agreed on several questions to be asked to the members of the focus group. Each researcher submitted his or her own set of questions, which later were discussed by the whole team. The research team consensually agreed on the most suitable questions for the study. Many questions were inspired by a set of questions in a study of microaggressions toward Asian Americans (see Sue, Bucceri, et al., 2007). For example, one question read: "Describe a time when you may have unintentionally discriminated against someone of a different racial group." Follow-up questions were asked, with examples including the following: "How did you react?" "How did they react?" and "How did it make you feel?" These follow-up questions were used to better understand the mental health impacts on whites, as well as their perceived impact on people of color.

PROCEDURE

This study was approved by the Institutional Review Board of the college. Participants were recruited in two ways. First, undergraduate students from the Research Experience Program of the college participated in this study for research credit that was required for their introductory psychology classes. Second, community members were recruited through the Web site www.craigslist.org. These participants were awarded $10 for their participation. Data collection took place for two months during the winter of 2009. Each focus group lasted approximately 60 to 90 minutes.

All focus groups were audio recorded. The participants read and signed informed consent forms before beginning the focus group, which also notified them they were being audio recorded. At the start of the session, the interviewer began by making introductions of the researchers in the room and stating the purpose of the group. The participants were handed the informed consent forms and a demographic sheet to read and complete. The demographic sheet asked the participants to identify their gender, age, race, ethnicity, sexual orientation, religion, occupation, the highest educational level completed, place of birth, and years spent in the United States.

The focus group proceeded after the informed consent forms were signed. The interviewer stated verbally that the focus group would be confidential and that only the researchers will have access to the audiotapes and the forms. The interviewer then asked the participants to keep all the information confidential and obtained verbal agreement from each of the participants. The interviewer then began asking the first questions, which inquired about participants' experiences as recipients of overt and subtle discrimination. These initial questions were asked intentionally to gain a rapport within the group and reduce defensiveness from participants. Then, the interviewer asked questions about participants' experiences as witnesses or enactors of overt and subtle discrimination. The interviewer was trained in maintaining nonjudgmental facial expressions, body language, and tone of voice to reduce any bias, judgment, or emotion in their questioning. Interviewers also used additional probes to allow participants to elaborate on their answers.

After the completion of the focus group, each audio file was transcribed by three researchers (the interviewer and two observers). After transcription, the CQR method was followed (see Hill et al., 1997; Hill et al., 2005). First, each researcher independently analyzed the transcribed document to produce domains, or broad categories to organize the data. A cross-analysis occurred whereby the researchers convened to consensually agree on the domains. The team then sent their ideas to the auditor who provided feedback about the domains. The researchers reconvened and accepted the auditor's feedback. A similar cross-analysis was conducted for themes that fit under each domain. The researchers worked independently, convened and discussed their analyses, and reached consensus on themes; these themes were then approved by the auditor. A final stage occurred in which the researchers worked (independently and then as a team) to organize examples under each theme. The auditor agreed with these examples and sent them back to the researchers, who then organized the domains into a final, orderly document. Because of the utilization of focus group interviews, the labeling of responses as "typical" or "variant" were not applied in ways traditionally used by CQR. The group of analysts consensually agreed, however, that a response was a typical response based on the number of times that the theme was mentioned in the focus groups, as well as the nonverbal reactions of participants. For example, observers documented when participants nodded their heads, smiled in agreement, or conveyed other forms of support with regard to others' statements.

RESULTS

Based on the focus group transcripts and CQR analysis, the research team agreed on five domains and several themes under each domain. The five domains included (1) Defense Mechanisms and other Cognitive Reactions Regarding Racial Microaggressions, (2) Emotional Reactions Regarding Racial Microaggressions, (3) Influences of Racial Bias, (4) Microaggressions toward People of Color, and (5) Microaggressions toward White People. To be considered a theme, more than one example was necessary, and only those categories that had definite examples were used. Several responses were considered significant, but because they could not be classified into any of the themes, they were grouped under the category Underdeveloped Incidents/Responses. The following section will report domains, themes, and examples of themes.

Domain 1: Defense Mechanisms and Other Cognitive Reactions Regarding Racial Microaggressions

Theme 1: Rationalization When questioned about their feelings or beliefs, participants shared many explanations or rationalizations to justify their racial prejudices and stereotypes. Instead of admitting to having racist thoughts or biases, almost all participants shared excuses for their thoughts and behaviors. For example, when questioned about his racist feelings, one participant stated:

> Why do you think I feel the way I do? Because I'm a racist just like every other white person. It's how I was brought up. The best you can do is make a conscious effort not to act on these thoughts. You figure you're racist and you try and deal with it.

Instead of taking responsibility for their beliefs, many of the participants chose to blame others (particularly their family, parents, friends, or society as a whole). Almost all participants communicated their racist attitudes and behaviors were unchanging, but were a direct result of an external force. Despite this, when asked whether they would try to change their beliefs, almost all participants denied any desire to do so, sharing there the idea that they could do little to change a racist society.

Theme 2: Denial of Individual Racism   Denial was a primary defense mechanism that was exhibited by participants when admitting to enacting or observing microaggressions. Many claimed a lack responsibility for their actions and beliefs (for example, stating that they were not racist), and many participants explained that they were never to blame for their microaggressive behavior. This was exemplified by one participant who stated, "It's not that I'm a racist, I'm just saying it's influenced by the world." This statement conveys that it is not the participant's fault that he has racial biases or prejudices; rather it is the fault of society and those around him. Additionally, he states that he is not the only one who holds these beliefs, but shares the idea that others around the world also feel similarly. This participant is deflecting personal responsibility and uses denial as a defense mechanism, so he can feel less guilty and convince himself that he is one of many with similar beliefs. Such beliefs allow him to continue his behavior without change or concern for others.

Theme 3: Endorsement of Stereotypes   The ability to blame a personal belief on an existing stereotype was another cognitive reaction frequently endorsed in the focus groups. As one participant pointed out:

> It's hard to admit it, but I feel like a lot of the stereotypes that we hear about are not really stereotypes because a lot of them turn out to be true in the majority . . . we call them stereotypes because people are scared to call it the truth.

The participants reported feeling relief in knowing that their beliefs were widely held stereotypes. When participants experienced people of color who fulfilled these racist stereotypes, participants reported becoming more secure and less guilty in their beliefs. Even when a single member of a minority group fulfilled their corresponding stereotype, the participants felt more confident in the notion that these assumptions were true. For example, if participants believed that African Americans were dangerous, they felt a sense of relief when an African American criminal was portrayed in the news media. These singular instances helped to alleviate participants' guilt for feeling such stereotypes. Some participants claimed that they would not alter their beliefs because they continually find individuals to fit into their stereotype. None of the participants, however, reported interacting with people of color who contradict negative racial stereotypes completely.

Theme 4: Humor   Humor was a common defense mechanism among the participants. Many participants reported dealing with their racist thoughts by laughing or joking with their family and friends. For example, when asked about his racial biases, one male participant shared, "I don't know, it's not really like unintentional, [but my friends and I] say 'I have a lot of black friends. . . .' And we just joke around and we just say it as a joke to each other." Instead of being able to deal with the discomfort of having racial biases, this participant chooses to laugh and tell others that he has friends of different racial groups. In doing so, he does not have to admit to having racial biases; meanwhile, he and his peers can continue to discuss race and racism at a superficial or humorous level, instead of dealing with more difficult emotions or conflicts.

Humor was also used when engaging in racist language. Participants reported using racial slurs and jokes toward friends of different racial groups; such behavior was perceived as "acceptable" as long as "everyone did it to each other." Participants stated that these types of racial jokes and statements were viewed as humorous, harmless, and excusable. As one participant describes, "I have a couple of black friends too and they're okay with the fact that we call them 'Nigga' but you can't call them 'Nigger' . . . they may care about that, but we joke around with each other." Participants reported saying "I'm just kidding" when making racist jokes with friends, which may provide these individuals with the illusion that their behaviors are harmless or excusable.

Theme 5: Passive Attitude toward Racism   A significant theme discovered among all focus groups was the participants' passive attitude toward racism. As white individuals living in the United States, participants shared that it was hard for them to believe that racism (blatant or subtle) even existed. A few participants cited President Obama's election as proof that the United States is no longer a racist society. Some admitted that racism may still exist in some ways, but minimized its existence or impacts on people of color. One participant pointed out, "It's bad, but it is what it is, you know? There's no extreme racism today, but still, bad things happen." This statement exemplifies the worldview that racism is not a problem that warrants serious attention or discussion, particularly for these participants who may not deal with the oppressive end of racism. Discussions in the groups ensued about not dwelling on subtle racism, particularly because the participants do not experience or witness blatant racism themselves.

Theme 6: Sensitivity and Compensation   Many of the participants in the focus groups discussed an awareness of the differences between themselves and members of other racial groups in particular situations. They discussed incidents in which they altered their behavior to fit the norms of the group they were among. Sometimes, participants shared that they changed their behaviors to compensate for their anxiety with race or their discomfort with their racial biases. Several participants talked about instances of heightened sensitivity and awareness of their surroundings. One woman explained this feeling while being in high school:

> I remember one instance in high school we were reading *Huck Finn* and there was one black girl in my class and it's obviously a very racially motivated book. And so reading it I felt everyone in the class, not just myself, were very aware and self-conscious about the things they said.

Although several participants claimed to be unaware of the existence of racial microaggressions, their statements imply they were aware of racial dynamics when engaging with members of other racial groups. Altering their behaviors under certain circumstances demonstrates an awareness of race or discomfort when confronted with race-related situations. Although many participants claimed that they did not think about race on a regular basis, many of their statements conveyed an awareness of racism and racial discrimination, particularly when certain situations caused them anxiety.

Domain 2: Emotional Reactions Regarding Microaggressions

Theme 1: Guilt   Almost all participants expressed feelings of guilt regarding their personal biases and beliefs about people of color. In fact, the words "guilt" or "feeling bad" was used consistently throughout all of the focus groups by almost all of the participants. Several shared that they felt "bad" or "guilty" about believing and assuming stereotypes (for example, feeling guilty for believing that all African Americans were dangerous). One participant describes concerns over being mugged by an African American, "I have the same dark feeling and I hate feeling like that because I know I can just as easily be mugged or beaten by a white person." Another participant discusses the guilt (and regret) after making a racist joke: "I just remember being like, feeling . . . bad, feeling . . . stupid, like I could have thought of seven other jokes I could have said." Both of these participants appear to admit to their guilt to alleviate the anxiety of possessing racist thoughts. Despite this, these participants (and others who expressed guilt) reported no desire to change or make attempts at changing their beliefs or behaviors. Although they realized they could try to change how they feel about others or their behaviors, they preferred to apologize for their feelings instead of further exploring the meaning behind their biases or investigating what they could do to change them.

Theme 2: Anger   Anger was a common emotional reaction discovered in each focus group. Although many participants expressed anger over what they viewed as racism toward the white group, a few participants expressed outrage over microaggressions they had witnessed toward people of color. One participant shared:

> When there was that news story about the sign on the Philly cheese steak place in Philly that said "You're in America now, speak English only," I heard a lot of white people in Colorado say "Yeah, that's awesome." People really supported that. That disgusted me because we're one of the few countries that do not have bilingual standards in schools. We're one of the only uni-language countries and that disgusts me.

This statement (and similar statements by participants) demonstrates that whites do have an existing knowledge about racial microaggressions and their influences on people of color. In this instance, this participant recognized that there was something inherently wrong with the idea of demanding that others change to fit another group's norms; however, she believed that she was a lone voice and that her opinion was different from most of her peers.

Theme 3: Sadness   Feelings of sadness were expressed by a few of the participants who empathized with people of color and their experiences with racial discrimination. Many shared occasions in which they were saddened by witnessing their parents, family, friends, or strangers engaging in racist jokes, remarks, behaviors, or assumptions. When participants had personal relationships with the victim or recipient of racial microaggressions, they were especially saddened by the experience. This was demonstrated by one participant stated:

> That's not fair . . . just because it's stereotyping on where you live based on race . . . and I remember it made me upset and I think the reason why it made me upset was because I had a relationship with someone of a different race.

Although some participants expressed this sadness, not one participant stated that they questioned or challenged other whites who enacted racial microaggressions or defended the people of color who were the recipient of the microaggression. They recognized the severity of the situation and its impact on the victim, but they never stated that they assertively spoke up against the aggressor. Many shrugged it off as humor as exemplified by one participant who stated "That's just the way the person is." This statement demonstrates that white individuals may feel sad about certain situations involving race, but choose to avoid conflict when such situations occur.

Domain 3: Influences of Racial Bias

Theme 1: Effect of Family Values and Upbringing   Participants discussed how they learned about racial bias from their family members, particularly through the values they were taught and the environments in which they were raised. When asked why they think or act the way they do, most participants placed responsibility on the families that raised them. As one participant observed, "It's hard for us to notice [racist attitudes] because that's how we were brought up." Many participants explained they simply were following an unquestioned tradition; whatever their parents taught them while growing up was the unquestionable truth. Again, instead of searching for meaning and further understanding of their behaviors, participants seemed to excuse their actions by blaming their existence on outside sources (for example, their parents or family members). Participants shared that it was markedly hard for them to question their parents and any authority figure. Instead of standing up for something they felt to be wrong, participants reported a choice to be bystanders, avoid conflict, and accept the reality that was created for them.

Theme 2: Consequences of Historical Racism   Another common theme exemplified in most focus groups was that historical racism influenced participants' racist thoughts and behaviors. Many participants reasoned that they could not do anything about the present because they could not change the past. One participant stated:

> I think history has proven that there have been some really shitty things that have happened so time can't erase that . . . I mean, I really don't think there will ever be a cure to it. . . . I think we'll get more and less PC, but it's a sad situation.

Many of the participants argued that the United States has an unchangeable history and therefore altering behaviors and beliefs now is impossible. Participants shared they have inherited a long line of attitudes and feelings about race that contribute to an inability to change society. Many participants reported that they simply were "following tradition," which allows individuals to perpetuate their racist thoughts and behaviors in contemporary times. Again, instead of advocating for change or social justice, these participants appear to be complacent in their racist behaviors and externalize blame onto others.

Domain 4: Microaggressions toward People of Color

Theme 1: Use of Racist Language   Participants were asked specifically to provide examples of microaggressions toward people of color, and many concrete examples involved the use of racist language. For example, one participant shared an experience from high school: "Our quarterback and someone else on their team started fighting and our quarterback was calling him a 'nigger,' 'you're a piece of shit,' 'you don't belong in our football league anymore,' and a huge fight actually started." Participants were able to identify instances in which racial slurs were used by others, as these were examples of blatant racism, as well as racist acts that others engaged in. Participants also were asked to discuss times in which they had used racial epithets or slurs, which was much more difficult for them to admit to or recognize. A male participant discussed one such experience, stating the following:

> One time, I was late for work and this guy was getting on the on-ramp to go on the highway and he was going so slow that I rushed around him and said "you f'in chink!" and flew right past him.

In using such language, the individual who enacted the microaggression against the person of color reported using racist language as a way of putting others down in a hurtful way. These actions were intentional and malicious, and participants knew that using such words could be used to upset victims, even when the specific situations were not race related. In retrospect, participants were conscious of these behaviors and were able to easily identify these acts as racist (even though they reported not wanting to admit to them).

Theme 2: Assumption of Inferiority   Another theme to emerge was that people of color were assumed to be inferior to whites. Participants shared examples of racial microaggressions in which the white individual exhibited a sense of superiority or implied that the person of color was not equal to their group. For instance, a female participant shared an experience that she witnessed:

> I work at a high-end swim club back home where there's expensive membership and we don't have many people of color who are members. We have one family. And so usually when they have friends over or people [of color] looking into memberships, they're often watched more carefully in the pool because they're not sure if they can swim or on the tennis court because they're not sure they know what they're doing.

In this example, the participant shared that the people of color were perceived differently because of their race. She states that this instance was influenced by others' perceptions that people of color would not be capable of swimming or playing tennis, which could be viewed as an assumption of an inferior social class status. People of color are often viewed as having a lower socioeconomic status, and therefore are stereotyped as incapable of participating in sports or activities that typically are pursued by people in higher social classes. While this is the perception that the participant shared, it is also possible that these people of color were observed because they were viewed as exotic (that is, they were the only people of color at the swim club) or as criminals (that is, people were afraid the people of color might do something illegal or wrong). Exoticization and assumption of criminality are microaggressions discussed in the taxonomy on racial microaggressions (see Sue, Capodilupo, et al., 2007), as well as research on microaggressions with people of color (Rivera et al., in press; Sue, Bucceri, et al., 2007; Sue, Capodilupo, et al., 2008; Sue, Nadal, et al., 2008).

Participants shared instances in which they were the enactors of microaggressions that assumed inferiority of persons of color. One participant shared a microaggression that he was involved in at his workplace:

> I used to be a bike messenger for a restaurant and one time I was in a big hurry. I needed to tell the dishwasher in the kitchen something . . . and I told him really quickly and he didn't understand me . . . so I told him in Spanish and he got really pissed off . . . because he didn't *not* understand me because it was in English; it was because I was speaking so quickly. I thought he would understand better if I said it in Spanish.

In this instance, the participant had assumed that his co-worker had misunderstood him because as he was Latino and that he must not have spoken English. This was implied by the participant's choice to repeat his message in Spanish, rather than repeating it unhurriedly. This is also exemplified in an instance described by another participant: "Say you get like Chinese takeout or something like that. Like I would walk in maybe speaking a little bit, like, speaking English a little slower and more articulate thinking that they don't understand really well." Such microaggressions are typical of Asian Americans and Latinos who have been found to experience microaggressions where they are treated like "aliens in their own land" (Rivera et al., in press; Sue, Bucceri, et al., 2007).

Theme 3: Assumption of Criminality   Participants also shared that they witnessed or participated in microaggressions in which people of color were assumed to be criminals. When asked to recall incidents in which an individual of color was the recipient of a microaggression, numerous examples of an individual being treated as dangerous or unlawful emerged. Some incidents that were discussed involved a certain behavior that assumed criminality. For example, a male participant said:

> One time, me and [my mom] were just walking and this black guy started walking towards us and automatically she just grabs her purse, just to hold it. I'm like, I start laughing at her, I'm like "you serious dude?"

This type of microaggression has been supported as being common experiences for African Americans and Latinos, who often are assumed to be dangerous (Rivera et al., in press; Sue, Nadal, et al., 2008). In fact, the aforementioned microaggression literature uses this very example of women holding their purses closer to them as a clear example of a microaggression. Another participant shared a similar experience, "If I'm in a bad neighborhood and there's a bunch of black people standing on the corner and I'm in my car, my father and my friends will lock the doors just in case something happens." The message conveyed in these instances is that people of color are dangerous, even when they are not doing anything indicative of criminal behavior.

Many participants shared the cognitions that may lead to assumptions of criminality. For example, one participant shared:

> Every time I come home from work, I'm walking down a street and I'll see a figure come my way and it's like 4 or 5 in the morning, there's relief that comes over me when I see a white face in the distance. I think "cool, good."

Although this example may not be an actual microaggression because it does not take a verbal or behavioral form, it is important to note that these types of racial biases influence behaviors. Because of these thoughts, some participants reported that their stereotypes about people of color as criminals are reasonable or warranted. For example, one male participant shared:

> I come home late at night, see a bunch of kids on one side of the street, [and] cross to the other side just walk on the other side of the block . . . just trying not to cross their path or get in anyone's way sure. That's just me being racist, or safe, I'm not sure which one.

This statement conveys that the individual recognizes that his behavior may have racial connotations. However, because of his biases toward people of color, he may not view such behaviors as being unjustified or irrational. Despite this, previous research has found that African Americans who are on the receiving end of this microaggression (that is, notice a white person cross to the other side of the street) perceive the behavior as being race related and may have negative emotional reactions because of such microaggressions (Sue, Nadal, et al., 2008).

Theme 4: Expectations of Conformity   Participants also reported microaggressions in which they expected people of color to conform to white norms or values. Participants shared having witnessed or participated in behaviors in which white individuals expected people of color to speak, act, or dress like whites. For example, a female participant spoke of a recurrent instance at her job:

> When I worked at [a museum], there were a lot of mostly women that lived in the projects in the Bronx and there have been times when I was

talking with other white people who were like, "How can she come to work and speak like that?"

This example implies that the white women expected the black woman to speak more like them or speak more "white" when at work. This implies that there is only one way of speaking and that having an accent or using non-white vernacular is inferior or improper. Another female participant displayed such an expectation when sharing a time when she saw a person of color come in to work for an interview: "Take the rag off your head, pull your pants up, you know? I don't know if that's necessarily a race thing, 'be like white people,' but be like a respectable person." This quote indicates the participant's belief that there is only one appropriate way of dressing, while also asserting that dressing in a different way is less "respectable" or even inferior. Expecting people of color to conform to white American values, behaviors, dress, and even hair has been found to be a common experience for Asian Americans (Sue, Bucceri, et al., 2007), Latinos (Rivera et al., in press), and African Americans (Sue, Nadal, et al., 2008).

Domain 5: Microaggressions toward White People

Theme 1: Use of Racist Language   Participants were asked to identify examples in which they were the recipients of microaggressions as whites. A female participant stated, "I live in Washington Heights and before that I lived in Harlem. So almost every day I walk down the street and get 'Oooh, hey whitey!' or 'Hey snowflake! Hey snow bunny.'" An additional example was given by a male participant who discussed common practices before a sporting event at his high school: "Before the game would start the black players would come out and they'd have this chant that they'd say: 'Vanilla ice cream tastes good.'" In both of these instances, racist language is used to undermine the targeted individual and the group to which they belong. While participants reported feeling uncomfortable in such situations, there were very few examples across all focus groups in which individuals were the recipients of racist language.

Theme 2: Feeling Like an Alien in Own Land/Minority   Participants shared a few experiences in which they felt as though they were treated as an outsider or an inferior person when they were white individuals within communities of color. One male participant stated:

I was trying to buy cigarettes. [The store] was really Hispanic. And this guy ahead of me was buying cigarettes, they were the same ones that I was getting and they charged him 7 bucks and then I had to pay $9.50. I'm pretty sure because I was a white dude they charged me higher.

A female participant shared her experience as a white person moving into a predominantly non-white area:

I moved to Harlem this year from Jersey and it's predominantly black, and obviously I stick out a lot . . . and one day in class we were talking about Harlem actually and one of the students said "all the white folk are moving in" or something to that effect. I mean it affected me because like I said, I moved here from Jersey and grew up in a predominantly white small town so for me I never felt like the outsider or minority or invading someone else's space and when she made that comment I felt like maybe I was invading their space.

In both incidents, the white individuals were viewed or treated as outsiders and were consequently given the message that they were not liked, they were unwelcome, or they deserved differential treatment. In both of these instances, however, participants admitted that these were insular occasions; participants recognized that they could avoid communities of color altogether and choose to reside only in white neighborhoods and communities.

Theme 3: Perceived Disadvantages   A number of participant responses regarding microaggressions toward whites highlighted disadvantages that they as white individuals felt they had to endure. For instance, one participant shared:

I know my friends work for the government and they said you have less of a chance of getting hired if you're white because they have all these quotas that they have to fill and they actually prefer to hire minorities. If you're a minority you have a better chance of getting hired.

Furthermore, another participant said:

Colleges too. I mean when I was applying, the application processes have a quota to fill basically. So I felt as a white female there were some times that I've been more disadvantaged than you know the minorities and other races because I came from a middle-class family so my parents made enough money to not receive financial aid but made too little money to be able to pay for my entire tuition.

In these examples, the participants expressed that they felt cheated or disadvantaged in other areas in the sense that someone less worthy of obtaining a job or getting into a college may get the spot over themselves due to that individual's status as a minority. These instances seemed to be limited, however, in that participants had difficulty recounting these experiences and did not report these experiences to have major impacts on their mental health.

UNDERDEVELOPED INCIDENTS AND RESPONSES

A few responses proved important to the contribution of understanding microaggressions from the perspective of the white American individual but did not fit under any of the aforementioned domains and themes, because of the limited number of examples, the lack of examples across all focus groups, or the lack of consensus by the research analysts in categorizing such responses. First, some participants expressed their feeling toward microaggressions as being unfair. For example, in response to witnessing a microaggression toward a black acquaintance, a female participant said, "I remember it just specifically made me feel really upset because I felt like it was really unfair." Second, participants felt that people of color could enact microaggressions against white individuals, particularly through comedy. One participant shared: "My brother-in-law always jokes that he can't say anything but Chris Rock could say whatever he wants." Another example was given, "Carlos Mencia, you ever see his comedy? He has no qualms. He'll attack everyone but if he was white I don't know if he could do that. I don't know if it would be so accepted to do that." In these examples, the participants feel a sense of unfairness that people of color can "get away" with microaggressions through comedy but that it is less likely to be accepted if white individuals were to do the same thing.

DISCUSSION

The results of this study support and extend the racial microaggression taxonomy put forth by Sue, Capodilupo, and colleagues (2007). As discussed, previous literature regarding microaggressions from the perspective of whites has been limited. Moreover, literature involving the processes of whites who enact, witness, or observe microaggressions has been mostly anecdotal. This is the first known study that examines how whites react to microaggressions, as well as the first study that examines the processes and struggles of dominant group members in general. Results from the study support the notion that whites are able to recognize some racial microaggressions toward people of color, particularly when such statements or behaviors are blatant (for example, use of racist language). It appears, however, that the degree to which white participants were able to recognize racial microaggressions that are more subtle or covert depends on various variables like racial identity status or the physical reactions of the microaggression recipient.

To understand perceptions of microaggressions further, it may be beneficial to review Helms' (1995) White Racial Identity Development model. Some participants' statements appear to coincide with Status 1: Contact, in which they are unaware of the existence of race and the ways that race may influence their everyday lives. This lack of awareness can be exemplified in participants who claimed that "racism doesn't exist anymore." Because these individuals may claim to be "colorblind," they may be unable to recognize when racial microaggressions do occur, or they may deny that certain interpersonal interactions had racial implications. Other participants' statements seemed to uphold Status 2: Disintegration, in which they are conflicted over racial moral dilemmas and view such dilemmas as irresolvable. This can be demonstrated by participants who (1) state that they cannot change racism or (2) are uncomfortable when their family or friends make racist jokes but do not say anything. Some responses illustrated characteristics of Status 3: Reintegration; these individuals may expect people of color to conform and behave similarly to whites. As mentioned, many participants shared instances in which they expected people of color to dress "respectably" or act "appropriately" at work, all of which convey that only one way of being is acceptable and that whiteness is the norm. Some participants' statements expressed traits of Status 4: Pseudo-Independence, in which they are able to understand white privilege, bias, prejudice, and discrimination in some basic intellectualized ways. For example, some participants were able to understand the historical consequences of race and recognize that they are whites who benefit from a racist world. Some statements by participants suggested attributes of Status 5: Immersion/Emersion, in that they connect to some emotions regarding race (for example, feeling guilty for holding onto stereotypes about people of color). Finally, none of the participants' statements palpably demonstrated features of Status 6: Autonomy, in that none of the participants conveyed that they thought about race regularly, that they were committed to social justice, or that they explored their emotions regarding race in deep or meaningful ways.

One's racial identity status may influence how one may practically react to racial microaggressions. For example, participants with a disintegration status may choose not to say anything when something racist occurs, whereas someone with a pseudo-independent status may confront an individual through humor. If participants reflected an autonomy status, they may have confronted whites who enacted microaggressions on either interpersonal or systemic levels. One's racial identity status also appeared to affect one's emotional processes with microaggressions. For example, participants who may exhibit the contact or reintegration statuses did not appear to have many emotional reactions about microaggressions. Because these participants believed that racism no longer existed or believed that people of color should conform to white norms, their negative feelings were minimal. Conversely, participants who maintained a disintegration status, a pseudo-independent status, or an immersion-emersion status seemed to connect more clearly with their emotions of guilt, sadness, or anger.

Few of these whites were confronted on their microaggressions (either directly or indirectly) by people of color. Out of the examples shared, the only time a person of color confronted the white individual on her or his behavior was when the Latino man expressed anger when his white co-worker assumed he did not understand or speak English well. In this case, the participant conveyed a sense of guilt or shame after being confronted. It is unclear whether he would have recognized the microaggressive behavior (and connected to the subsequent feelings involved) if he was never confronted on the situation. Given this, it is necessary to notice that these participants reported only those microaggressions that they were aware that they committed or observed. This finding suggests that whites typically become aware of racial microaggressions in one of two ways: (1) if the incident is blatant and obviously race related and (2) if they are confronted about the behavior by the recipient or person of color.

Participants shared that they, too, are the recipients of blatant and subtle discrimination as whites. Participants, however, did not report a sense of psychological or emotional distress as a result of these instances. This is in great contrast to the studies on people of color (Rivera et al., in press; Sue, Bucceri, et al., 2007; Sue, Capodilupo, et al., 2008; Sue et al., 2009; Sue, Nadal, et al., 2008; Watkins et al., in press), which have demonstrated that being the recipients of microaggressions may cause immediate emotional reactions (for example, frustration, sadness, anger), and have lasting cumulative effects on mental health (for example, depression, anxiety, trauma). Similar studies have yielded comparable findings for women (Capodilupo et al., in press; Nadal, Lyons, Hamit, Wienberg, & Corman, 2010); lesbian, gay, and bisexual people (Nadal, Issa, et al., in progress); and persons with disabilities (Keller et al., in press). This study (taken with the other microaggression studies) suggests that microaggressions may have damaging mental health impacts on members of target or oppressed groups, while having minimal effects on the mental health of privileged or dominant groups.

LIMITATIONS

While gaining insight into the perspective of whites with regard to racial microaggressions, both as victims and as enactors of microaggressions, it is important to identify the limitations of the current study. First, the sample is restricted in size, with a total of 15 participants, as well as in demographics. For example, the majority of participants were in their 20s and were students, thus limiting the sample's representativeness and consequent generalizability. As this study was qualitative in nature, the answers given by participants as well as the interpretations of the researchers involved in the analyses may be biased or influenced by additional factors. The researchers discussed what biases they may hold before conducting the study, but these predispositions may have influenced the analyses in the identification of domains and themes. Additionally, within the focus groups, participants may have been influenced by group dynamics to provide answers that were in agreement with what others shared rather than creating dissonance. Furthermore, the racial nature of the discussion may have prevented some participants from feeling comfortable enough to speak openly with regard to their opinions of microaggressions and specifically about instances in which they were enactors of racial microaggressions.

IMPLICATIONS FOR WORKPLACE SETTINGS

This study has many implications for the study of workplace and institutional discrimination. First, it contributes to the literature on microaggressions and provides the perspective of the dominant group. To prevent microaggressions from occurring on societal and interpersonal levels, it is necessary to explore the experiences of those from the dominant group to advocate for knowledge, awareness, and change. This study advocates for increased education about microaggressions, not just for the recipients of microaggressions, but also for those who may enact or observe those microagressions. Because race has become subtle in the United States, such education about microaggressions can be implemented in earlier, more formative years (elementary school, middle school, or high school), which would allow individuals to become aware of microaggressions before adulthood. Second, because previous research has found that microaggressions occur in the classroom (Sue et al., 2009), academic institutions and training programs must ensure that microaggressions are included in educational programs to prevent these instances from transpiring.

Education about microaggressions should be integrated into multicultural competence training models in all workplace settings and other institutions (Nadal, 2008). While it is important for employees to learn about blatant forms of racism, they also must become conscious of ways that subtle microaggressions may manifest in their professional relationships. Human resources departments must train their employees to become knowledgeable of microaggressions by teaching about the ways that microaggressions may manifest and the meanings behind them. Supervisors must become aware of microaggressions; they must recognize how racial (and other) dynamics may affect their interactions with their employees and how they may direct microaggressions toward them. Such supervisors and other workplace leaders should learn to enact and model effective interpersonal skills in coping with microaggressions; for example, they can learn to address microaggressions when they occur, or to react nondefensively when confronted by an employee or co-worker on microaggressive behaviors. Finally, institutional policies and skills may be implemented to prevent microaggressions while also promoting healthy workplace climates. For example, openly discussing multicultural issues (including discrimination and microaggressions) during staff meetings allows employees to feel safe in addressing such issues when they become salient. Moreover, instilling procedures and guidelines involving microaggressions must be advocated for as well. Many workplace settings have policies involving harassment and blatant discrimination, but other subtle forms of discrimination also must be addressed as well.

REFERENCES

Capodilupo, C. M., Nadal, K. L., Corman, L., Hamit, S., Lyons, O., & Weinberg, A. (in press). The manifestation of gender microaggressions. In D. W. Sue (Ed.), *Microaggressions and marginalized groups in society: Race, gender, sexual orientation, class, and religious manifestations.* New York: John Wiley & Sons.

Dovidio, J. F., Gaertner, S. L., Kawakami, K., & Hodson, G. (2002). Why can't we all just get along? Interpersonal biases and interracial distrust. *Cultural Diversity and Ethnic Minority Psychology, 8,* 88–102.

Helms, J. E. (1995). An update of Helm's white and people of color racial identity models. In J. G. Ponterotto, J. M. Casas, L. A. Suzuki, & C. M. Alexander (Eds.), *Handbook of multicultural counseling.* Thousand Oaks, CA: Sage.

Hill, C. E., Thompson, B. J., Hess, S. A., Knox, S., Williams, E. N., & Ladany, N. (2005). Consensual qualitative research: An update. *Journal of Counseling Psychology, 52,* 196–205.

Hill, C. E., Thompson, B. J., & Williams, E. N. (1997). A guide to conducting consensual qualitative research. *The Counseling Psychologist, 25,* 517–572.

Keller, R. M., Galgay, C. E., Robinson, L. L., & Moscoso, G. (in press). Microaggressions experienced by people with disabilities in U.S. society. In D. W. Sue (Ed.), *Microaggressions and marginalized groups in society: Race, gender, sexual orientation, class, and religious manifestations.* New York: John Wiley & Sons.

McConahay, J. B. (1986). Modern racism, ambivalence, and the Modern Racism Scale. In J. F. Dovidio, & S. L. Gaertner (Eds.), *Prejudice, discrimination, and racism* (pp. 91–126). Orlando, FL: Academic Press.

Nadal, K. L. (2008). Preventing racial, ethnic, gender, sexual minority, disability, and religious microaggressions: Recommendations for promoting positive mental health. *Prevention in Counseling Psychology: Theory, Research, Practice, and Training, 2*(1), 22–27.

Nadal, K. L., Issa, M. A., Leon, J., Wideman, M., Meterko, V. M., & Wong, Y. (in progress). Sexual orientation microaggressions: A qualitative study (copy on file with authors).

Nadal, K. L., Lyons, O., Hamit, S., Weinberg, A., & Corman, L. (2010). Gender microaggressions: Perceptions, processes, and coping mechanisms. Manuscript submitted for publication (copy on file with authors).

Rivera, D. P., Forquer, E. E., & Rangel, R. (in press). Microaggressions and the life experience of Latina/o Americans. In D. W. Sue (Ed.), *Microaggressions and marginalized groups in society: Race, gender, sexual orientation, class, and religious manifestations.* New York: John Wiley & Sons.

Seal, D. W., Bogart, L. M., & Ehrhardt, A. A. (1998). Small group dynamics: The utility of focus group discussions as a research method. *Group Dynamics: Theory, Research, and Practice, 2*(4), 253–266.

Sears, D. O. (1988). Symbolic racism. In P. A. Katz, & D. A. Taylor (Eds.), *Eliminating racism: Profiles in controversy* (pp. 53–84). New York: Plenum.

Sue, D. W., Bucceri, J. M., Lin, A. I., Nadal, K. L., & Torino, G. C. (2007). Racial microaggressions and the Asian American experience. *Cultural Diversity and Ethnic Minority Psychology, 13*(1), 72–81.

Sue, D. W., Capodilupo, C. M., & Holder, A. M. B. (2008). Racial microaggressions in the life experience of black Americans. *Professional Psychology: Research and Practice, 39*, 329–336.

Sue, D. W., Capodilupo, C. M., Torino, G. C., Bucceri, J. M., Holder, A. M. B., Nadal, K. L., et al. (2007). Racial microaggressions in everyday life: Implications for clinical practice. *The American Psychologist, 62*, 271–286.

Sue, D. W., Lin, A. I., Torino, G. C., Capodilupo, C. M., & Rivera, D. P. (2009). Racial microaggressions in the classroom. *Cultural Diversity and Ethnic Minority Psychology, 15*, 183–190.

Sue, D. W., Nadal, K. L., Capodilupo, C. M., Lin, A. I., Torino, G. C., & Rivera, D. P. (2008). Racial microaggressions against black Americans: Implications for counseling. *Journal of Counseling and Development, 86*, 330–338.

Watkins, N. L., LaBarrie, T. L., & Appio, L. M. (in press). Black undergraduates' experiences with perceived racial microaggressions. In D. W. Sue (Ed.), *Microaggressions and marginalized groups in society: Race, gender, sexual orientation, class, and religious manifestations*. New York: John Wiley & Sons.

APPENDIX A

Organizations Dealing with Workplace Discrimination and Harassment

Susan Strauss and Michele A. Paludi

We have compiled a listing of resources dealing with workplace discrimination and harassment. We believe this listing is a good starting point for organizations seeking additional information about workplace issues. This list is neither complete nor exhaustive. These resources should not be viewed as substitutes for legal advice or counseling.

All Business Network
www.all-biz.com

American Association of University Women
www.aauw.org

American Association on Intellectual and Developmental Disabilities
www.aamr.org

American Psychological Association
www.apa.org

Business and Professional Women's Organization
www.bpwusa.org

Business.Gov
www.business.gov

Center for Reproductive Rights
www.reproductiverights.org

Center for Women and Work, Rutgers University
www.cww.rutgers.edu

Disabled Businesspersons Association
www.disabledbusiness.com

Employee Assistance Professional Association
www.eapassn.org

Equal Employment Opportunity Commission
www.eeoc.gov

Equality Now
www.equalitynow.org

Families and Work Institute
www.familiesandwork.org

Feminist Majority Foundation
http://feminist.org

Job Accommodation Network
www.jan.wvu.edu

Leadership for the Employment of Americans with Disabilities
www.eeoc.gov/initiatives/lead/index.html

National Alliance on Mental Illness
www.nami.org

National Institute for Occupational Safety and Health
www.cdc.gov/niosh

National Institute of Mental Health
www.nimh.nih.gov

National Organization for Women
www.now.org

National Organization on Disability
www.nod.org

National Partnership for Women and Families
www.nationalpartnership.org

National Resource Center on Domestic Violence
www.nrcdv.org

National Sexual Violence Resource Center
www.nsvrc.org

Occupational Safety and Health Administration
www.osha.org

Office of Violence Against Women, U.S. Department of Justice
www.ojp.usdoj.gov/vawo

Project Return to Work, Inc.
www.return2work.org

Safe at Work Coalition
www.safeatworkcoalition.org

Society for Human Resource Management
www.shrm.org

U.S. Department of Labor
www.dol.gov

Work and Family Connection
www.workfamily.com

Worksupport
www.worksupport.com

APPENDIX B

Sample Policies and Procedures

Michele A. Paludi

Contributors to chapters in this volume have provided recommendations for training programs in workplace discrimination as well as sample outlines of such programs. This appendix presents sample policies and procedures for preventing and dealing with workplace discrimination. These resources are intended to provide employers with suggestions for developing or modifying their workplace discrimination management program. They are based on case law, the Equal Employment Opportunity Commission's (EEOC) guidances, human resource management practices, and empirical research in the social sciences that have been cited throughout both volumes of this book set.

These policies are educational tools to assist organizations in eliminating stereotypes and associated fears about workplace discrimination. The policies also help make employees feel secure that they will not be fired from their jobs should they be a party to a complaint of workplace discrimination. Furthermore, the policies provide employees with their rights and responsibilities for filing a complaint of discrimination or harassment, being accused of discrimination, or being a witness to an internal act of discrimination or harassment. Also included are the types of sanctions, corrective actions, and sample organizational policy prohibiting retaliation toward parties to a complaint. Employees are informed by the policies that investigations will be completed promptly, thoroughly, and by an impartial investigator, according to EEOC recommendations.

Contributors to these volumes, for example, Human Resources Management Solutions, have used these policies when consulting with workplaces. These policies may be adapted to meet the unique needs of businesses, including unionized companies, companies with on-site Employees Assistance Programs, and in states that include additional protected categories, for example, sexual orientation (see volume 1).

This appendix includes policies on hate crimes, bullying, and religious observances because differences among employees are often at the root of hate crimes. Hate crimes are crimes which in whole or part are motivated by the offender's bias toward the victim's status. Hate crimes are intended to intimidate individuals because they are perceived to be "different" with respect to their sex, race or color, age, genetic information, religion, national orientation, sexual orientation, or disability.

This appendix also includes sample policies on workplace violence and intimate partner violence as a workplace issue considering the work cited in this volume by Nadal, Griffin, Vargas, Issa, Lyons, and Tobio (chapter 15), Dziech (chapter 14), and Paludi, D'Aiuto, and Paludi (chapter 7) regarding the continuum of microaggressions, harassment and discrimination, and workplace violence.

Employers should ensure that all their policies and procedures as well as training programs are reviewed by their legal counsel.

Additional policies may be found in the following resources:

- Paludi, M. (2008). *Understanding and preventing campus violence.* Westport, CT: Praeger.
- Paludi, M., Nydegger, R., & Paludi, C. (2006). *Understanding workplace violence: A guide for managers and employees.* Westport, CT: Praeger.

Some of the policies in this book set were adapted from these works and were reproduced with permission of ABC-CLIO.

SAMPLE B.1. WORKPLACE DISCRIMINATION MISSION STATEMENT

(Name of Company) is an Equal Opportunity Employer. This means that we extend equal opportunity to all individuals without regard for race or color, religion, sex, national origin, age, genetic information, pregnancy, or disability.

This policy affirms (Name of Company) commitment to the principles of fair employment and the elimination of all vestiges of discriminatory practices that might exist. We encourage all employees to take advantage of opportunities for promotion as they occur.

The mission of (Name of Company) is to promote a deep understanding and appreciation among the diverse members of this firm to result in equality in employment opportunities as well as to lead efforts to create an inclusive work environment.

I am personally counting on all management and employees to provide enlightened leadership and cooperation in support of diversity, equity, and affirmative action so that we can all be enriched by the experience of working in an integrated environment.

(Name of Company)'s Equal Opportunity Program is responsible for the monitoring of civil rights, laws, guidelines, policies, and programs at the federal and state levels.

Policies and training programs to prevent discrimination on the basis of sex, race, gender, national origin, genetic information, pregnancy, age, religion, and disability are included in the mission of (Name of Company).

Along with the proactive programs, (Name of Company) is also responsible for reactive efforts: complaint investigation and resolution. We have procedures in place to ensure that employees who are members of protected classes are not harassed or discriminated against because of their protected class status.

(Name of Company) has policy statements and investigatory procedures for sexual harassment, discrimination, Americans with Disabilities, workplace violence, religious observances, hate crimes, bullying, and HIV/AIDS.

I encourage all job applicants and employees to discuss their concerns about equal opportunity with me or (Name of Investigator). Neither applicants nor employees will experience any retaliation for coming forth with questions or filing complaints.

This program will be reviewed annually.

(Name of President)

SAMPLE B.2. NONDISCRIMINATION POLICY STATEMENT AND PROCEDURES

(Name of Company) is committed to maintaining a working environment that supports equal rights for all employees. Employment decisions will be based only on merit, performance, and legitimate professional criteria.

(Name of Company) prohibits discrimination on the basis of age, disability, equal compensation, genetic information, national origin, pregnancy, race or color, religion, sex, and sexual harassment in the recruitment or treatment of employees, and in the operation of its activities and programs, as specified by federal and (Name of State) laws. A separate policy on sexual harassment is included in this employee handbook.

Application to (Name of Company)

With respect to recruitment, recruitment sources will be advised in writing of (Name of Company's) policy, and commitment to equal opportunity and must acknowledge their compliance with the program. Applicants are considered with regard to their skills, education, performance, and other bona fide qualifications. Nonmeritorious factors, such as age, disability, equal compensation, genetic information, national origin, pregnancy, race or color, religion, and gender may not be considered.

Right to Redress

All job applicants and employees have the right to redress possible injustices or wrongs done to them. Employees who believe they have been discriminated against because of age, disability, equal compensation, genetic information, national origin, pregnancy, race or color, religion, gender, and sexual harassment may file an oral or written complaint with (Name of Investigator) stating the nature of the perceived discrimination, the alleged perpetrator, witnesses, and recommended remedy needed to correct the situation. A complaint form is included at the end of this policy.

Investigation of Complaints

Complaints will be investigated in the following manner:

1. Upon receipt of a written complaint, the investigator will ask whether the individual has any witnesses he or she would like to be interviewed on their behalf. Individuals will complete a form providing names of witnesses as well as the issues the witnesses may address. Complainants will provide a signed statement giving permission to contact these witnesses.
2. The investigator will immediately forward a copy of the complaint, along with a copy of (Name of Company's) Nondiscrimination Policy Statement

and Procedures, to the individual complained against and request a meeting with this individual within three business days.

3. During the meeting with the respondent, the investigator will ask whether the individual has any witnesses he or she would like to be interviewed on their behalf.

   Individuals will complete a form providing names of witnesses as well as the issues to which the witnesses may address. Complainants will provide a signed statement giving permission to contact these witnesses.

4. Names or other identifying features of witnesses on behalf of the complainant and respondent will not be made known to the opposing party. This will help ensure participation by witnesses in the investigation.

5. All complaints of discrimination will be investigated impartially, promptly and confidentially. To the maximum extent possible, the investigation will be completed within two weeks from the time the formal investigation is initiated.

6. All information provided during the investigation will be treated in a confidential manner. Parties to the complaint will be asked to sign a confidentiality form in which they state they will keep the complaint and complaint resolution confidential. They will also be asked to sign a form indicating they will not retaliate against any party to the complaint.

7. A safe environment will be set up for the complainant, respondent, and witnesses to discuss their perspectives without the fear of being ridiculed or judged.

8. No conclusions about the veracity of the complaint will be made until the investigation is completed.

9. All documents presented by the parties to the complaint will be reviewed. Documents include, but are not limited to, the following: letters and notes.

10. Following the completion of an investigation, one of the following determinations will be made:
    - Sustain the Complaint: A finding of discrimination has been made and recommendations for corrective action will be identified, including reprimands, relief from specific duties, transfer, or dismissal.
    - Not Sustain the Complaint: A finding of no discrimination has been made.
    - Insufficient Information: Insufficient information exists on which to make a determination. All parties will be reinvestigated.

Following any determination and recommendations for corrective action, the investigator will issue a written decision with findings to (President of Company), who will correspond with the complainant and person complained against of the findings of the investigation and recommendations for corrective action. (Name of President of Company) will make appropriate statements of apology to individuals involved in the complaint.

If complainants are not satisfied with either internal procedure, they may seek redress through other sources, for example, the Equal Employment Opportunity Commission of (Name of State). Any party to a complaint resolution may do so without fear of reprisal.

Each complaint against the same individual will be handled independently. Similarly, knowledge that the complainant has filed complaints against other individuals in the past will not enter into the investigative process. Such information may be taken in to account in determining sanctions for violation of the nondiscrimination policy.

Policy Review

The firm will review this policy on Equal Opportunity annually to ensure its completeness and accuracy in light of changing legislation and conditions.

Training

(Name of President of Company) will be responsible for facilitating training programs for all administrators and employees on this Equal Opportunity Policy.

Discrimination Complaint Form

Your name:

Date:

Telephone numbers:

Description of discrimination problem:

What was said/done/shown to you?

Who was the person(s) involved:

Any witnesses who observed/heard the comments/touching, etc?

How did you feel when this incident (these incidents) occurred?

What do you want (Name of Company) to do to resolve this situation?

SAMPLE B.3. POLICY ON SEXUAL HARASSMENT

(Name of Company) has an obligation to create a work environment for all employees that is fair, humane, and responsible—an environment that supports, nurtures, and rewards career progress on the basis of such relevant factors as work performance.

All employees of (Name of Company) have a responsibility to cooperate in creating a climate at (Name of Company) where sexual harassment does not occur. We have a zero tolerance for sexual harassment of our employees. All employees at all levels of (Name of Company) must not engage in sexual harassment.

The following policy statement is designed to help employees of (Name of Company) become aware of behavior that is sexual harassment and the procedures (Name of Company) will use to deal with sexual harassment in a way that protects complainants, witnesses, and respondents.

What Is Sexual Harassment?

Sexual harassment is legally defined as "unwelcome sexual advances, requests for sexual favors, and other verbal or physical conduct of a sexual nature" when any one of the following criteria is met:

- Submission to such conduct is made either explicitly or implicitly a term or condition of the individual's employment
- Submission to or rejection of such conduct by an individual is used as the basis for employment decisions affecting the individual
- Such conduct has the purpose or effect of unreasonably interfering with an individual's work performance or creating an intimidating, hostile or offensive work environment

Two types of sexual harassment situations are described by this legal definition: (1) quid pro quo sexual harassment and (2) hostile environment sexual harassment.

Quid pro quo sexual harassment involves an individual with organizational power who either expressly or implicitly ties an employment decision to the response of an employee to unwelcome sexual advances. Thus, a supervisor may promise a reward to an employee for complying with sexual requests (for example, a better job, promotion, raise) or threaten an employee's job for failing to comply with the sexual requests (for example, threatening to not promote the employee, threatening to give an unsatisfactory performance appraisal).

Hostile environment sexual harassment involves a situation in which an atmosphere or climate is created in the workplace that makes it difficult, if not impossible, for an employee to work because the atmosphere is perceived by the employee to be intimidating, offensive, and hostile.

For purposes of this policy, sexual harassment includes, but is not limited to the following:

- Unwelcome sexual advances
- Sexual innuendos, comments, and sexual remarks
- Suggestive, obscene, or insulting sounds
- Implied or expressed threat of reprisal for refusal to comply with a sexual request
- Patting, pinching, or brushing up against another's body
- Sexually suggestive objects, books, magazines, posters, photographs, cartoons, e-mail, or pictures displayed in the work area
- Actual denial of a job-related benefit for refusal to comply with sexual requests

Thus, sexual harassment can be physical, verbal, visual, or written. These behaviors constitute sexual harassment if they are committed by individuals who are in supervisory positions or co-workers. And, these behaviors constitute sexual harassment if they occur between individuals of the same sex or between individuals of the opposite sex. (Name of Company) prohibits these and other forms of sexual harassment. Any employee who engages in such behavior will be subject to disciplinary procedures.

What Isn't Sexual Harassment?

Sexual harassment does not refer to relationships between responsible, consenting adults. Sexual harassment does not mean flirting. Giving compliments does not mean sexual harassment. Sexual harassment refers to unwanted, unwelcome behavior. Not every joke or touch or comment is sexual harassment. The key is to determine whether the behavior is unwanted and unwelcome. Furthermore, sexual harassment interferes with an employee's ability to get their work done.

Costs of Sexual Harassment

High costs are associated with the sexual harassment to individuals. They include depression, feelings of helplessness, headaches, anxiety, sleep disturbances, and disordered eating. The cost of sexual harassment to this company includes decreased productivity, absenteeism, and decreased morale.

What Should Individuals Do If They Believe They Are Being Sexually Harassed?

Employees who have complaints of sexual harassment, including any supervisor, co-worker, vendor, client, or visitor are urged to report such conduct to (Name of Investigator) so that (s)he may investigate and resolve the problem. Employees are encouraged to bring their concerns to (Name of Investigator) within 60 days of the alleged incident(s).

(Name of Investigator) will investigate all complaints as expeditiously as possible in a professional manner. The confidentiality of the investigative procedures will be maintained. The complaint will be investigated and resolved typically within a two-week period.

Complainants and those against whom complaints have been filed will not be expected to meet together to discuss the resolution of the complaint.

Investigatory procedures have been developed and are fully explained in another memorandum: (Name of Company) Sexual Harassment Complaint Procedure.

Any employee who is found to have engaged in sexual harassment will be subject to disciplinary action, as indicated in (Name of Company) complaint procedure.

Retaliation

(Name of Company) and its employees will not retaliate against employees for reporting sexual harassment or assisting (Name of Investigator) in the investigation of a complaint. Any retaliation against such individuals is subject to disciplinary action, including verbal and written reprimands, transfers, demotions, and dismissal.

False Complaints

If after investigating any complaint of sexual harassment it is discovered that the complaint is not bona fide or that an individual has provided false information regarding the complaint, that individual may be subject to disciplinary action, including verbal and written reprimands, transfers, demotions, and dismissal.

Recommended Corrective Action

The purpose of any recommended corrective action to resolve a complaint will be to correct or remedy the injury, if any, to the complainant and to prevent further harassment. Recommended action may include the following: a private or public apology; written or oral reprimand of the individual who engaged in sexual harassment; or relief from specific duties, suspension, transfer, or dismissal of the individual who engaged in sexual harassment.

If complainants are not satisfied with the attempts to resolve the sexual harassment, they may seek resolution through other sources, for example, the (Name of State) Division of Human Rights or the Equal Employment Opportunity Commission.

Policy Review

This policy will be reviewed periodically by (Name of Investigator) and by (Name of President), who welcome comments on the policy, its interpretation or implementation.

For additional information regarding sexual harassment, contact (Name of Investigator) or (Name of President). They have been trained in complaint resolution and receive additional education about sexual harassment law and its management and psychological applications. Both (Name of Investigator) and (Name of President) will be responsible for a program of information and education concerning this policy and procedures relating to sexual harassment.

Office Numbers and Phone Numbers:

(Of Investigator)
(Of President)

SAMPLE B.4. SEXUAL HARASSMENT COMPLAINT PROCEDURES

Employees of (Name of Company) who have complaints of sexual harassment by anyone at this Company, including any supervisors, are encouraged to report such conduct to (Name of Investigator) so that (s)he may investigate and resolve the problem. Individuals who feel subjected to sexual harassment should report the circumstances orally or in writing within 60 days to (Name of Investigator).

(Name of Investigator) will maintain confidentiality in her/his investigation of complaints of sexual harassment.

Any employee pursuing a complaint may do so without fear of reprisal.

Resolutions of Complaints

If an employee wishes to pursue the matter through a formal resolution, a written complaint must be submitted to (Name of Investigator), giving details of the alleged harassment, including dates, times, places, name(s) of individual(s) involved, and names of any witnesses. The complaint must be addressed to (Name of Investigator).

Formal complaints will be investigated in the following manner:

1. Upon receipt of a written complaint, (Name of Investigator) will immediately forward a copy of the complaint, along with a copy of (Name of Company) Sexual Harassment Policy Statement and Procedures, to the individual complained against and request a meeting within three days.
2. The investigation will be limited to what is necessary to resolve the complaint or make a recommendation. If it appears necessary for (Name of Investigator) to speak to any individuals other than those involved in the complaint, (s)he will do so only after informing the complainant and person complained against.
3. (Name of Investigator) will investigate all complaints of sexual harassment expeditiously and professionally. To the extent possible, the investigation will be completed within two weeks from the time the formal investigation is initiated.
4. (Name of Investigator) will maintain the information provided to her/him in the complaint and investigation process confidential. The only other employee of (Name of Company) who will be informed about the investigation is (Name of President), President of (Name of Company).
5. (Name of Company's) first priority will be to attempt to resolve the complaint through a mutual agreement of the complainant and the person complained against.
6. If an employee making a formal complaint asks not to be identified until a later date (for example, until the completion of a performance appraisal), (Name of Investigator) will decide whether or not to hold the complaint without further action until the date requested.
7. If a formal complaint has been preceded by an informal investigation, (Name of Investigator) shall decide whether there are sufficient grounds to warrant a formal investigation.
8. The names or other identifying information regarding witnesses for either party involved in the complaint will not be made known to the opposing party.

9. Referrals for therapists and medical personnel for all individuals involved in an investigation will be made available upon request.
10. Following the completion of an investigation, (Name of Investigator) will make one of the following determinations:
    - Sustain the Complaint: A finding of sexual harassment has been made and recommendations for corrective action will be identified. Recommended corrective action may include an apology; written or oral reprimand; or relief from specific duties, suspension, dismissal, or transfer of the employee found to have engaged in sexual harassment.
    - Not Sustain the Complaint: A finding of no sexual harassment has been made.
    - Insufficient Information: Insufficient information exists on which to make a determination. (Name of Investigator) will reinvestigate all parties named in the complaint.
11. Following any determination and recommendations for corrective action, (Name of Investigator) will issue a written decision with findings of fact and reason to (Name of President). (Name of President) will correspond with the complainant and person complained against of the findings of the investigation and recommendations for corrective action. Appropriate statements of apology will be made to employees involved in the complaint by (Name of President).

If complainants are not satisfied with the attempts to resolve their complaint of sexual harassment, they may seek resolution through other sources, for example, the (Name of State) Division of Human Rights or the Equal Employment Opportunity Commission.

For additional information regarding (Name of Company's) zero tolerance of sexual harassment, contact (Name of Investigator) or (Name of President).

Name of Investigator

Office Number

Phone Number

Name of President

Office Number

Phone Number

Both (Name of Investigator) and (Name of President) are trained in complaint resolution and receive additional education about sexual harassment law and its management and psychological applications.

In addition, (Name of President) and (Name of Investigator) will be responsible for a program of information and education concerning sexual harassment in general and (Name of Company's) policy and procedures.

SAMPLE B.5. DISABILITY NONDISCRIMINATION POLICY

(Name of Company) does not discriminate on the basis of disability in the recruitment, hiring and retention of employees.

Defining "Disability"

An individual with a disability is defined by law as someone who meets the following criteria:

- Has a physical or mental impairment that substantially limits one or more major life activities
- Has a record of having such an impairment
- Is regarded as having such an impairment

Learning disabilities is a general term that refers to a heterogeneous group of disorders manifested by significant difficulties in the acquisition and use of listening, speaking, reading, writing, reasoning, or mathematical abilities. These disorders are intrinsic to the individual, presumed to be due to central nervous system dysfunction, and may occur across the life span.

Reasonable Accommodation

(Name of Company) will make an accommodation to the known disability of a qualified applicant or employee if it would not impose an "undue hardship" on the firm. Undue hardship is defined by law as an action requiring significant difficulty or expense when considered in light of such factors as size, financial resources, and the nature and structure of its operation.

Reasonable accommodation may include, but is not limited to the following:

- Making existing facilities used by employees readily accessible to and usable by employees with disabilities
- Acquiring or modifying equipment or devices, adjusting training materials and policies, and providing qualified readers or interpreters

A modification or adjustment is "reasonable" by law if it "seems reasonable on its face, that is, ordinarily or in the run of cases." Thus, the request is reasonable if it appears to be plausible or feasible. A reasonable accommodation enables an applicant with a disability to have an equal opportunity to participate in the application process and to be considered for hire in the firm. In addition, a reasonable accommodation permits an employee with a disability an equal opportunity to enjoy the benefits and privileges of employment that employees without disabilities enjoy.

Requesting a Reasonable Accommodation

An individual with a disability must request a reasonable accommodation when she or he knows that a barrier is preventing her or him, due to a disability, from effectively performing their duties. (Name of Company) recommends that an individual request a reasonable accommodation before their performance suffers or conduct problems occur.

(Name of Company) requests that employees with a physical disability, psychiatric disability, or learning disability provide professional verification by a licensed health care provider who is qualified to diagnosis the disability. This verification must reflect the employees' present level of functioning of their major life activity affected by the disability. The verification must provide detailed data that support the requests for any reasonable accommodation.

Applicants or employees must pay the cost of obtaining the professional verification. The firm has the discretion to require supplemental assessment of a disability. The cost of the supplemental assessment shall be borne by the employee or applicant. If the firm requires an additional assessment for purposes of obtaining a second professional opinion, then the firm shall bear any cost not covered by any third party.

Employees who are recuperating from temporary injuries or illnesses may request interventions during this stage of recovery. Verification of the temporary impairment must be obtained by employees. The cost of obtaining the professional verification shall be borne by the employee.

Someone other than the individual with a disability may request a reasonable accommodation on behalf of the individual. Thus, a family member, friend, health professional, or other representative may request a reasonable accommodation on behalf of an applicant or employee.

Requests for reasonable accommodation do not need to be in writing.

All requests for reasonable accommodation will be dealt with expeditiously by (Company).

Applicants and employees may be asked about their ability to perform specific functions. (Name of Company) will not ask applicants or employees about the existence, nature, or severity of a disability.

SAMPLE B.6. HIV/AIDS POLICY AND PROCEDURES

(Name of Company) does not unlawfully discriminate against applicants or employees living with or affected by the Human Immunodeficiency Virus (HIV) or Acquired Immune Deficiency Syndrome (AIDS) in terms of recruitment, hiring, advancement, discharge, compensation, training, performance appraisals, or other terms, privileges, and conditions of employment. In addition, the firm will not ask nor require applicants to submit to a medical examination before receiving a conditional job offer.

HIV and AIDS: Research Findings

HIV is a blood-borne virus and is spread only through intimate contact with blood, semen, vaginal secretions, and breast milk. Scientists continue to make new discoveries about HIV infection and AIDS. But one piece of information has never changed—how the disease spreads. Scientists have recognized this fact since 1982. The basic facts about HIV transmission and prevention are sound.

The firm is committed to maintaining a safe and healthy learning and work environment for all employees. This commitment stands on the recognition that HIV, and therefore AIDS, is not transmitted through any ordinary workplace contact.

Reasonable Accommodations

The firm recognizes that HIV infection and AIDS, the most serious stage of disease progression resulting from HIV infection, pose significant and delicate issues for (Name of Company). The firm will treat HIV infection and AIDS in the same manner as other illnesses in terms of all of its employee policies. Employees living with or affected by HIV infection and AIDS will be treated with compassion and understanding, as would employees with other disabling conditions.

In accordance with the law, the firm will provide reasonable accommodations for employees and applicants with disabilities who are qualified to perform the essential functions of their positions. This applies to employees and applicants living with HIV infection and AIDS, and is especially relevant in light of new treatments for HIV infection that may allow people living with AIDS to return to work after periods of disability leave.

The firm will make an accommodation to the known disability of a qualified applicant or employee if it would not impose an "undue hardship" on the firm. Undue hardship is defined by law as an action requiring significant difficulty or expense when considered in light of factors such as size, financial resources, and the nature and structure of its operation. Reasonable accommodation may include, but is not limited to, the following: making existing facilities used by employees readily accessible to and usable by employees with disabilities; acquiring or modifying equipment or devices, adjusting training materials, and policies, and providing qualified readers or interpreters; and providing flexible work schedules for employees to meet medical appointments and tests as well as counseling appointments.

Generally, employees with HIV/AIDS have the responsibility to request an accommodation. It is the firm's policy to respond to the changing health status of employees by making reasonable accommodations. Employees may continue to work as long as they are able to perform their duties safely and in accordance with performance standards. Employees are asked to contact (Name of Person Charged with Americans with Disabilities Act Compliance) for assistance in making reasonable accommodations.

A modification or adjustment is "reasonable" by law if it "seems reasonable on its face, that is, ordinarily or in the run of cases." Thus, the request is reasonable if it appears to be plausible or feasible. A reasonable accommodation enables an applicant with HIV/AIDS to have an equal opportunity to participate in the application process and to be considered for hire in the firm. In addition, a reasonable accommodation permits an employee with HIV/AIDS to enjoy the benefits and privileges of employment that employees without HIV/AIDS enjoy. The firm requests that employees with HIV/AIDS provide professional verification by a licensed health care provider who is qualified to diagnosis the disability. This verification must reflect the employees' present level of functioning of their major life activity affected by the disability. The verification must also provide detailed data that support the requests for any reasonable accommodation.

Applicants or employees must pay the cost of obtaining the professional verification. The firm has the discretion to require supplemental assessment of a disability. The cost of the supplemental assessment shall be borne by the employee or applicant. If the firm requires an additional assessment for purposes of obtaining a second professional opinion, then the firm shall bear any cost not covered by any third party.

Requests for reasonable accommodation do not need to be in writing. All requests for reasonable accommodation will be dealt with expeditiously by the firm.

Applicants and employees may be asked about their ability to perform specific functions. The firm will not ask applicants or employees about the existence, nature, or severity of their HIV/AIDS status.

Confidentiality of Procedures

Information about an employees' medical condition is private and must be treated in a confidential manner. In most cases, only administrators directly involved in providing a reasonable accommodation or arranging benefits may need to know an employee's diagnosis. The firm will protect the confidentiality of employees' medical insurance information. Others who may acquire such information, even if obtained personally from the individual, should respect the confidentiality of the medical information.

HIV/AIDS Discrimination and Harassment

Employees are expected to continue working relationships with any employee who has HIV infection or AIDS. Individuals who refuse to work with, withhold services from, harass, or otherwise discriminate against an employee with HIV infection or AIDS will be subject to the same disciplinary procedures that apply to other policy violations. Applicants or employees who believe they have experienced discrimination because of their real or perceived HIV/AIDS status should report their experiences to (Name of Investigator).

Investigation of Complaints

Complaints will be investigated in the following manner:

1. Upon receipt of a written complaint, the investigator will ask whether the individual has any witnesses he or she would like to be interviewed on their behalf. Individuals will complete a form providing names of witnesses as well as the issues to which the witnesses may address. Complainants will provide a signed statement giving permission to contact these witnesses.

2. The investigator will immediately forward a copy of the complaint, along with a copy of the firm's HIV/AIDS Policy Statement and Procedures, to the individual complained against and request a meeting with this individual within three business days.

3. During the meeting with the respondent, the investigator will ask whether the individual has any witnesses he or she would like to be interviewed on their behalf. Individuals will complete a form providing names of witnesses as well as the issues to which the witnesses may address. Complainants will provide a signed statement giving permission to contact these witnesses.

4. Names or other identifying features of witnesses on behalf of the complainant and respondent will not be made known to the opposing party. This will help ensure participation by witnesses in the investigation.

5. All complaints of discrimination will be investigated expeditiously and professionally. To the maximum extent possible, the investigation will be completed within two weeks from the time the formal investigation is initiated.

6. All information provided during the investigation will be treated in a confidential manner. Parties to the complaint will be asked to sign a confidentiality form in which they state they will keep the complaint and complaint resolution confidential. They will be asked to sign a form indicating they will not retaliate against any party to the complaint.

7. A safe environment will be set up for the complainant, respondent, and witnesses to discuss their perspectives without the fear of being ridiculed or judged.

8. No conclusions about the veracity of the complaint will be made until the investigation is completed. All documents presented by the parties to the complaint will be reviewed. Documents include, but are not limited to, letters and notes.

9. Following the completion of an investigation, one of the following determinations will be made:
   - Sustain the Complaint: A finding of discrimination has been made and recommendations for corrective action will be identified, including reprimands, relief from specific duties, transfer, or dismissal.
   - Not Sustain the Complaint: A finding of no discrimination has been made.
   - Insufficient Information: Insufficient information exists on which to make a determination. All parties will be reinvestigated.

Following any determination and recommendations for corrective action, the investigator will issue a written decision with findings to (Name of President) who will correspond with the complainant and person complained against of the findings of the investigation and recommendations for corrective action. (Name of President) will make appropriate statements of apology to individuals involved in the complaint. If complainants are not satisfied with either internal procedure, they may seek redress through other sources, for example, the (Name of State)'s Equal Employment Opportunity Commission. Any party to a complaint resolution may do so without fear of reprisal.

Each complaint against the same individual will be handled independently. Similarly, knowledge that the complainant has filed complaints against other individuals in the past will not enter into the investigative process. Such information may be taken in to account in determining sanctions for violation of the nondiscrimination policy.

Policy Review

The firm will review this policy on HIV/AIDS annually to ensure its completeness and accuracy in light of changing legislation and conditions.

Training

(Name of President) will be responsible for facilitating training programs for all administrators and employees on this HIV/AIDS policy.

SAMPLE B.7. RELIGIOUS OBSERVANCES POLICY

(Name of Company) does not discriminate against applicants or employees because of religion. We define the term religion to include all aspects of religious observance, practice and belief.

(Name of Company) will make reasonable accommodation for religious beliefs or practices. Any employee whose religion conflicts with an employment requirement has a duty to inform (Name of Human Resource Director) of any conflict in a timely manner. Once informed of a religion-based conflict, (Name of Company) will initiate every effort to accommodate the employee, including flexible scheduling, voluntary substitutions, and lateral transfers.

An accommodation that creates an undue hardship on this firm is not a reasonable accommodation by law, for example, if it infringes on other employees' job rights, impairs workplace safety, or if the accommodation conflicts with another law.

An individual with a religious observance must request a reasonable accommodation by contacting (Name of Human Resource Director). Written notification of the decision will be mailed to the employee or applicant. The decision can be appealed within 10 days by submitting a written request to (President of Company). This decision will be communicated to the individual. There will be no further appeal.

(Name of Company) will not retaliate against an individual for filing a religious discrimination complaint or participating in an investigation of religious discrimination at (Name of Company).

SAMPLE B.8. POLICY ON HATE CRIMES

(Name of Company) fosters a civil, open, and interactive community.

At (Name of Company) we are committed to maintaining an environment free of discrimination and all forms of coercion that diminish the dignity of any member of the firm. It is the policy of (Name of Company) not to discriminate against any individual on the basis of race, color, religion, genetic information, national origin, pregnancy, equal compensation, sex, age, or disability in matters of recruitment or employment in accordance with civil rights legislation. (Name of Company) has issued separate policies on discrimination and sexual harassment.

What Is a Hate Crime?

Hate crimes are against the law. Employees found to be involved in hate crime–related incidents are subject to legal action. Hate crimes are a violation of (Name of Company) rules and regulations. Weapons of any kind are prohibited on the property except for those carried by sworn police officers on official business.

A hate crime generally can be defined as a crime that in whole or part is motivated by the offender's bias toward the victim's status. Hate crimes are intended to hurt and intimidate individuals because they are perceived to be different with respect to their race, color, religion, national origin, sexual orientation, sex, or disability.

Legislation list specific crimes that are identifiable as a hate crime, including murder, manslaughter, robbery, aggravated assault, burglary, motor vehicle theft, arson, forcible and nonforcible sex offenses, intimidation, destruction, damage or vandalism of property, and other crimes involving injury to any person or property in which the victim is intentionally selected because of the actual or perceived race, sex, religion, ethnicity, or disability of the victim.

Bias-Motivated Incidents

When the behavior does not fall into one of the listed criminal categories identified above, hate offenses are referred to as bias-motivated incidents.

These incidents may include cases of verbal slurs and other behavior, and be precursors to more serious hate-motivated violence.

Impact of Hate Crimes on Individuals

Research has identified that victims of hate crimes are vulnerable to subsequent attacks and feelings of alienation, helplessness, suspicion, and fear. Hate crimes affect the ability to work at (Name of Company) and depart from the standard for civility and respect.

Procedure for Dealing with Hate Crimes and Bias-Motivated Incidents

An employee of (Name of Company) who is involved in or witnesses behavior that poses imminent danger should immediately contact the police. In situations that do not involve imminent danger or for advice on the appropriate course of action, a member of the community is to notify (Name of Investigator).

The sanctions imposed for violations of these regulations include, but are not limited to, fines, restitution for damages, probation, suspension, and termination from employment.

Visitors, vendors, and the families of members of employees are expected to comply with the provisions of this policy. Noncompliant behavior leads to removal from the premises.

Guidance for identifying potential threatening or violent behavior and for the best ways to deal with incidents may be obtained from (Name of Investigator).

SAMPLE B.9. BULLYING POLICY

Bullying is defined as repeated inappropriate verbal or physical behavior that is conducted by one or more individuals against another person. This behavior violates (Name of Company's) ethics code, which clearly states that discrimination and harassment of any kind will not be tolerated.

Workplace bullying often involves an abuse of misuse of power. Bullying intimidates, degrades, offends, and humiliates individuals, possibly in front of other employees, clients or vendors.

The purpose of this policy is to communicate to all employees that (Name of Company) will not in any instance tolerate bullying behavior. Employees found in violation of this policy will be disciplined, up to and including termination.

(Name of Company) considers the following types of behavior examples of bullying:

- Verbal Bullying: slandering, ridiculing, or maligning a person; persistent name calling that is hurtful, insulting, or humiliating; using a person as the butt of jokes; abusive and offensive remarks
- Physical Bullying: pushing, shoving, kicking, poking, tripping, assault or threat of physical assault, damage to a person's work area or property
- Gesture Bullying: nonverbal threatening gestures, glances that can convey threatening messages
- Exclusion and Shunning: socially or physically excluding or disregarding a person in work-related activities

Examples of bullying include, but are not limited to, the following:

- Persistent singling out of one person
- Shouting or raising your voice at an individual in public or in private
- Using verbal or obscene gestures
- Personal insults and use of offensive nicknames
- Public humiliation in any form
- Constant criticism on matters unrelated or minimally related to the person's job performance or description
- Repeatedly accusing someone of errors that cannot be documented
- Spreading rumors and gossip regarding individuals
- Manipulating the ability of someone to do their work (for example, overloading, underloading, withholding information, setting meaningless tasks, setting deadlines that cannot be met, giving deliberately ambiguous instructions)

Reporting Bullying

The firm requires prompt and accurate reporting of all bullying incidents. Any employee who has a complaint of bullying is encouraged to report such conduct to (Name of Investigator) so that the complaint may be investigated and resolved promptly.

Complainants and those against whom complaints have been filed will not be expected to meet together to discuss the resolution of the complaint.

Employees who file a complaint of bullying may do so orally or in writing. A standardized form for filing complaints of bullying is included with this policy.

Investigating Complaints of Bullying

The firm will investigate the complaint of bullying. The investigation will be limited to what is necessary to resolve the complaint. If it appears necessary for them to speak to any individuals other than those involved in the complaint, they will do so only after informing the complainant and the person against whom the complaint is made.

The firm will endeavor to investigate all complaints of bullying expeditiously and professionally. In addition, they will make every attempt to maintain the information provided to them in the complaint and investigation process as confidentially as possible. If warranted, the investigator will work with local police officials in resolving the complaint of bullying.

After the investigation of the complaint, (Name of President) will institute discipline and corrective action if warranted.

(Name of Company) and its employees will not retaliate against employees for reporting bullying or assisting the investigator in the investigation of a complaint. Any retaliation against an employee is subject to disciplinary action, up to and including termination.

If after investigating any complaint of bullying it is discovered that the complaint is not bona fide or that an employee has provided false information regarding the complaint, the employee may be subject to disciplinary action.

Bullying Complaint Form

Name:

Date:

Date/Time of Incident(s):

Name(s) of Individuals Present:

Employee Who Engaged in Act of Perceived Bullying:

Type of Action(s) Employee Engaged in (verbal bullying, physical bullying, gesture bullying, or exclusion):

Impact of Actions on You (physical health, emotional well-being, work-related consequences):

What Do You Want (Name of Company) to Do to Rectify This Problem?

Additional Information You Would Like to Share:

SAMPLE B.10. POLICY ON WORKPLACE VIOLENCE

Employees of (Name of Company) must be able to work in an atmosphere of mutual respect and trust. As a place of work, the firm should be free of violence and all forms of intimidation and exploitation. The firm is concerned and committed to our employees' safety and health. We refuse to tolerate violence in the workplace and will make every effort to prevent violent incidents in this workplace. All employees at all levels must not engage in violence in the workplace and will be held responsible for ensuring that the firm is free from violence. Any employee who engages in such behavior will be subject to disciplinary procedures.

(Name of Company) has a zero tolerance for workplace violence.

What Is Workplace Violence?

Workplace violence includes, but is not limited to, verbal threats, non-verbal threats, pushing, shoving, hitting, assault, stalking, murder, and related actions. These behaviors constitute workplace violence whether they are committed by employees who are in a supervisory position or by co-workers, vendors, clients, or visitors. And, these behaviors constitute workplace violence if they occur between employees of the same sex or between employees of the opposite sex.

Reporting Workplace Violence

The firm requires prompt and accurate reporting of all violent incidents whether or not physical injury has occurred. Any employee who has a complaint of workplace violence is encouraged to report such conduct to (Name of Investigator) so that the complaint may be investigated and resolved promptly.

Complainants and those against whom complaints have been filed will not be expected to meet together to discuss the resolution of the complaint.

Employees who file a complaint of workplace violence may do so orally or in writing. A standardized form for filing complaints of workplace violence is included with this policy.

Investigating Complaints of Workplace Violence

The firm will investigate the complaint of workplace violence. The investigation will be limited to what is necessary to resolve the complaint. If it appears necessary for the investigator to speak to any individuals other than those involved in the complaint, they will do so only after informing the complainant and the person against whom the complaint is made.

The firm will endeavor to investigate all complaints of workplace violence expeditiously and professionally. In addition, they will make every attempt to maintain the information provided to them in the complaint and investigation process as confidentially as possible. If warranted, the investigator will work with local police officials to resolve the complaint of workplace violence.

After the investigation of the complaint, (Name of President) will institute discipline and corrective action, if warranted.

(Name of Company) and its employees will not retaliate against employees for reporting workplace violence or assisting the investigators in the investigation of a complaint. Any retaliation against an employee is subject to disciplinary action, up to and including termination.

If after investigating any complaint of workplace violence it is discovered that the complaint is not bona fide or that an employee has provided false information regarding the complaint, the employee may be subject to disciplinary action.

Inspection of Company for Workplace Violence

(Name of Company) will review previous incidents of violence at the firm. They will review existing records identifying patterns that may indicate causes and severity of assault incidents as well as identify changes necessary to correct these hazards.

Training

The firm will provide training on workplace violence annually to all employees.

Workplace Violence Complaint Form

Name:

Date:

Date/Time of Incident(s):

Name(s) of Individuals Present:

Employee Who Engaged in Act of Perceived Violence:

Type of Action(s) Employee Engaged in (verbal threats, pushing, hitting, stalking):

Impact of Actions on You (physical health, emotional well being, work-related consequences):

What Do You Want (Name of Company) to Do to Rectify This Problem?

Additional Information You Would Like to Share:

SAMPLE B.11. POLICY ON INTIMATE PARTNER VIOLENCE AS A WORKPLACE CONCERN

Employees of (Name of Company) must be able to work in an atmosphere of mutual respect and trust. As a place of work, (Name of Company) should be free of violence and all forms of intimidation and exploitation. (Name of Company) is concerned and committed to our employees' safety and health. The firm refuses to tolerate violence in the workplace.

(Name of Company) has issued a policy prohibiting violence in the workplace. We have a zero tolerance for workplace violence.

(Name of Company) also will make every effort to prevent violent acts in this workplace perpetrated by spouses, mates, or lovers. The firm is committed to dealing with intimate partner violence as a workplace issue. (Name of Company) has a zero tolerance for intimate partner violence.

Intimate Partner Violence: Definition

Intimate partner violence—also referred to as battering, spouse abuse, spousal assault, and domestic violence—is a global health problem. This victimization is defined as violence between adults who are intimates, regardless of their marital status, living arrangements, or sexual orientations. Such violence includes throwing, shoving, and slapping as well as beatings, forced sex, threats with a deadly weapon, and homicide.

Intimate Partner Violence: Myths and Realities

Myth: Intimate partner violence affects a small percentage of employees.

Reality: Approximately 5 million employees are battered each year in the United States. Intimate partner violence is the leading cause of injury and workplace death to women in the United States.

Myth: People must enjoy the battering since they rarely leave the abusive relationship.

Reality: Very often victims of battering do leave the relationship. Women and men remain in a battering relationship not because they are masochistic, but for several well-founded reasons, including the following:

- Threats to their lives and the lives of their children, especially after they have tried to leave the batterer
- Fear of not getting custody of their children
- Financial dependence
- Feeling of responsibility for keeping the relationship together
- Lack of support from family and friends
- The batterer is not always violent
- They still love the batterer

Myth: Individuals who batter abuse their partners because they are under a great deal of stress, including being unemployed.

Reality: Stress does not cause individuals to batter their partners. Society condones partner abuse. In addition, individuals who batter learn they can achieve their goals through the use of force without facing consequences.

Myth: Children are not affected by watching their parents in a battering relationship.

Reality: Children are often in the middle of domestic violence. They also may be abused by the violent parent. Children may grow up to repeat the same behavior patterns they witnessed in their parents.

Myth: Battering presents no long-term consequences.

Reality: Significant long-term consequences result from battering, including depression, anger, fear, anxiety, irritability, loss of self-esteem, feelings of humiliation and alienation, and a sense of vulnerability.

Myth: Intimate partner violence only occurs in poor and minority families.

Reality: Intimate partner violence occurs among all socioeconomic classes and all racial and ethnic groups.

Services Offered by (Name of Company) for Employees Who Are Victims of Intimate Partner Violence

(Name of Company) will offer the following services for our employees who are victims of intimate partner violence:

- Provide receptionists and building security officer with a photograph of the batterer and a description of the batterer

- Screen employee's calls
- Screen employee's visitors
- Accompany the employee to her or his car or subway
- Permit the employee to park close to the office building, if required
- When a restraining order is issued, (Name of President) will send a formal notification to the batterer that indicates that his or her presence on the firm's premises will result in arrest
- Referrals for individual counseling

About the Editor
and Contributors

EDITOR

MICHELE A. PALUDI, Ph.D., is the series editor for Women's Psychology and for Women and Careers in Management for Praeger. She is the author/editor of 34 college textbooks, and more than 170 scholarly articles and conference presentations on sexual harassment, campus violence, women and leadership, workplace diversity, psychology of women, gender, and discrimination. Her book, *Ivory Power: Sexual Harassment on Campus* (1990, SUNY Press), received the 1992 Myers Center Award for Outstanding Book on Human Rights in the United States. Dr. Paludi served as Chair of the U.S. Department of Education's Subpanel on the Prevention of Violence, Sexual Harassment, and Alcohol and Other Drug Problems in Higher Education. She was one of six scholars in the United States to be selected for this subpanel. She also was a consultant to and a member of former New York State Governor Mario Cuomo's Task Force on Sexual Harassment. Dr. Paludi serves as an expert witness for court proceedings and administrative hearings on sexual harassment. She has had extensive experience in conducting training programs and investigations of sexual harassment and other Equal Employment Opportunity (EEO) issues for businesses and educational institutions. Dr. Paludi is President of Human Resources Management Solutions. In addition, she has held faculty positions at Franklin & Marshall College, Kent State University, Hunter College, Union College, and Union Graduate College, where she directs certificate programs in human resource management and leadership and management. She is on the faculty in the School of Management and was recently named "Woman of the Year" by the Business and Professional Women in Schenectady, New York.

CONTRIBUTORS

LAURA G. BARRON graduated with her bachelor of arts degree from Oberlin College and her doctorate in industrial/organizational psychology from Rice University in 2009. She is an assistant professor of psychology at University of Wisconsin–Stout. Her research focuses on diversity and discrimination and she is particularly interested in legal issues related to diversity. She recently was awarded two external grants to study these issues.

JENNIE D'AIUTO graduated from Southern Vermont College located in Bennington, Vermont with her bachelor's degree in business administration and a concentration in criminal justice. She graduated from Union Graduate College, where she earned her MBA and human resources certificate. Her career goals include human resource management.

BILLIE WRIGHT DZIECH, Ph.D., professor of language arts at the University of Cincinnati, co-authored *The Lecherous Professor: Sexual Harassment on Campus* (1984, 1990). This examines the conditions that allow sexual harassment to flourish on campus and the costs that it exacts from students, faculty, and administrators. In 1989, she published *On Trial: American Courts and Their Treatment of Sexually Abused Children.* This is the first book to examine the experiences of child victims and their families seeking justice in America's courts. She has lectured and consulted at higher education institutions and businesses across the country and in Canada and has appeared on numerous radio and television shows. Her work has been discussed, reviewed, and published in publications as diverse as the *New York Times*, the *Chronicle of Higher Education*, the *Wall Street Journal,* and *People* magazine. Dr. Dziech was the 1994 recipient of the Cohen Award, the University of Cincinnati's highest recognition for excellence in teaching and of her institutions' 1998 Award for Outstanding Scholarly and Professional Activity.

MARIE FUDA graduated from Siena College in 2008 with a bachelor of science in marketing and management. In 2009 she received her masters in business administration from Union Graduate College and earned a certificate in human resource management from Union Graduate College in 2010.

MARÍA FERNANDA GARCIA, Ph.D., received her doctorate in management from Texas A&M University in 2004. She is an assistant professor in the Department of Marketing and Management at the University of Texas at El Paso. Her current research interests include diversity issues at work, responses to mistreatment in work settings, and international human resources issues.

CAREN B. GOLDBERG, Ph.D., is a renowned human resource management professor. Her research, which focuses primarily on diversity and sexual harassment, has appeared in such journals as *Journal of Applied Psychology, Human Resource Management, Sex Roles, Psychology of Women Quarterly, Journal of Organizational Behavior*, and *Group and Organization Management*. She also has contributed several chapters to books. She was honored last year by the Society for Human Resource Management as one of 100 thought leaders at the Leadership Summit on Diversity and Inclusion. Dr. Goldberg recently completed a three-year associate editor term at *Group and Organization Management* and serves on the editorial boards of *Group and Organization Management* and *Human Resource Management.* She has appeared on *Dateline, NBC* and has been quoted in numerous magazines and newspapers. Dr. Goldberg serves as an expert witness in discrimination and harassment cases for both the plaintiff and defense sides. She has provided written or oral testimony in *Sullivan v. Brodsky, Kayne, and Morgan Stanley; Apsley, et al. v. The Boeing Company, The Onex Corporation, and Spirit Aerosystems; EEOC v. Xerxes Corporation; Wilson v. Virgin Islands Water and Power Authority;* and *Penn v. USF Holland, Inc.*

KATIE E. GRIFFIN is a master's student in forensic psychology at the John Jay College of Criminal Justice–City University of New York. Her research interests include microaggressions and mental health, as well as hate crimes and associated legislation.

LISA M. V. GULICK is a doctoral student in industrial-organizational psychology at George Mason University. She received a bachelor's degree in psychology from the University of Washington. Her research aims to contribute to methods of developing and preparing leaders to work effectively across cultures, and also seeks to improve ways of successfully embracing diversity in the workplace.

HARRY R. HAYES, J.D., has been the director of human resources and human resources consulting for Jaeger & Flynn Associates in Clifton Park, New York. He was a labor and employment attorney before entering a career in human resource management. He is a designated Professional in Human Resources from the Human Resource Certification Institute. Mr. Hayes provides clients in various business areas with assistance in recruitment strategies, preemployment screening, interview techniques, best practices to comply with employment laws, employee training, development and retention strategies, and handbook policies.

MIKKI HEBL, Ph.D., graduated with her bachelor of arts degree from Smith College and her doctorate from Dartmouth College. She joined the psychology faculty at Rice University in 1998, was given the endowed title of the Radoslav Tsanoff Assistant Professorship in 2000, and promoted to associate professor in 2004. Her research focuses on the manifestation and remediation of discrimination against a variety of stigmatized groups. She currently has more than 75 publications and is a consulting editor for several applied journals.

MARIE-ANNE ISSA is a Ph.D. candidate in forensic psychology at John Jay College of Criminal Justice–City University of New York. She received her master's degree in psychology from the American University of Beirut, Lebanon, and master's degree in forensic psychology from the John Jay College of Criminal Justice. Her research interests include psychopathy, juvenile justice, violence, forensic assessment, stereotypes and prejudice, and cross-cultural issues.

MICHAEL KAUFMAN, Ph.D., is a public speaker, educator, and writer focused on gender equality and ending violence against women, including workplace harassment. He has worked with organizations in 45 countries, including extensively with the United Nations, as well as numerous governments, corporations, universities, and nongovernmental organizations. Dr. Kaufman is the co-founder of the White Ribbon Campaign, the largest effort in the world of men working to end violence against women. He is the author or editor of six books on gender issues, on democracy and development studies, as well as an award-winning novel. His articles have been translated into Italian, French, Spanish, German, Portuguese, Italian, Russian, Turkish, Hungarian, Estonian, Chinese, and Japanese. He previously taught at York University.

EDEN B. KING, Ph.D., is an assistant professor in the Department of Psychology at George Mason University. She received her doctorate from Rice University in 2006. Her research integrates organizational and social psychological theories in conceptualizing social stigma and the work-life interface. This research addresses three primary themes: (1) current manifestations of discrimination and barriers to work-life balance in organizations, (2) consequences of such challenges for its targets and their workplaces, and (3) individual and organizational strategies for reducing discrimination and increasing support for families.

DAVID A. KRAVITZ, Ph.D., is professor of management in the School of Management at George Mason University. He received a bachelor's degree from Carleton College, master's degree and a doctorate from the University of Illinois at Urbana, and postdoctoral training at Bowling Green State University. His primary research interests involve public beliefs about and attitudes toward affirmative action and diversity management. His recent activities have focused on bridging the research-practice gap in diversity management.

PAULA K. LUNDBERG-LOVE, Ph.D., is a professor of psychology at the University of Texas at Tyler (UTT) and was the Ben R. Fisch Endowed Professor in Humanitarian Affairs for 2001–2004. Her undergraduate degree was in chemistry and she worked as a chemist at a pharmaceutical company for five years before earning her doctorate in physiological psychology with an emphasis in psychopharmacology. After a three-year postdoctoral fellowship in nutrition and behavior in the Department of Preventive Medicine at Washington University School of Medicine in St. Louis, she assumed her academic position at UTT where she teaches classes in psychopharmacology, behavioral neuroscience, physiological psychology, sexual victimization, and family violence. Subsequent to her academic appointment, Dr. Lundberg-Love pursued postgraduate training and is a licensed professional counselor. She is a member of Tyler Counseling and Assessment Center, where she provides therapeutic services for victims of sexual assault, child sexual abuse, and domestic violence. She has conducted a long-term research study on women who were victims of childhood incestuous abuse, constructed a therapeutic program for their recovery, and documented its effectiveness upon their recovery. She is the author of nearly 100 publications and presentations and is co-editor of *Violence and Sexual Abuse at Home: Current Issues in Spousal Battering and Child Maltreatment* as well as *Intimate Violence against Women: When Spouses, Partners, or Lovers Attack.* As a result of her training in psychopharmacology and child maltreatment, her expertise has been sought as a consultant on various death penalty appellate cases in the state of Texas.

OLIVER B. LYONS holds a master's degree in forensic psychology from John Jay College of Criminal Justice–City University of New York. His areas of interest include the etiology of juvenile conduct problems, noninstitutionalized psychopathy, and the contribution of everyday discrimination to mental illness and antisocial behavior.

JENNIFER L. MARTIN, Ph.D., is the department head of English at a public alternative high school for at-risk students in Michigan and a lecturer at Oakland University where she teaches graduate research methods in the Department of Educational Leadership; feminist methods and introduction to Women and Gender Studies (WGS) in the Department of Women and Gender Studies. She is not only a feminist teacher, but a feminist activist. She has volunteered as an assault responder and engaged in political action for feminist causes. Currently she is the Title IX Education Task Force Chair for the Michigan National Organization for Women in order to advocate for Title IX compliance in Michigan's schools. She has conducted research and written articles on the topics of peer sexual harassment, teaching for social justice, service learning, and the at-risk student.

KENNETH W. MOORE is the president of Ken Moore Associates. He specializes in quantitative strategic business and organizational development leading to improved corporate performance. His expertise helps people to develop their financial and nonfinancial skill sets and link their work to the business plan and other performance drivers established for the organization. His experience in industry and in government includes proactive employee relations, leadership and technical training, compensation and employee benefit program design and strategic human resources planning. Before his consulting work, he was employed by Lord Corporation, Bunzl, PLC, and TD Banknorth. Mr. Moore is an adjunct professor in the business schools of the State University of New York at Albany and the Union Graduate College. He previously taught at Purdue University, the College of St. Rose, and the New School for Social Research. A native of Albany New York, he received a bachelor's degree in French from Nasson College in Maine and a master's degree in Education from the University of Southern California. He is the author of numerous human resources and strategic management articles that have been published in such journals as the *Indianapolis Business Review, Hoosier Banker, HR Now*, HR.com, ManagementFirst.com, and *HR Dergi*, the magazine of the Turkish Human

Resources Society. Many of his articles explore the changing nature of the human resources management as an internal, value-adding asset to the corporation. Two of his articles have been accepted as White Papers by the Society of Human Resources Management.

KEVIN LEO YABUT NADAL, Ph.D., is a professor, psychologist, performer, activist, and author who received his doctorate in counseling psychology from Columbia University. As an assistant professor of psychology and mental health counseling at John Jay College of Criminal Justice–City University of New York, he has published several works focusing on Filipino American, ethnic minority, and LGBTQ (lesbian, gay, bisexual, transgendered, queer) issues in the fields of psychology and education. He is the author of *Filipino American Psychology: A Handbook of Theory, Research, and Clinical Practice*.

CARMEN A. PALUDI, Jr., holds advanced degrees in electrical engineering from Clarkson University and Syracuse University, and has conducted graduate studies in applied physics and electronics engineering at the University of Massachusetts, and engineering management at Kennedy Western University. His 32-year career spans work for the Department of Defense in federal civil service as well as the private sector. He has held positions as senior principle engineer, member of the technical staff, and senior scientific advisor for the United States Air Force, Sanders Associates, The MITRE Corporation, Titan Corporation, and L-3 Communications, Inc. He has over 20 technical publications in refereed journals, and presents at international symposia and conferences. Mr. Paludi was an adjunct faculty at New Hampshire Technical College and a guest lecturer at the Advanced Electronics Technology Center at the University of Massachusetts. He frequent lectures at the Union Graduate College. He is a capability maturity model integration (CMMI) trained and certified appraisal team member by the Software Engineering Institute at Carnegie Mellon University. He has developed and presented in-house training programs in requirements management, requirements development, and risk management. He has more than 30 years of program management experience.

CHRISTOPHER P. ROSEMAN received a Ph.D. from the University of Toledo in counselor education and supervision. His research interests have focused on an offender's lack of shame and guilt and the impact that has on empathy development as well as using victims and survivors in innovative offender treatment programming to enhance empathy development. He is an assistant professor in the University of South Dakota Counselor Education Program and director of the Counseling and School Psychological Services Center.

LYNDA M. SAGRESTANO, Ph.D., is the director of the Center for Research on Women at the University of Memphis. She earned her doctorate in social psychology from the University of California–Berkeley and held National Institute of Mental Health (NIMH)-funded postdoctoral fellowships at the University of California–Los Angeles and the University of Illinois, Chicago. Her research interests include maternal and prenatal health, adolescent sexual behavior, HIV prevention, domestic violence, and gender and work stress. She is currently involved in several projects in Memphis, including a study of sexual harassment in middle and high school; the evaluation of Community Voice, a community-based infant mortality reduction intervention; and a study of barriers to economic self-sufficiency for single female heads of household in Tennessee. She is a consulting editor of *The Psychology of Women Quarterly* and serves on the advisory boards of several local organizations.

WILLIAM E. SCHWEINLE, Ph.D., received his doctorate from the University of Texas at Arlington in experimental (social and quantitative) psychology. His research has focused on the social psychology of men's wife-directed aggression and men's sexual harassment of women, among other areas. He is an assistant professor in the University of South Dakota Physician Assistant Program and chair of the South Dakota Medical Internal Review Board.

TIMOTHY R. STACEY holds a master's degree in clinical psychology with a specialization in neuropsychology from The University of Texas at Tyler. He completed his bachelor's degree of science in psychology at Texas Christian University in Fort Worth. Mr. Stacey plans to become a licensed professional counselor.

MARGARET S. STOCKDALE, Ph.D., completed her doctorate in industrial and organizational psychology at Kansas State University. She is a professor of psychology and program director for applied psychology at Southern Illinois University at Carbondale, and associate editor of *Psychology of Women Quarterly.* Her primary research concerns gender issues in the workplace, primarily sexual harassment. Her research articles have appeared in *Psychology, Public Policy and the Law, Law and Human Behavior, Psychology of Women Quarterly, Journal of Vocational Behavior, Basic and Applied Social Psychology,* and *Psychology of Men and Masculinity.* In addition, she is co-author or editor of five books. Dr. Stockdale is an active applied psychology consultant and has conducted training programs for major corporations, local agencies, and businesses. Dr. Stockdale teaches graduate and undergraduate courses in workplace diversity, organizational behavior, industrial and organizational psychology, and applied social science research methods.

SUSAN STRAUSS, R.N., Ed.D., is a national and international speaker, trainer, and consultant. Her specialty areas include harassment, workplace bullying, organization development, and management/leadership development. Her clients are from business, education, health care, law, and government organizations, both public and private sectors. Dr. Strauss has authored book chapters, articles in professional journals, written curriculum and training manuals, and the book, *Sexual Harassment and Teens: A Program for Positive Change.* She has been featured on *The Donahue Show, CBS Evening News,* and other television and radio programs as well as interviewed for newspaper and journal articles by such publications as the *Times of London, Lawyers Weekly,* and *Harvard Education Newsletter.* She has presented at international conferences in Botswana, Egypt, Thailand, Israel, and the U.S., and conducted sex discrimination research in Poland. She has consulted with professionals from other countries such as England, Australia, Canada, and St. Martin.

MICHAEL TOBIO is a master's student in forensic psychology at John Jay College of Criminal Justice–City University of New York. He plans to pursue a doctorate in clinical psychology.

MARÍA DEL CARMEN TRIANA, Ph.D., is an assistant professor in the Management and Human Resources Department at the University of Wisconsin–Madison. She earned her doctorate in management at Texas A&M University. Her research interests include diversity at work, organizational justice, and human resources selection.

VIVIAN M. VARGAS is a master's student in forensic psychology at John Jay College of Criminal Justice–City University of New York. She has conducted research focusing on various topics ranging from racial microaggressions to experiences of sex workers.

Index

United Nations Educational,
Scientific, and Cultural
Organization, 40
University of Phoenix, xxix

Values of generations, 104
Veteran generation, 103–107, 122
Video Only, xxviii
Videos in training, 119

Walker, Madame C. J., 74
Web-based pedagogy, 119
Witnesses, in investigations of
workplace discrimination, 9
Women's liberation, 130

Work/life balance, 73; programs
for, 100
Workplace discrimination
and harassment policies,
181–183; legislation, xxix–xxx
Workplace violence, 49–58;
examples, 49; impact of, 50;
policy, 58; training program,
52–57
World Food Program, 39

Zero tolerance, 135
Zero tolerance policy
for discrimination,
99, 100